ENGLISH G

HIGHLIGHT

3

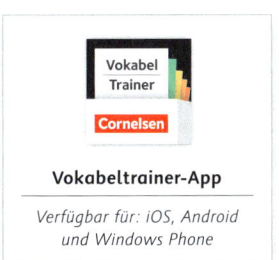

Vokabeltrainer-App

*Verfügbar für: iOS, Android
und Windows Phone*

Cornelsen

English G · Highlight · Band 3

Im Auftrag des Verlages herausgegeben von
Frank Donoghue, Nenagh, Irland

Konzepterarbeitung von
Susan Abbey, Nenagh, Irland
Wolfgang Biederstädt, Köln
Frank Donoghue, Nenagh, Irland

Erarbeitet von
Sydney Thorne, York
Susan Abbey, Nenagh, Irland
Frank Donoghue, Nenagh, Irland

in Zusammenarbeit mit der Englischredaktion
Susanne Döpper (Projektleitung), Silvia Wiedemann
(koordinierende Redakteurin), Britta Bensmann,
Eva Baumgart (Bildredaktion) sowie Jenny Dames,
Michael Dunkel, Sandhya Gupta, Annegret Hauser,
Anne Linder, Karin Wedepohl

Vokabelanhang
Ingrid Raspe, Düsseldorf

Beratende Mitwirkung
Armin Düpmeier, Warendorf; Petra Klein, Villmar;
Christa Lüdemann, Hannover; Tobias Pfeifer,
Dossenheim; Stefan Royl, Lörrach; Dagmar Wengh,
Ankum; Ellen Wiegard-Kaiser, Bielefeld sowie
Herbert Willms, Herford

Layoutkonzept und technische Umsetzung
Klein & Halm Grafikdesign, Berlin

Umschlaggestaltung
Cornelsen Verlag Design unter Verwendung
der Entwürfe von Klein & Halm Grafikdesign, Berlin
und kleiner & bold, Berlin

www.cornelsen.de

Druck und Bindung: Livonia Print, Riga

1. Auflage, 6. Druck 2023
broschiert
978-3-06-032758-4

1. Auflage, 5. Druck 2023
gebunden
978-3-06-032759-1

978-3-06-032818-5 (E-Book)

Dein Englischbuch enthält folgende Teile:

Unit 1 bis 4	Die vier Kapitel des Buches
In Ireland	Ein fakultatives, kurzes Kapitel zum Abschluss
Diff-Bank	Weitere Aufgaben – unterschiedlich schwer
Wordbank	Zusätzliche Wörter zu bestimmten Themen
Text file **TF**	Interessante Texte, passend zu den Units
Skills file **SF**	Beschreibung wichtiger Lern- und Arbeitstechniken
Language file **LF**	Zusammenfassung wichtiger Sprachregeln
Vocabulary	Wörterverzeichnis zum Lernen der neuen Wörter
Dictionary	Alphabetisches Wörterverzeichnis zum Nachschlagen (*English-German* und *German-English*)

Die Units bestehen aus diesen Teilen:

Lead-in	Einstieg in die neue Unit
Theme 1 / Theme 2	Neue Themen mit vielen Aktivitäten und Übungen
Story	Eine Geschichte zum Lesen
Skills training	Hören|Listening (L) – Lesen|Reading (R) – Sprechen|Speaking (S) – Schreiben|Writing (W) – Sprachmittlung|Mediation (M) – Hör-Sehverstehen|Viewing (V)
Focus on language	Texte und Aufgaben zum Entdecken von Regeln und Üben wichtiger Strukturen
STOP! CHECK! GO!	Üben, Vertiefen, Lernfortschritt feststellen

In den Units findest du diese Symbole:

👥 👥👥	Partnerarbeit / Gruppenarbeit
🎧 🎧	Nur auf CD / Auf CD und im Schülerbuch
🎥	Filme auf der DVD
MK	Aufgaben zur Schulung von Medienkompetenz
○ ●	Leichtere Übungen / schwierigere Übungen
○ // ●	Bei dieser Aufgabe gibt es eine leichte Variante in der Unit und eine schwierigere in der Diff-Bank.
More help p.125	Hilfen zu einer Aufgabe in der Diff-Bank
More practice 1 p.123	Weitere Übungen in der Diff-Bank

INHALT

	Lerninhalte	Your task (Lernaufgabe)	Texte
Unit 1 I love London 	· etwas über London erzählen · seine Meinung zu Mode äußern · Zustimmung und Ablehnung ausdrücken · sagen, was man tun muss, kann oder soll	**London plans** Ein Poster zum Thema *A Great Day in London* gestalten (S. 13) 	**Quiz** *What do you know about London?* (S. 8) **Magazine** *What's special about London?* (S. 10) **Advert** *London adverts* (S. 12) **Story** *Clever Sherlock!* (S. 14–15)

*Revision (simple past)

	Lerninhalte	Your task (Lernaufgabe)	Texte
Unit 2 Country life 	· über das Leben auf dem Land und in der Stadt sprechen · sagen wie etwas geschah · einen Kommentar verfassen · ein Bild beschreiben · sagen, dass man etwas schon einmal oder noch nie gemacht hat	**Find out about students in your class** Eine Umfrage durchführen (S. 41) 	**Picture story** *This isn't a park!* (S. 31) **Article** *Well done, Molly!* (S. 32) **Story** *The country detectives* (S. 34–35) **Internet forum** *My ideal place* (S. 37)

*Revision (will-future)

	Lerninhalte	Your task (Lernaufgabe)	Texte
Unit 3 Liverpool – the world in one city 	· Liverpool und seine Geschichte kennen lernen · sich mit Problemen in der Schule auseinander setzen · über Essen sprechen · seine persönliche Meinung ausdrücken · sagen, was passiert, wenn … · Vergleiche anstellen	**Are you good at business?** Einen Geschäftsplan entwickeln und vorstellen (S. 53) 	**Letter** *A letter from school* (S. 51) **Dialogue** *What's wrong?* (S. 52) **Story** *Something special* (S. 54–55) **Article** *Liverpool girls want to be like Tasha!* (S. 56)

*Revision (simple present)

INHALT

	Lerninhalte	Your task (Lernaufgabe)	Texte
Unit 4 Scotland is different	· Fotos beschreiben · sich mit drohender Arbeitslosigkeit auseinander setzen · ein Zimmer buchen · Personen oder Dinge näher beschreiben	**Find out about Scotland** Informationen selbstständig erarbeiten (S. 69)	**Article** *Another Inverness shop closes (S. 70)* **Dialogue** *Hard times (S. 71)* **Website** *Bed and breakfast next to Loch Ness (S. 72)* **Jigsaw** *Ghosts don't exist (S. 74–75)* **Song** *Amy Macdonald, Pride (S. 77)*
*In Ireland	· Erfahrungen bei einem Schüleraustausch austauschen · Dublins Sehenswürdigkeiten entdecken		**Story** *A German student in Dublin (S. 86–88)*

Die Angebote des Schülerbuches sind nicht obligatorisch abzuarbeiten. Die Auswahl der Übungen und Übungsteile richtet sich nach den Schwerpunkten des schulinternen Curriculums.

* fakultativ

I love London

1 👥 **What do you know about London?**

Do this quiz with a partner. Pick A , B or C .

If you don't know the answer, just guess. Then check on pages 116–117.

THE LONDON QUIZ

1 Who lives at Buckingham Palace?

A The King. B The Queen. C The President.

2 On the Tube you can travel by ...
A bus.
B train.
C car.

3 In books and films Sherlock Holmes is a famous London ...
A detective.
B film star.
C singer.

5 What's the name of this famous football stadium?
A Westminster. B Wimbledon. C Wembley.

4 The name of the bell in this famous clock is ...
A Big Tom. B Big Bill. C Big Ben.

6 Tourists are on the London Eye for …
A five minutes. B thirty minutes.
C two hours.

7 London buses are red. But London taxis are …
A red. B yellow. C black.

▶ Workbook 1, p. 3   ▶ Text file 1, pages 116–117

2 **PEOPLE AND PLACES** **A London tour**
a) Watch the film and enjoy the tour.
b) Then watch the film again and follow the tour on the map.

c) Watch the film a third time. What's the right information?
1 The best bus for tourists is number 11 / 21.
2 Buses are free for London children under 14 / 16.
3 Tower Bridge can open for big boats / buses.
4 You can feed birds / sheep in St James's Park.
5 The London Eye is 35 / 135 metres high.
6 Buckingham Palace has 775 windows / rooms.

d) 👥 What do you think? Talk to a partner.

I think	London the film	is looks	boring • cool • exciting • fun • funny • great • interesting • OK

I agree.

I don't agree. I think …

Young Londoners

 1 **What's special about London?**

a) Read about four young Londoners. Who would you like to meet? Why?

I'd like to meet ... because he / she is ... / looks ... / ... likes ... / says ...

buzz **a magazine for Fulham and Hammersmith**

Why do we ❤ London?

by our young reporter, Sam Holmes

Find out what young Londoners really think of their city.

Ruby Philips

I love fashion, and in London you can see the hottest clothes before they're in the magazines. I also really like London's shopping centres and markets. The markets are cheaper – and they're really cool ☺. I like Camden Market best. I'm allowed to go there with my friends sometimes.

Sam Holmes

I live in London and I love it here! I've lived here all my life. But what's so special about London? And what's the downside of London?
I asked some of my friends.

Tally O'Connor

I love the different cultures in London. My mum's family is Greek. (My real name is Talia – that's Greek.) My dad is Irish and Scottish. With so many different cultures the food in London is amazing.
And it's a great place for music and concerts. There's only one problem. I'm only allowed to go to concerts with mum or dad ☹.

Alfie Harper

There's one good thing about London: Londoners are very friendly. I made friends very quickly when we came here from Plymouth two years ago. But the best thing about London is the football. There are two big football clubs near where I live – Chelsea and Fulham. I'm a big Chelsea fan. (My friend Tally is a Fulham fan, but nobody is perfect!) The downside is that London is noisy and very expensive.

b) Match the headings A–E with Sam, Ruby, Tally and Alfie's texts.
Careful! One sentence doesn't fit.

A London isn't cheap.

B I've never lived in a different town.

C You can see great new clothes in London.

D Arsenal is the best London football club.

E London is great because lots of different people live there.

c) True or false?
1 Sam doesn't like London very much.
2 Sam is a reporter for **buzz**.
3 Ruby says that London is special for clothes.
4 Ruby thinks that shopping centres are better than markets.
5 Tally likes the food of different cultures.
6 Tally goes to concerts alone.
7 Alfie says that Londoners aren't friendly.
8 Alfie thinks that London has no downsides.

2 **What do you know about London now?**
Pick a) or b).

a) ◯ Copy and complete the sentences.
All the information is on pages 8–11.
1 Wembley is famous for its football …
2 Sherlock Holmes is a London …
3 London buses are free for …
4 Camden has a famous …
5 Chelsea and Fulham are London football …
6 Buckingham Palace is the home of …
7 Big Ben is the name of a big …
8 The London Eye is … metres high.

b) ● What information about London was new for you? Write a list.
London has many different cultures. …
👥 Partner check: Compare your list with a partner. Did he/she write the same things?

Camden Market

Amazing London – for teens

1 **London adverts**

Which adverts (A–G) are about music, shopping, sport or transport?

A AN AMAZING NIGHT!

THE MUSICAL

BOOK NOW

VICTORIA PALACE THEATRE

B

Chelsea stadium tours –
Stamford Bridge

See the dressing rooms and walk through the players' tunnel

Book a tour and visit the museum.

C

London Travelcard

Buy a one-day Travelcard and travel on the Tube and by bus all day with only one ticket.

D ## CAMDEN MARKET

Hundreds of stalls, shops, restaurants and cafes.
London's number 1 address for fashion.
Open 7 days a week.

E TODAY at the O2 London

ONE DIRECTION
Britain's biggest boyband

Songs: *What makes you beautiful • One thing • More than this • Up all night*

F Visit:

The Queen Elizabeth Olympic Park, London

Scene of the 2012 Olympic Games

G ## OXFORD STREET

Britain's favourite high street. • More than 300 shops. •
One of the busiest streets in Europe.

More practice 1 p. 93

2 👥 YOUR TASK London plans

You are going to give young people tips for a great day in London. First you'll work alone, then in a group. You'll also make a poster. Follow steps 1–5.

Step 1: Find ideas: What can tourists in London do? Where can they go?
Work alone. Look at pages 8–12 and 116–117. Write two or more good ideas:
Young tourists can …
They can also …

Young people can go to the London Eye.

The London Eye? Maybe it's very expensive.

Step 2: Agree with partners in a group.
Work in a group. Talk to your partners and agree on three (or more) ideas. Write them down.

🔵 Write why it's a good idea.

But it's a great idea!

More help p.93

Look. The concert is in the evening.

Step 3: Find out more.
Work with your partners. Go to www.cornelsen.de/highlight and put in the webcode: *High-3-13*. Make notes, for example: – When does it open / start?
– How much are the tickets?
– How can you get there?

Great. So they can go to Oxford Street before the concert.

A GREAT DAY IN LONDON

Visit Big Ben. It's free!

Buy presents in Oxford Street. Go there by Tube.

Step 4: Make your poster.
Write your London tips on a poster.
– Put information on the poster.
– Get photos on the internet.
– Draw some pictures.
– Write captions.

Great shop!

Step 5: Reading circle
Put your poster on the classroom wall. Then look at the other posters. Put a smiley ☺ on the best poster.

And in the evening?
Go to the O2 Arena for a fantastic concert!

1 **Before you read**

👥 Look at the pictures. Where do the friends go? What do they do?

They go to the Tube.

They go to a …

They play …

🎧 ## Clever Sherlock!

1 **About me**

My name is Sam Holmes.
But everybody calls me
Sherlock. Like Sherlock
5 Holmes – the great
detective!

Everybody calls me a geek because I like things like books,
history, museums. My friends like normal things –
shopping, music, football. But I don't like normal things.
10 They're too … normal!

geeky things　　　**normal things**

Saturday plans

So when I met my friends (Ruby, Alfie and Tally) last
Saturday, I wanted to go to the
I love the dinosaurs there. But of
15 course my friends laughed.
They said: "BORING!"

My friend Ruby wanted to go shopping.
I said "BORING",
but the others said, "OK".
20 I said: "We have no money, so we can't go shopping."
"Very clever, Sherlock," Ruby answered.

NATURAL HISTORY MUSEUM

Disaster on the Tube

We went to the Tube station
in Fulham. We ran down to our
25 train, but Alfie was too slow.
The train left and poor Alfie
was still on the platform.

FULHAM BROADWAY

We tried to phone Alfie,
but our mobiles didn't
30 work on the Tube.

Then I had an idea.
"We'll get out at the next
station and wait for the
next train." And that's what we did. Ten minutes
35 later the next train came and Alfie was on it.
He was happy to see us.
"That was very clever,
Sherlock," Tally said.
So I was happy too.

I like Tally!

40 **Shopping disaster**

So our shopping
adventure began.
But we didn't go to a normal shop!
No, we went to
45 the most famous
shop in London!

Harrods

When we went through the door, Ruby said, "We have
to go in quickly. They don't like groups of kids here."

This was a very expensive shop!

50 Alfie had a rucksack with
a football in it. And that
was the next disaster.
The security man came and said,
"You aren't allowed to have
55 a rucksack in Harrods. And
if you're under 15, you aren't allowed in the shop
without an adult."

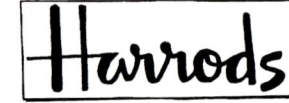

£2000

Then I had an idea. I saw a woman in the shop and
I shouted, "MUM, we're here." The woman looked
60 surprised. The security man looked surprised too.
We left the shop quickly.
"Very clever, Sherlock!" Tally said to me.

Disaster in Hyde Park

So next we went to Hyde Park. We played football, but
65 we didn't see the teenagers behind a tree.
They drank something ...

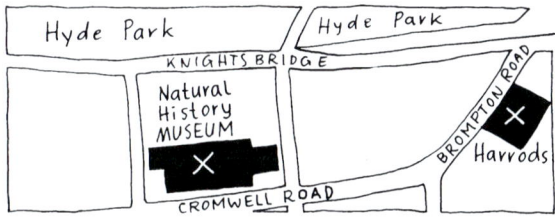

Then Alfie kicked the
football into their picnic.
"Hey, you idiot!" a big boy
70 shouted. "We're keeping
your football!"

Then I had an idea. I went behind a
tree and took out my mobile. A LOUD
noise came from it – like the noise of
75 a police car. The teenagers heard it,
ran away – and left the football!.

"Very clever again, Sherlock," Tally said.
I felt like a million dollars!

In the museum, at last

80 So we were in Hyde Park with NO money and NO more
ideas. "Erm ...," I said. "The Natural History Museum
is near here – and it's free."
So we went there. First we went to see the dinosaurs –
and my friends loved them.

85 And they all loved the earthquake room too. You
can really feel the earthquake there! It's amazing
and everybody loved it. And now
everybody loves the museum –
especially Tally. So I think that
90 I am a VERY clever Sherlock!

2 ○ **What places are in the story?**
1 a Tube station 2 a hospital 3 a shop
4 a park 5 a post office 6 a museum

3 **Who thought this in the story?**
Alfie, Tally, Ruby, Sherlock – or all of them?
1 I want to see the dinosaurs.
2 I want to go shopping.
3 I can get the next train!
4 Sherlock was very clever in Harrods.
5 Thanks, Sherlock. I have my football back.
6 The earthquake room is great!

More practice 2 p. 93

4 ● **Why and what?** More help p.94
Copy and complete the sentences.
1 Sam's friends call him *a geek* because ...
2 His friends said "BORING!" when ...
3 Alfie missed the Tube train because ...
4 They had a problem at Harrods because ...
5 The teens in the park ran away when ...
6 They went to the museum because ...

More practice 3 p. 94   More practice 4 p. 95

Collect ideas before you write

Before you write, collect ideas from texts in your English book.
▸ *Skills file 8, p. 133*

1 Ideas for a text about your neighbourhood

a) First collect ideas from texts in your book.
For example read this text: Who likes Fulham and why? *... likes Fulham because ...*

Is Fulham a great place for young people? Tell buzz what you think!

The best thing about Fulham is the river. Also, there's an amazing market near our house and there are lots of nice cafes here too.

Darren

I don't like Fulham much. We live near a busy road. And we aren't far from Heathrow Airport, so we hear the planes too.

Livvy

I think Fulham is great! You can go shopping in the Westfield shopping centre. And you can watch great football at Fulham Stadium.

Ruby

We live next to a big hospital. There aren't any parks near us and our nearest Tube station is 15 minutes away. I think it's boring here.

Josh

b) 👥 WORDS Work with a partner. Collect words for your neighbourhood from the buzz texts. Make lists or a network:

My neighbourhood

transport	shopping	sport	other
...	market	...	river
...	...	...	...

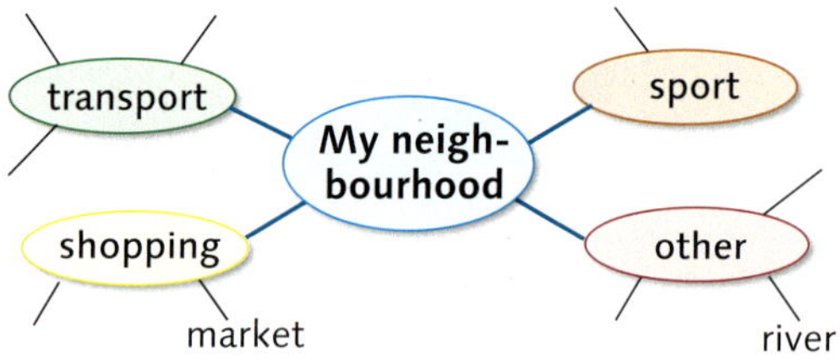

Write as many words as you can. **More help** p. 95
School, post office, ...

▸ *Wordbank 1, p. 146*

c) Collect sentences for your text.
Read these sentences from the **buzz** texts. Then change the words in orange and write about **your** neighbourhood.

1 The best thing about Fulham is the river. → *The best thing about my town is the park.*
2 There's an amazing market near our house. → *There's ...*
3 There are lots of nice cafes here.
4 You can go shopping in the shopping centre.
5 There aren't any parks near us.
6 Our nearest Tube station is 15 minutes away.

2 NOW YOU **More help** p. 95
Now tell Ruby or Darren from **buzz** about your neighbourhood.
Write about 40 words (● 60 words).
Put your text in your DOSSIER.

Make your text more interesting
– with words from 1b),
– with sentences from 1c).

Understanding new words

1   Word building

a) Look at the words in black.
Match each word with a photo A–D.

> Sometimes words that you know can help you to understand new words.
>
> For example you know *work*. So *worker* = *work* + *-er* is someone who works *(Arbeiter/in)*. That's easy!
>
> ▶ *Skills file 2, p. 125*

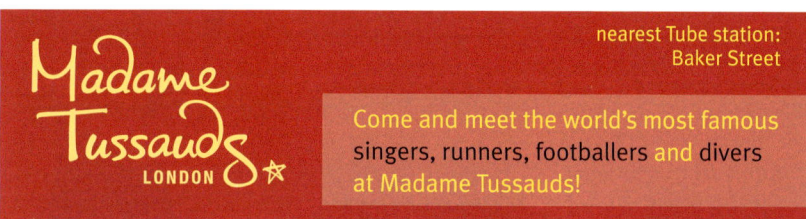

nearest Tube station:
Baker Street

Come and meet the world's most famous singers, runners, footballers and divers at Madame Tussauds!

b) 👥 What could these new words mean?
Talk to a partner and write your ideas. Then check in a dictionary.

1 driver
2 reader
3 listener
4 walker
5 writer
6 skiver
7 dancer
8 talker

> Driver: I think it comes from *drive*.

> So in German it's ...

c) Look at these examples: **sun ➜ sunny, cloud ➜ cloudy, rain ➜ rainy.**
The red words below are like these words. What do they mean in German?

The walkers started early, so they were a bit sleepy.

Hampstead, in the north of London, is hilly and has a big park.

d) Some words have two parts. Look at these examples:
bus stop = bus *(Bus)* + stop *(anhalten)*   → *Bushaltestelle*
postcard = post *(Post)* + card *(Karte)*   → *Postkarte, Ansichtskarte*
What's a *bus driver*? And what's a *postman* or a *postwoman*?

2   From the newspaper

What do these red words mean?
👥 Partner check: Compare with a partner.

More practice 5 p. 96

Young swimmers and divers from all parts of Britain were at the Olympic swimming pool yesterday. One winner was John Burns. He said in a TV interview, "I was ill yesterday. It was a long car trip and I was travelsick. But today I'm OK."

1 Is fashion important?

a) Serena and Andy are talking about shopping and fashion. Listen to them.   More help p.96
Do you agree with Andy or Serena?

I'm going shopping.

That's rubbish!

But you don't have to spend a lot of money on fashion.

You're wrong! I always buy cheap clothes.

Fashion is a waste of money.

I don't agree.

You're right.

Oh!!! Not again!

Serena

b) Work with a partner. Take roles. Listen to Serena and Andy again.
Repeat the sentences in the speech bubbles with as much feeling as you can.   More practice 6 p.97

2 PLACEMAT   What things are most important for teenagers?

Step 1: Work in groups of four. Every student writes three ideas in one corner of the placemat.

Step 2: Read out your ideas to the group.

Step 3: Talk about the ideas. Agree on three things that most students in your group think are important. Write them in the middle of your placemat.

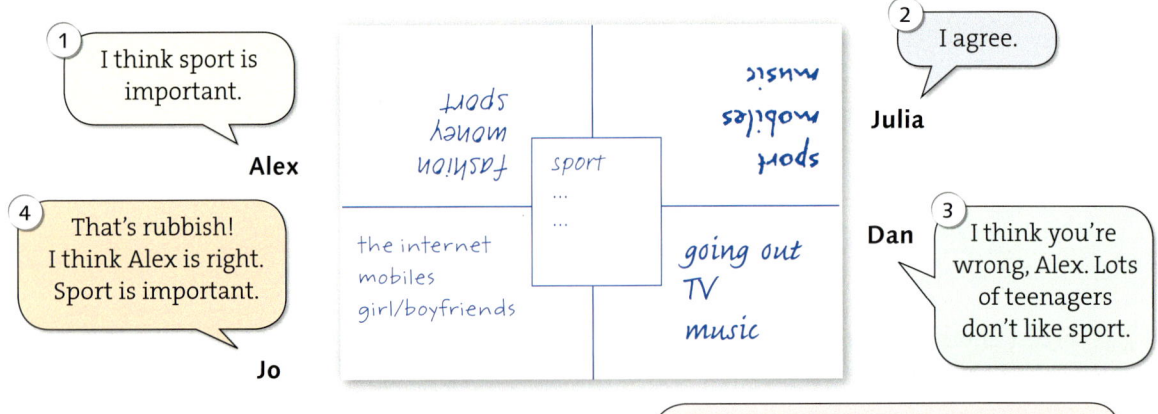

1 I think sport is important.

Alex

2 I agree.

Julia

4 That's rubbish! I think Alex is right. Sport is important.

Jo

Dan

3 I think you're wrong, Alex. Lots of teenagers don't like sport.

Step 4: Tell the class about your group's ideas.
Do the rest of the class have the same ideas?
What are the most popular ideas in your class?

We think that the most important thing for teenagers is …
Number two on our list is …

1 Before you watch

a) Look at the photos from the new DVD in exercise 2.

Think about these questions:
1 Is the DVD in Plymouth or London? How do you know?
2 Who is in the film?
3 Where will the people go in the film? (to a shop, cafe, park, market, stadium, …?)
4 What will happen?

b) 👥 **Pair:** Talk about the questions in a) with a partner.

c) **Share:** Tell the class what you and your partner think.

> I think the film is in …

> Yes, you're right. And …

> We think that the people will go to …

2 The funny ringtone

a) ⭕ Watch the film. Then put the photos in the right order.

b) Watch the film a second time. Then answer these questions:
Who goes to the cafe? What do they drink? Where do they go then? Who has a problem?

c) Now watch the film again and check your answers.

3 👥 What can you remember?

Ask your partner three questions about the film.
Can he / she answer them?

Who	lives in London SW6?
	gives Ruby her phone?
	has a smoothie / cup of tea?
	buys clothes at Camden Market?
	puts on a hat?
	loses something?
	…?

1 Tips for visitors to London

a) ◯ Match the parts of the brochure (1–3) with the pictures (A–C).

Stay safe in the city!

Like in all cities, you have to be careful when you're in London. But London is a very safe place, so you don't have to be nervous.

1 Crossing the road: When you cross the road, you have to look right, then left, then right again. You should use the subways, so you don't have to cross busy roads.

2 Pickpockets: Sometimes there are pickpockets in shops or on buses and trains. Please be very careful if you have to open your bag or use your mobile.

3 On the Tube: Please stand on the right on the escalators. Then other people can walk past you on the left.

b) Look again at these sentences from the text and complete the FOCUS-box.

1 You have to be careful.
2 You have to look right, then left.
3 You don't have to be nervous.
4 You don't have to cross busy roads.

> **FOCUS**
>
> • Mit ... sagst du, was jemand tun muss.
> • Mit ... sagst du, was jemand nicht zu tun braucht.

▸ *Language file 7, p. 143*

2 School rules

Alfie is talking about his old school and his new school in London.

a) Listen. Which school is stricter – Alfie's old school or his new school in London?

b) Listen again and take notes.

	old school	new school
wear a tie	✔	✗
wear a blazer		
wear normal shoes		
stay at school all day		

c) ⬤ Use your notes and complete the sentences.
At Alfie's old school the students have to ..., but at his new school they don't ...

3 *Can, should* or *have to*?

a) Match the sentences on the left with the speech bubbles.

1 Du willst sagen, was jemand tun kann oder darf.

2 Du willst jemandem raten, etwas zu tun.

3 Du willst sagen, dass jemand etwas tun muss.

4 Du willst sagen, dass jemand etwas nicht tun muss.

a) You have to do it.

b) You don't have to do it.

c) You can do it.

d) You should do it.

▶ *Language file 7 , p. 143*

b) 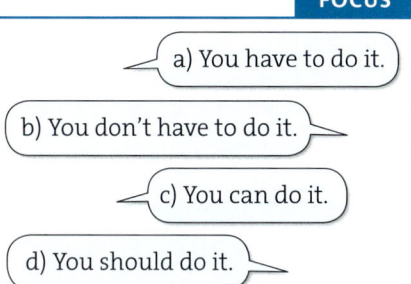 Now look again at the tips for visitors on page 20.
Tell your partner these tips in German.

1 You have to be careful in London.
2 You should use the subways.
3 You don't have to be nervous.

4 You have to look right, then left.
5 Stand on the right on the escalators,
   then people can go past you on the left.

4 A letter to **buzz**

a) ◯ Complete the letter with the correct form of the verb. // ● p. 97

Dear buzz
My friend often visits me in the evening, but then she has to / doesn't have to (1) walk home alone. Her mum and dad can't pick her up because they have to / don't have to (2) work in the evenings. The problem is that she has to / doesn't have to (3) walk along dark streets. She says that I have to / don't have to (4) worry about her, but I worry a lot. I have to / don't have to (5) be sure that she's OK, so I phone her on her mobile.
A nervous friend

b) Complete with *should / shouldn't*.

Dear nervous friend
Your friend really … (1) walk along dark streets. She … (2) walk on busier streets. If someone says something unfriendly to her, she … (3) answer. She … (4) say nothing and walk away quickly. If she's very scared, she … (5) ask for help.

buzz

5 Tips for visitors in Germany

Copy and complete these tips for British visitors to Germany.

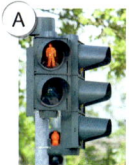

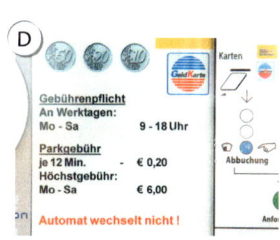

You … wait when the man is red.

You … cross when the man is green.

Currywurst is popular – you … try it!

It's 7 pm. You … pay.

More practice 7 p. 97

1 REVISION   My class trip

A German student is on a class trip to London. She wrote an email to her cousin in Canada. Write the verbs in the simple past.

Example: *We arrived in London …*

Ein Lösungsblatt für die Aufgaben 1–4 und 6 kannst du von deiner Lehrerin/deinem Lehrer erhalten. Die Audio-Datei für Aufgabe 3 findest du online bei den Dateien zum Workbook.

Hello Pinar

We … **(1 arrive)** in London three days ago. My English family … **(2 be)** at Heathrow airport. They're really nice – especially Kate. At first I … **(3 have)** problems because they all … **(4 talk)** so fast. I … **(5 not understand)** anything! But it's OK now.

On the first day I … **(6 not see)** the German students in my class. I … **(7 go)** with Kate to her friend's house and we … **(8 play)** computer games.

Yesterday I … **(9 meet)** the other German students at the Tower of London. It was really cool.
 … you … **(10 visit)** the Tower when you were in London last year? … you … **(11 like)** it?

See you soon
Sandra xx

► *Language file 3, p. 140*

2 WORDS   Travel in London

a) Copy this table.
Then write the words from the box in it.

transport	people	places
boat	adult	bus stop
…	…	…

adult • bike • *boat* • bridge • bus • bus driver • *bus stop* • car • child • detective • drive • escalator • football fan • ferry • harbour • hill • king • market • plane • platform • queen • river • ride • road • sea • security man • shopping centre • stadium • street • taxi • ticket • traffic lights • train • train station • tourist • travel • Tube

b) Find one word to complete **all** three phrases.
1 Cross the …   Walk along the …   Go to the end of the … and turn left.
2 Go by … to town.   Wait for the … on the platform.   The … is leaving the station.
3 Buy a … from the bus driver.   A … to London, please.   You can get a … at the station.
4 The cars must stop at the …   Turn left at the …   The … are red.
5 Sit on the …   The best … for tourists is number 11 …   Wait at the … stop.
6 See boats on the …   See fish in the …   Cross the … on a bridge.

c) ● Write sentences about you and travel – as many as you can. Some ideas:
I often travel by … to …   *I get on the … at …*   *When it's raining I …*
Sometimes I go to town by …   *For our summer holidays we …*   *Yesterday I …*

🎧 3 LISTENING   Travelling in London

a) Listen to the three scenes and match them with the photos. The sounds can help you.

b) Listen again and answer the questions.
1 a) When is the train going to leave?   **A** 11.00   **B** 11.40   **C** 3 pm
  b) Which station is Waterloo?   **A** the first station   **B** the second station   **C** the third station.
2 a) The woman can take the bus number 9 to   **A** the Strand   **B** Covent Garden   **C** Harrods.
  b) How often does the number 9 bus come? Every   **A** 2 or 3 minutes   **B** every 4 or 5 minutes
   C every 6 or 7 minutes .
3 a) Where do the people want to go?   **A** to the Tower   **B** to Big Ben   **C** to Baker Street.
  b) Why do they want to be there by 2.30?   **A** to see the Queen   **B** to meet their children
   C to buy a ticket.

4 MEDIATION   Staying with a family

Während eurer Klassenfahrt nach London bist du in einer englischen Gastfamilie. Hilf deinem Freund Paul, die Hinweise der Gastmutter Mrs Green zu verstehen.

Mrs Green	Welcome to our home. We hope you'll enjoy your stay in London. We usually have dinner at 7.30, so you should be here at around 7.
Paul	Was war das mit dem Abendessen?
You	Abendessen ist gewöhnlich um halb acht, deshalb ... (1)
Mrs Green	You don't have to walk home after your activities. Just phone me when you're ready and I'll pick you up in the car.
Paul	Was war das mit anrufen?
You	Nach unseren Ausflügen ... (2) laufen. Wir sollen Mrs Green anrufen und sie ... (3)
Mrs Green	After dinner you aren't allowed to go out again alone. You have to stay at home.
Paul	Dürfen wir nach dem Abendessen ausgehen?
You	Nein, ... (4)
Mrs Green	There isn't a TV in your bedroom. But of course, you are allowed to watch TV in the living room with us.
Paul	Was ist mit Fernsehen?
You	Wir ... (5)
Mrs Green	We only have one bathroom, so nobody should stay in there too long.
Paul	Ich habe leider nur *bathroom* verstanden – worum ging es genau?
You	Da es nur ein Bad gibt, ... (6)

5 WRITING My day in London

Look at the pictures. These young people spent a day in London.

Molly

Anna

Luke

a) Molly, the girl in the first picture, wrote about her day. Read her text.

On Saturday I went to London. I went with my friend Andy. We travelled by bus. I was hungry when we arrived, so we went to a cafe, had breakfast and chatted.

After breakfast we looked at the shops in Oxford Street. I felt especially happy because I found a T-shirt for Andy's birthday.

In the afternoon we had a ride on the London Eye. The weather was perfect and we saw the river, the bridges, Big Ben ... It was great!

After that we felt a bit tired, so we went to Covent Garden. We bought a sandwich and a drink, and sat and listened to a guitarist. And then it was time to take the bus back home.

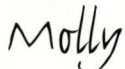 Molly

I really liked the London Eye!

b) Now imagine you're Anna or Luke. You're going to write about your day. Decide who you are and collect ideas about the day in London. Look at Molly's text for help.

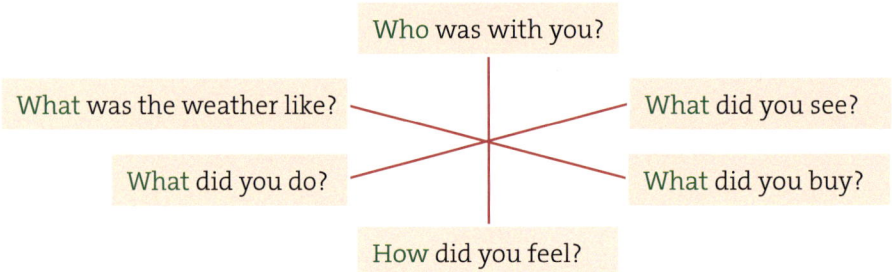

Who was with you?

What was the weather like?

What did you see?

What did you do?

What did you buy?

How did you feel?

c) Can you use Molly's sentences for your text too?
Example: I went with my friend Andy. => *I went with my friend Kate.*
1 I was hungry when we arrived, so ...
2 I felt especially happy because ...
3 The weather was ... and we ...
4 We bought ... and ..., and sat and ...

d) Now write your text. Write as many sentences as you can.

e) 👥 Partner check: Read and correct your partner's text. He/She corrects your text.

► *Skills file 8, pp. 132–134*

6 READING Tally's blog

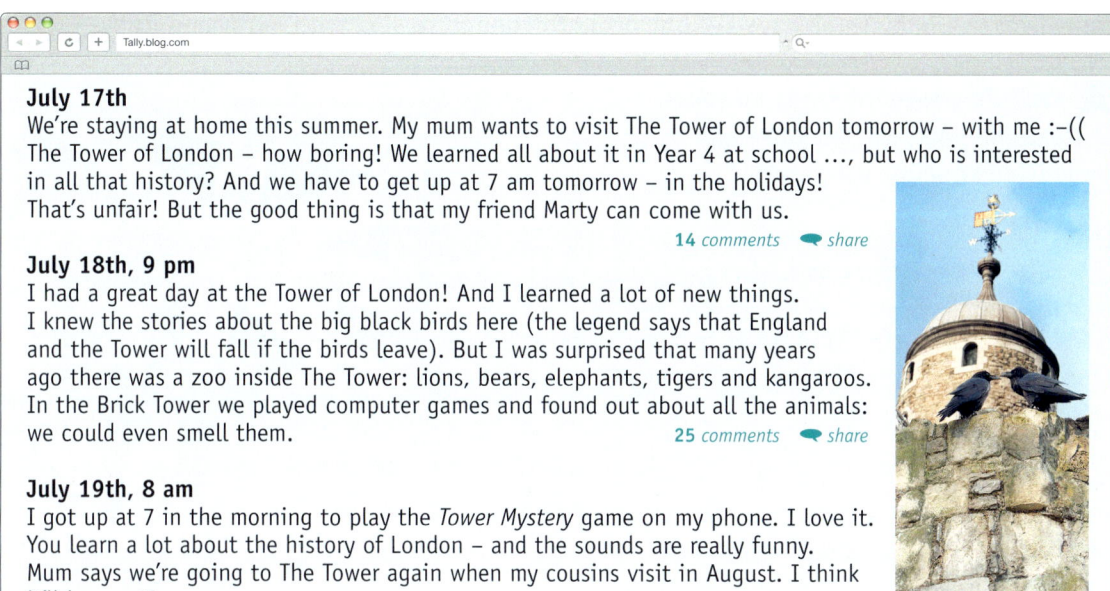

July 17th
We're staying at home this summer. My mum wants to visit The Tower of London tomorrow – with me :-((
The Tower of London – how boring! We learned all about it in Year 4 at school …, but who is interested in all that history? And we have to get up at 7 am tomorrow – in the holidays!
That's unfair! But the good thing is that my friend Marty can come with us.

14 *comments* 💬 *share*

July 18th, 9 pm
I had a great day at the Tower of London! And I learned a lot of new things.
I knew the stories about the big black birds here (the legend says that England and the Tower will fall if the birds leave). But I was surprised that many years ago there was a zoo inside The Tower: lions, bears, elephants, tigers and kangaroos. In the Brick Tower we played computer games and found out about all the animals: we could even smell them.

25 *comments* 💬 *share*

July 19th, 8 am
I got up at 7 in the morning to play the *Tower Mystery* game on my phone. I love it.
You learn a lot about the history of London – and the sounds are really funny.
Mum says we're going to The Tower again when my cousins visit in August. I think it'll be great!

2 *comments* 💬 *share*

a) Match three of these sentences with the parts of Tally's blog (17th, 18th or 19th):

1 I didn't know about the wild animals! 3 Do I want to go again? Yes, please!

2 Tower of London? No, thanks! 4 Tower of London? Never again!

b) Pick the correct answer.

1 On July 17th Tally is happy because **A** she likes visiting the Tower of London.
 B she can sleep late. **C** her friend Marty is going to be with her.

2 The Tower of London legend says the big black birds **A** are bad for England and the Tower.
 B are good for England and the Tower. **C** must leave the Tower.

3 On July 19th Tally **A** plays the *Tower Mystery* game in the Brick Tower.
 B doesn't want to go to The Tower of London again. **C** doesn't sleep late.

7 My learner log

Copy and complete your learner log. You can put it in your DOSSIER.

My learner log for Unit 1

Now I can …
– talk about the good and bad things where I live: …
– take ideas from a text when I write: 😀 😐 🙁
– talk about things I can, should and have to do: …
– talk about things I don't have to do: …
– say if I agree or don't agree with somebody: …

After Unit 1:
– I know a lot of city words, for example …
– Some places I want to visit in London are …
– These pages in the Unit were easy: …
– These pages in the Unit were difficult: …

My progress in English is: GREAT! 👍 / OK 👊 / NOT VERY GOOD 👎

A visit to a city – using the simple past

Emily lives in Leeds. Three days ago she came to London to stay with her friend Ruby.

1 **Emily's postcard from London**

a) Read the postcard. Do you think
Emily liked London? Why (not)?

> Hi!
> I arrived here in London three days ago. On
> the first day Ruby and I visited all the famous
> places. They were great! We walked for miles
> and miles! So we were tired and we didn't do
> very much in the evening.
> On the second day we went shopping in Oxford
> Street. Did you go there last year? I bought
> some cool presents. (One for you – surprise!)
> In the evening we saw some famous bands at
> a free concert in Hyde park. It was fantastic!
> See you soon! Emily

LONDON-Postcards © kleinundhalm.de

b) The simple past

Regelmäßige Verben enden auf **-ed**.
1 Copy three examples from the postcard.

Unregelmäßige Verben enden **nicht** auf **-ed**.
2 Copy four examples from the postcard:
were, …

Verneinungen verwenden das Wort **didn't**.
3 Copy one example from the postcard.

Fragen beginnen mit dem Wort **Did …?**
4 Copy one example from the postcard.

▶ *Language file 3, p. 140*

2 **Emily and Ruby**

a) Emily is telling a friend about her time in London.
Pick the right verbs 1–8 from the box.

> came • had • made • played •
> told • wanted • went • wore

> Last week I visited my friend Ruby. Ruby is really nice and she … (1) a cake
> when I arrived in London! One day we … (2) to a park. We … (3) badminton
> and then we bought ice creams. Ruby … (4) me lots of funny stories and
> I laughed a lot! On the last day Ruby's mum took us to a concert. I … (5)
> my new dress. We … (6) to come home by Tube, but Ruby checked the time
> and it was too late. So we drove home in a London taxi!
> I … (7) a great time with Ruby and I was really sad when I left London
> and … (8) home.

b) Now find the simple
past forms of these
verbs. They're all in the
speech bubble.

1	visit *visited*	5	buy *bought*
2	arrive	6	take
3	laugh	7	drive
4	check	8	leave

3 ● Emily's photos

Now Emily is showing photos of her trip to London.
Copy and complete the sentences. Use the right verb forms.

1 I didn't travel into London by bus because it was quicker by Tube.

I travelled by bus.
I didn't travel by train. *(no -ed)*

I went to London.
I didn't go to Paris.

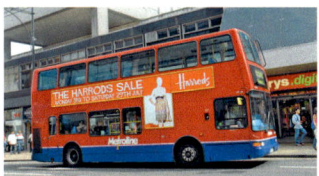

1 I ... (not travel) into London by bus because it was quicker by Tube.

2 I took photos of Buckingham Palace, but I ... (not see) the Queen.

3 I was at Big Ben at 18.20, so I ... (not hear) the famous bell.

4 I ... (not visit) the Tower of London because the tickets were expensive.

5 We went to the zoo, but we ... (not see) the tigers.

6 We ... (not go) on a boat trip on the river because we ... (not have) time.

4 NOW YOU

a) Write an email to Emily about a visit to a city. Write as many sentences as you can.

Hi!
I hope you're OK.
Last week I was in Berlin / Hamburg / ...
I stayed with a friend / in a hotel / ...
On the first day ...
On the second day ...
On the last day ...

You can use some sentences in exercises 1, 2 and 3 and change them for your text:
On the first day Ruby and I visited all the famous places.
=> On the first day I visited the Brandenburger Tor.

b) 👥 **Partner check:** Show your email to a partner and check your partner's email.

5 An elephant's trip to London

a) Copy and complete the rhyme.

Elephant, elephant, where did you go?
I went to London two hours ago.
Elephant, elephant, what ... you ...? (see?)
I ... lots of people, but they ... me! (saw, not like)
Elephant, elephant, what happened then?
I ... a young woman the way to Big Ben. (ask)
Elephant, elephant, then what ... you ...? (do?)
I ... the wrong Tube and ... back at the zoo.
(take, arrive)

b) 👥 Say the rhyme with a partner.

Country life

Hills, fields and trees in the Cotswolds

Small towns like Chipping Campden have nice old houses.

Mickleton

Chipping Campden

The village of Mickleton

1 Young Lives

a) Listen to the radio programme *Young Lives*. Pick the right answer.

1 Molly talks about ...
  A her family.
  B where she lives.

2 Molly ...
  A likes living in the country.
  B wants to leave her farm.

b) Copy the notes. Then listen again and complete them with the words in the green box.

About Molly
1 lives on ...
2 goes to school in ...
3 goes to school by ...
4 goes shopping in ...
5 best friend's name: ...
6 dog's name: ...

A Alex
B a farm
C Stratford
D Chipping Campden
E Missy
F bus

c) Now check your notes with a partner: *Molly lives ... She goes ... Her dog's name is ...*

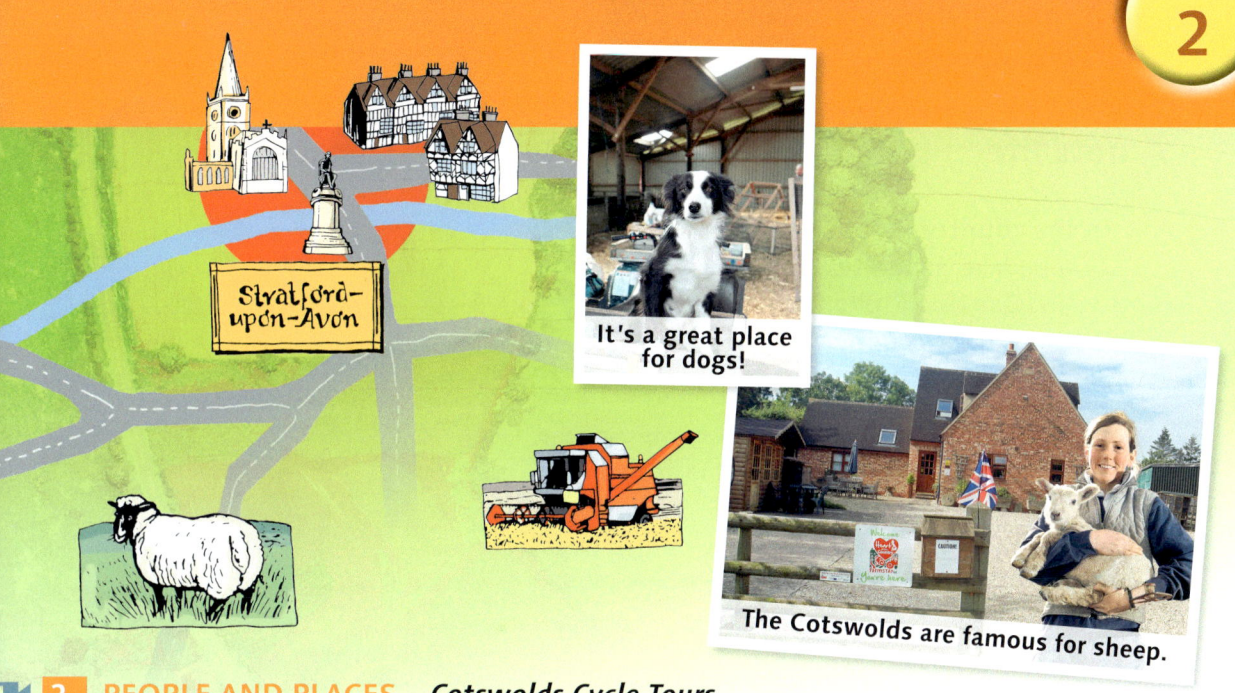

It's a great place for dogs!

The Cotswolds are famous for sheep.

2 PEOPLE AND PLACES   *Cotswolds Cycle Tours*

a) Look at these pictures. Which of the ten things can you see in the map and photos?

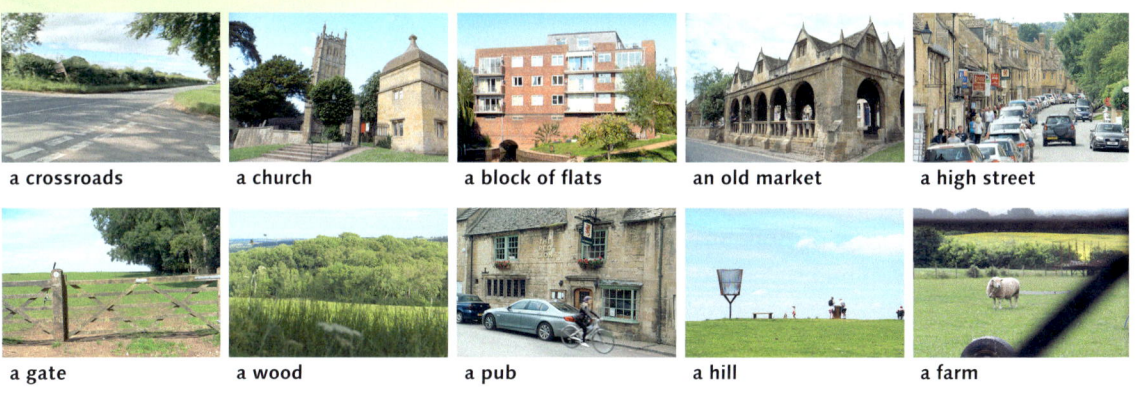

a crossroads   a church   a block of flats   an old market   a high street

a gate   a wood   a pub   a hill   a farm

b) Now watch the film. Which of the ten things was *not* in the film?

c) Look at the map of Chipping Campden.
Which route (red, green or blue) did Becky take? Watch the film again and check.

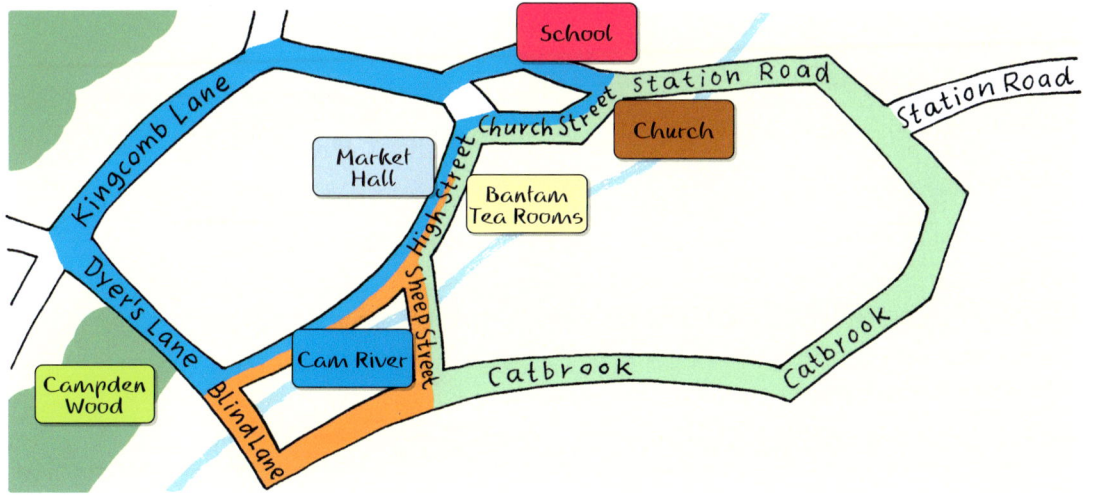

▸ *Workbook 1–2, p. 15*

A new life

🎧 1 In the country

a) ⭕ Rob Blake is from London. He's new in the Cotswolds. One day he phones his friend Alfie. Is Rob happy in the country? Why (not)?

Rob Blake   **Alfie Harper**

Rob	Hey Alfie. How are things in London?
Alfie	Hi Rob. All's good here. How are you? Are you busy?
Rob	You're joking! There's nothing to do here. This is the country.
Alfie	Oh come on! I like the country – remember!
Rob	Well ... we've bought a dog. His name is Wally. He's great.
Alfie	Cool!
Rob	And dad has started a new CCTV business. He has bought a new van. So he's happy.
Alfie	That's cool.
Rob	Mum is happy because she has found a job in the post office. And she has met nice people there.
Alfie	That's good. But you don't like your new life?
Rob	No – it sucks! The village is **really** small. There's **one** shop, the post office ... and that's all! No cinema, nothing! But school is OK.
Alfie	And have you met some nice girls???
Rob	No. Well ... No.
Alfie	I don't believe you!
Rob	Well, there's a girl on the school bus. She's a neighbour ... well, from the next farm. I've seen her, but I haven't spoken to her – yet!
Alfie	Sounds good!
Rob	Hey, I must go and cut the grass! What a pain!

COTSWOLD CCTV SERVICES

It sucks! and *What a pain!* are teenager talk.

It's not very good..

It sucks! What a pain!!

b) Read the dialogue again and finish these sentences.

1 Alfie still lives in ...
2 Wally is Rob's new ...
3 Rob's dad has a ... business.

4 Rob's village is really ...
5 Rob has seen a nice girl on ...
6 Rob now has to ..., but he doesn't want to!

c) What's new for Rob and his parents? Copy and complete the sentences.

> has bought • has found • has met • has seen • hasn't spoken • has started

1 Rob's dad ... a new business and he ... a new van.
2 Rob's mum ... a job at the post office and she ... nice people there.
3 Rob ... a girl on the school bus, but he ... to her yet.

More practice 1   p. 98

2 This isn't a park!

a) Look at the pictures. Then listen to **part 1** of the story and put pictures A–E in the right order.

A

B **ad at all times** Please close the gate.

C Heart of England Way

Come on, Wally!

D This isn't a park, you know!

OK, OK, take it easy!

E Come back, Wally!

b) Now listen to **part 1** and **part 2** of the story. Choose the correct answer.

1 Rob and Wally are   A in a park   B in a garden   C on a track   D at a zoo.
2 Wally is running after   A a cat   B a dog   C a sheep   D a rabbit.
3 The girl in the car is   A a friend   B a neighbour   C a sister   D a postwoman.
4 In the end the girl is   A friendlier   B worried   C scared   D angry.
5 The girl can drive   A on the farm   B on the road   C in the village   D in the city.
6 They'll meet again   A in town   B at school   C on the bus   D on the farm.

c) Who asks these questions – Rob or Molly?

1 Is that your car?
2 How old are you?
3 Can you drive?
4 Where are you from?
5 Do you like it here in Mickleton?

Listen to **part 2** of the story again and check your answers.

d) Find the right answers for the five questions in c). Say more than one word.

 p.99

Molly and the sheep

1 Molly is in the newspaper

a) Before you read: Look at the photo and the headline.
Who is the article about? Is it a happy or a sad story?

COTSWOLD POST

Well done Molly!

Last Wednesday Molly Taylor went to check her family's sheep near the village of Mickleton – but she found three of them in the river. Molly, 14, saw that she had to save them. First she quickly phoned home. But she couldn't wait for help. So brave Molly calmly walked into the water to help the sheep.

Later Molly said, "It wasn't dangerous for me because the water wasn't deep. But it was deep for the sheep. The sheep were really heavy because they were so wet. So I had to work hard."

Molly's father, John Taylor, spoke proudly about his daughter. "Molly did so well," he said.

Farmer's daughter, Molly Taylor, saved three sheep.

"She saved the sheep. We've never had an accident like this before."

The police think that dogs ran after the sheep and have asked people for help.

Police officer Dave Butler said: "Dogs often behave dangerously in fields where there are animals. Please tell us if you have seen dogs near the Taylors' farm."

b) Who was it? Match the people and animals (1–3) with actions from the green box.

1 Molly Taylor …
2 Molly's dad …
3 Dogs …

behave dangerously. • did well. • quickly phoned home. • spoke proudly about his daughter. • worked hard.

More practice 2 p. 99

More practice 3 p. 100

▸ *Language file 9, p. 144*

c) You saw a dog in the fields near Mickleton! Pick dog A or B.
Then tell the police about the dog. Your partner takes the role of the police.

Police __ What's your name?
You __ (give your name)
Police __ Can you spell that, please?
You __ (spell your name)
Police __ What's your address in Germany?
You __ (give your address)
Police __ Thanks. Can you describe the dog, please?
You __ Yes. The dog was … It had …

black / white / brown   long / short   leg / tail / ears

2 Can I take a message?

Rob wants to phone Molly.

a) Read and listen to the dialogue. Can he speak to her?

Mr Taylor	Hello.
Rob	Oh, hello. Is that the Taylors?
Mr Taylor	Yes, it is. Who's speaking?
Rob	This is Rob Blake. Can I talk to Molly please?
Mr Taylor	I'm sorry, Rob, Molly can't come to the phone right now. Can I take a message?
Rob	Oh yes, yes please. I read about Molly in the paper. I wanted to ask if she's OK. And I wanted to say "Well done."
Mr Taylor	That's very nice of you, Rob. I'll give her your message. She's fine now. I think she'll be at school tomorrow.
Rob	Great, I'll see her on the bus then. Thank you. Goodbye.
Mr Taylor	You're welcome. Bye.

b) Listen again. Then copy and complete the Taylors' notepad.

Messages

Who phoned?: ....

Wanted to
speak to: ....

Message: *Asked if Molly is ...*

3 ROLE-PLAY Talking on the phone

a) How can you say these things in English on the phone? Write your answers.
Look at exercise 2 for help.

1 Du bist am Telefon. Frage, mit wem du sprichst.
2 Sage, wer du bist.
3 Sage, dass du mit deinem Freund Adam sprechen möchtest.
4 Sage, dass er gerade nicht zum Telefon kommen kann.
5 Frage, ob du etwas ausrichten kannst.
6 Sage, dass du die Nachricht weitergeben wirst.

b) 👥 **Partner B:** Go to page 90.
Partner A: You're in England. You phone your host mother, Mrs Smith, because you won't be home at 4 pm. You're going on a trip and you'll be back at 8 pm.
First practise what you want to say:
Hello. This is ... Can I ... to Mrs Smith, please?
I won't ... at 4 o'clock.
I'm going ... trip.   I'll be ... at 8 o'clock.
Thank ...
Now phone partner B.

c) 👥 Copy the notepad. Then swap roles. Now you're the babysitter for the Smiths. Listen to your partner.
– Say Mr Smith can't come to the phone right now.
– Ask if you can take a message.
– Make notes on your notepad.

📞 **Messages**

Who phoned? _____

Wanted to
speak to: _____

Message: _____
_____
_____

🎧 1 I need help

Listen to the phone call. Are these sentences true or false?

1 Molly says she needs help.
2 Molly's dad is feeling well.
3 Rob can come now.
4 Rob is unhappy.

🎧 The country detectives

The country girl

Rob and Wally ran along the track and met Molly in her car. Then they all drove across the fields. Rob opened the gate when they came to a field with
5 lots of sheep. The sheep ran into the next field and Molly and her dog Missy came behind them.
"You're very good with the sheep, Molly," Rob said. Molly smiled. And Rob smiled too. He really liked her.

10 Bags in the bushes

Suddenly Wally put his nose into some bushes. "What is it, Wally?" Rob asked. Then he saw lots of big bags in the bushes. And they were full of rubbish.
15 "Molly, look at this," Rob shouted.
"Lots of people leave their rubbish here," she said angrily. "And the police can't catch them because they do it at night."
"I have an idea," Rob answered. "Dad could put
20 CCTV cameras on your farm. Then you could catch the stupid people! What a great advert for dad's business!"

Lights at night

Rob's dad was interested and the Taylors agreed
25 happily. On Saturday Rob and his dad put CCTV cameras in different places on the farm and a monitor in the farm office.
In the evening Molly's dad still didn't feel well, so he had to stay in bed. Molly and Rob watched
30 a DVD and then they checked the CCTV monitor. First there was nothing, but suddenly they saw a fox.
"Wow!" Rob said. "I've never seen a fox before."
"It has one of our chickens in its mouth!" Molly
35 shouted. "Come on!" They ran quickly to the chickens – but then they suddenly saw car lights!

A clever trick

"Rob," Molly said quietly, "you drive my car. Park at the end
of the track, in front of the gate, so they can't drive away.
I'll stay here and write down the car number."
Rob was a bit nervous. "Erm, Molly, last week I told you
I can drive …, but I can't really drive!"
"Oh Rob!" she said. "OK, I'll park the car. You stay here
and write down the number. Here's a pen."
Rob went nearer the lights. He wrote down the number
of the big black car. Then he went back to the farm
and waited for Molly.

Not so clever really

Later two police officers were at the Taylors' door. They spoke with
Molly's mother.
"Good evening. Do you have a car, number P399 DOJ?"
"That's my daughter's car," Mrs Taylor said. "Is there a problem?"
"Well, yes. We're trying to catch people who leave rubbish on your farm.
She parked her car at the end of the track and we can't go home."

That week there was an article in the
Cotswolds paper:

And Rob chatted on the internet with Alfie:

New business helps farmers

A new business in Mickleton has put CCTV
cameras on a farm to catch people who leave
their rubbish there. Lots of other farmers are
interested.
"It's a good idea," police officer Butler said. "But
if people see something, they should phone the

Rob:	Molly and I are good friends now.
Alfie:	Only good friends?
Rob:	Well …
Alfie:	And what about life in the country?
Rob:	It's great! I really like it now ☺.

2 ⬤ **You're a reporter!**  p.100

Put sentences A-H in the right order and tell the story for a newspaper.

A Rob ran to Molly's field with his dog.
B Molly phoned Rob.
C The two police officers couldn't drive home.
D The police said the CCTV was a good idea.
E Rob wrote the number of the car.
F Rob and Molly saw lights of a car at night.
G Rob's dad put CCTV cameras on the farm.
H Rob's dog, Wally, found some rubbish.

More practice 4 p.100

3 NOW YOU **What do *you* think?**

a) Read the sentences. Pick A or B, or write your own idea C.
1 Molly phoned Rob because A she needed help B she wanted to see Rob again C …
2 Molly's idea to park the car at the end of the track was A brave B stupid C …
3 Rob now likes life in the country because A he has a dog B he likes Molly C …

b) Compare with other students in your class. Did you have the same answers?

More practice 5 p.101

Talking about a picture

1 **In the town or in the country?**

A

in the foreground

B

in the background

a) Pick a picture (A or B) and describe it. Make notes. ► *Wordbank 2, p. 147*

1 Say where it is.

This is in a town / in the country.

2 What can you see?

I can see a van	in the middle of the picture.
There's a woman	on the left / on the right.
There are two horses	in the foreground / background.

3 What are the people doing?

A woman is	reading a … • chatting together. • waiting for … •
The men are	crossing the … • going shopping. • talking to … • …

4 Make a general comment.

I like I don't like	life in town the country	because	there are lots of … / there aren't any … you can meet … / go … / see … it's (too) quiet / noisy / busy / boring / …

b) Use your notes and prepare a short talk about your picture. Then practise your talk.

c) 👥 Now tell a partner about your picture.

Partner A:
Give your talk.
Remember steps
1–4 in the tip.

Partner B:
Listen to your partner's talk.
Does he / she talk about
points 1–4 in the tip?

Then swap roles.

> Remember the steps in 1 a):
> **1** say **where** it is,
> **2** say **what** you can see,
> **3** say what the people are **doing**,
> **4** make a general **comment**.

► *Skills file 9, p. 135*

Linkers and time phrases

 1 **Alfie's ideal place**

a) Alfie wrote this comment on the internet forum *My ideal place.*
Read his text. What does he think about London?

> Linkers and time phrases make your writing more interesting. You'll practise using them on this page.

▸ *Skills file 8, p. 133*

I came to London two years ago. At first I didn't really like it.
But now I think it's a great place. I'll tell you why.

In London you can go everywhere on the Tube or by bus.
That's cool because you don't need a car.

Also, I really like my neighbourhood. When I want to meet my friends,
I can walk to their houses. So we usually meet every evening.

And London is an amazing city for sport. I always go to football
games at the weekend.

So London is my ideal place to live.

b) Copy the table. Write the red words
in Alfie's comment in the table.

TIME WORDS	LINKERS
two years ago	But
...	...

 2   **Rob's ideal place**

a) Now read Rob's comment on the internet
forum. It doesn't have linkers and time phrases.
Write it again. Put the linkers and time phrases
from the box into the text at numbers 1–8.

> Also • because • But • For example • So •
> last August • every Saturday • At first

I moved to the Cotswolds (1). (2) I didn't like it here. (3) now I think it's cool.
The people are friendly. (4) the neighbours help you if you have a problem.
(5) the towns in the Cotswolds are nice. Stratford is a famous town.
I go to Stratford with my friends (6) (7) there are great shops there.
(8) the Cotswolds are my ideal place to live.

b) Is Rob happy in the Cotswolds now?

 3 **NOW YOU**  **p.101**

Now write your comment for the internet
forum *My ideal place*. Write as many sentences
as you can. Put your text in your DOSSIER.
Ideas: Is it in a town or in the country?
Why do you like it? What are the people like?

> Düsseldorf is a big city in the west of
> Germany. My uncle and aunt live there,
> and I think it's a great place to live.
> I like the shops ...

1 READING

Read sentences 1–5 and the notices A–F below. Then pick the best notice for each sentence.
You won't need one notice.

1 You're a tourist in the Cotswolds and you want to listen to music.
2 You're in the country and you have a problem with your bike.
3 You're 17 and you love sport.
4 You're tired and hungry. So you want a place to stay and something to eat.
5 Your little brother or sister would like a new pet.

A

KITTENS – 9 WEEKS OLD
ALL BOYS
NEED LOVING HOMES
READY TO GO.
01386 ~~xxxxx~~

B

The Bantam Tea Rooms

We offer home made cakes, biscuits, scones, tea cakes and toast all day (10 am – 5 pm).
At lunchtime we serve home made soup and sandwiches.

We also have a variety of teas, coffees and hot chocolate, and soft drinks, including local apple juice.
In summer months, sit in our garden and enjoy a slice of cake or a cream tea.

We also have rooms and can offer bed and breakfast accommodation. Please ask for details.

C

MOBILE BICYCLE
service and repair

We come to you.
Most services carried out on site at home/work.
Prices from £15 per bike.
Collection and delivery services available.
Call David
07927 ~~xxxxx~~

D

Listen to *North Cotswolds Community Radio* for up-to-the minute news, event information, lots of music and much more.

NCCR
Entertainment you'll love
Information you'll need

E

Mickleton Rangers FC

Training at 7 pm every Thursday at sports field Stratford Road.

If interested, phone Lewy: 841408

Players must be 16 or over.

F

Help! We need more actors for our Christmas pantomime, Dick Whittington.
Village Hall, Mondays 7.30 pm
The Mickleton Players

2 MEDIATION   On holidays in the Cotswolds

a) You're on holidays in the Cotswolds with your friend Arif. But Arif doesn't understand a lot of English. Look at the *Bantam Tea Rooms* notice and answer his questions – in German.

1 Wann haben sie geöffnet?
2 Es heißt *Tea Rooms*. Gibt es nur Tee oder auch andere Getränke? Welche?
3 Es ist jetzt Mittagszeit. Ich habe Hunger, möchte aber keinen Kuchen essen. Was gibt es sonst?
4 Es ist warm heute. Können wir draußen sitzen?
5 Es ist schön hier. Kann man hier vielleicht übernachten?

b) Tell your friend the most important information about *Mobile Bicycle* – in German.

▶ *Skills file 11, p. 137*

▶ *Text file 2, pp. 118–120*

1 A visit to grandad's farm

In this film our four friends from Unit 1 visit a farm.

Before you watch: Look at the photos in exercise 2, then think about these three questions:

1 What are the names of the four friends?
2 Where do the friends live? What will be new for them on the farm? Collect ideas.
3 Do you think they will like life on the farm? Why (not)?

2 Chill in the country

a) Watch the film.

b) 👥 Now work with a partner. Copy and complete the captions. Write as much as you can.

Scene 1: The four friends plan a visit to …

Scene 2: The friends arrive at …

Scene 3: The kids have …

Scene 4: But first they have to …

Scene 5: In the evening they …

Scene 6: The next morning they …

3 NOW YOU   What do *you* think?

a) Read the five sentences below.

1 The kids had a good time in the country.
2 They enjoyed the work on the farm.
3 Alfie's grandad wasn't very nice.
4 The kids had lots of fun in the evening.
5 They'll all come back again next weekend.

b) 👥 Now talk about the sentences with a partner. Do you agree?

● Say why you agree or don't agree.

I agree because …   I don't agree because …

Yes
I agree.
That's true.
You're right.

No
I don't agree.
That's rubbish.

1 Molly's questionnaire

Students in Molly's class are finding out about other students in their class.

a) Copy Molly's questionnaire.

		me	Partner 1: Hana	Partner 2: Ali	Partner 3: Noah
Have you ever	visited a farm?	lots of times!!			
	ridden a donkey?	once			
	been on a plane?	twice			
	moved house?	no			

b) Listen to Molly. Complete the answers for her three partners.

c) Now read her report. Find three mistakes in it.

> Two students have visited a farm and I live on a farm. But Noah hasn't visited a farm.
> Only one person has ridden a donkey – me! The others have never ridden a donkey.
> We have all been on a plane. Hana has been on a plane five times.
> Two students have moved house. I haven't moved house.

2 The present perfect

a) Complete the rule.

Das *present perfect* besteht aus zwei Teilen:

I You	have		visited a farm once.
			never mov... house.
He She It	has	**+**	
			been on a plane once.
We They	have		rid... a donkey twice.

Regelmäßige Verben erhalten die Endung ...

Einige Verben haben unregelmäßige Formen. Diese musst du lernen, z.B. *be* – ..., *ride* – ...

Mit dem *present perfect* sagst du, dass du etwas schon einmal, mehrmals oder noch nie gemacht hast. Signalwörter sind:
ever, never, once, twice, lots of times.

Statt ... kann auch die Kurzform *'ve* stehen.

b) Copy and complete the table for regular verbs.

I work	I've worked
I start	I've ...
I finish	...
I text	...
I open	...
I cook	...

c) Look at the list of irregular verbs on page 200 and complete the table.

I buy	I've bought
I meet	I've ...
I speak	...
I have	I've had
I am	I've been
I ride	...
I see	...
I find	...

▶ *Language file 4, p. 141*

3 Molly and Rob

a) Read the sentences and pick the right form of the verb.
1 I know that Rob has / have seen a fox once.
2 And I know that Molly has / have saved sheep from a river.
3 Molly and Rob has / have been to Stratford lots of times.
4 Rob and his sister has / have lived in a block of flats.
5 And Molly? No, she hasn't / haven't lived in a block of flats.

b) ○ **NOW YOU** What about you? Write six sentences about yourself. // ● p.102
I've ... once / a few times / lots of times. I've never ...

ridden a horse

spoken to a star

been to a beach

had a disaster

found money in the street

worked on a farm

More practice 6 p. 102

4 YOUR TASK Find out about students in your class

a) Make a questionnaire with four questions.
○ Use the questions below. ● Make your own questions.
Put your own information under *me*. Leave space for three partners.

		me	Partner 1: ...	Partner 2: ...	Partner 3: ...
Have you ever	lost money?	once			
	met a famous person?	no			
	been to the sea?	no			
	seen a game of rugby?	no			

No, I haven't.

Yes, I have. Lots of times!

b) 👥 **Walk around:** Ask the questions and make notes of your partners' answers.

c) Look at your notes and write what you have found out. Write sentences like this:

Only I Two / Three students	have	visited ... ridden... met ... been to ... had ... found ... talked ... played ...
One student / Nobody	has	

STOP! CHECK! GO!

Ein Lösungsblatt für die Aufgaben 1–4 kannst du von deiner Lehrerin/deinem Lehrer erhalten. Die Audio-Datei für Aufgabe 6 findest du online bei den Dateien zum Workbook.

1   WORDS   Town and country words

a) ⦿ Copy the diagram. Then put the words from the green box into your diagram.

block of flats • bushes • church • crossroads • farm • farm gate • *field* • high street • park • *pub* • sheep • stadium • station • track • van • river • village • wood

b) Can you find more words for your diagram?

c) 👥 Partner check: Compare your diagram with other students.

> Where is post office in your diagram?

> In the middle. You can find post offices in the town and in the country.

> Oh yes, that's right!

2   WORDS   How many differences can you find?

Partner B: Go to page 90.   **Partner A:** Look at this page.

a) ⦿ Make a list of eight things in the picture and write where they are:
in the foreground / background, in the middle, on the left / right, behind, in front of, next to, near, …

Things in the picture	Where in my picture?	In my partner's picture
a wood	in the background, on the left	
	…	

b) 👥 Now talk to your partner about your pictures.
Find at least five differences. Make notes in the third column of your table.

> There's a … in the background on the left.

> In my picture it's on the right.

3 LANGUAGE   A visit to *Cotswold Farm Park*

What's the missing word: *has* or *have*?

Rob's sisters Jodie and Evie are at *Cotswold Farm Park*. They … (1) seen
lots of things in the park. They're excited because Adam Henson … (2)
come into the farm park.

They know Adam, the owner of the park, from TV.

Jodie _____	Oh hello, Adam. We always watch you on TV!
Adam _____	Hi! … (3) you had a nice day so far? What … (4) you seen?
Evie _____	We … (5) just been to see the rabbits. They're so cute.
Jodie _____	And the pigs! I … (6) never been so near a pig before. They're cool.
Adam _____	Well, enjoy your visit. Nice to see you. Bye.
Jodie + Evie _	Bye, Adam.

Adam Henson

4   Telephone language

a) You're a tourist. You phone *Mobile Bicycle*.
What do you say? What does the other person say?
Write the dialogue.

> **MOBILE BICYCLE**
> **service and repair**
> We come to you.
> **Call David 07927** ~~542990~~

Tourist:	Mobile bicycle:
Hello. Can / I / please / to / David / talk /? (*Sage hallo und frage, ob du mit David sprechen kannst.*)	to the phone / he / can't / I'm sorry / come / right now. (*Sage, dass David gerade nicht ans Telefon kommen kann.*)
	I / a message / take / Can /? (*Frage, ob du etwas ausrichten kannst.*)
a problem / I / my bike / have / with (*Du hast ein Problem mit deinem Rad.*) Can / David / me / help /? (*Frage, ob David helfen kann.*)	give / your message / him / I'll (*Sage, dass du es ausrichten wirst*)
	your name / What's / where / and / are you? (*Frage nach dem Namen des Anrufers und wo er oder sie gerade ist.*)
(*Sage deinen Namen und buchstabiere ihn.*) in Chipping Campden / outside / I'm / the church (*Sage, wo du bist.*)	be / in an hour / David / will / there (*Sage, David wird in einer Stunde da sein.*)
(*Bedanke dich und verabschiede dich.*)	(*Sage: „Bitte, gern geschehen", und verabschiede dich.*)

b) 👥 Practise the dialogue with a partner. Swap roles.

5 A picture story

a) Look at the pictures A–F and put them in the right order.

A

- Mr Jones' dog found rubbish in the field next to the sheep.

B

Mr Jones phoned Rob's dad. "I'm busy", said Rob's dad • "I can come on Saturday."

C

- Mr Jones, a farmer, found a sheep in his field. It couldn't stand. • Its leg was sore.

D

- Mr Jones and his family talked about the problem.

E

- Mr and Mrs Jones watched the monitors. • They saw two people and a car.

F

- Rob's dad came with his cameras. • Mr and Mrs Jones put CCTV cameras in the fields.

b) Partner check: Now compare your answers with a partner.
- I think picture B is number 1.
- I don't agree! I think picture ... is number 1.

c) WRITING Copy and complete the story in A–F.

• = Write a time phrase • = Write a linker (*and, because, so, but, when, ...*)

One day in September, Mr Jones, a farmer, found a sheep ...

d) ◉ **WRITING** Finish the story. For help, look at the story on pages 34–35.

Mrs Jones ...

Mr Jones drove his tractor ...

"OK. We'll take these men".

6 LISTENING   Is it better to live in the country or in the city?

a) You're going to listen to a radio programme. Before you listen, copy these names in a list:

> *Anna:*
> *Thomas:*
> *Nina:*
> *Karan:*
> *Joe:*

b) Now listen and find out:
Where do the callers live?
(Make notes: co = country, ci = city)
Do they like living there?
(likes it = ☺, doesn't like it = ☹)
Example: *Anna: co, ☹*

c) Listen again and write down why they like it or don't like where they live:
Anna: co, ☹, bus to school – an hour

7 👥 APPOINTMENTS   Have you ever met a famous footballer?

a) Copy the table. Think of three more questions and add them. (They can be funny!)

Have you ever ...	me	1 o'clock partner	2 o'clock partner	3 o'clock partner
played tennis?				
visited another country?				
been to hospital?				
seen a real elephant?				
spoken to a famous person?				
...				

b) 👥 Answer the questions for yourself. Then make an appointment with three partners and ask them your questions. Note their answers. Yes = ✓ or no = ✗.
Have you ever ...   – Yes, I have. (✓) / No, I haven't. (✗)

c) ⬤ 👥 Tell another partner / the class what you have found out:
Malte has (never) been to hospital. Svenja has ...

8 My learner log
Copy and complete your learner log. Then put it in your DOSSIER.

My learner log for Unit 2

Now I can ...
– talk about pictures: 😆 🙂 😣
– take or give a message on the phone: ...
– say where I have been: ...
– say what I have never done: ...
– use time phrases and linkers: 😆 😐 😣

After Unit 2
– I know a bit about country life in the Cotswolds.
– I know some English teen language.
– These pages were easy: ...
– These pages were difficult: ...

After Unit 2 my English is: GREAT! 👍 / OK 👐 / NOT VERY GOOD 👎

Plans for next weekend – using the future tense

1 Plans

a) Read this email from your English friend Andy. What does he want to do in August?

b) The future

Die Zukunftsform bildest du mit *will* oder *'ll*.

1 Copy four examples from Andy's email.

Verneinungen verwenden das Wort *won't*.

2 Copy two examples from Andy's email.

Fragen beginnen mit *Will…?*

3 Copy one example from Andy's email.

▶ *Language file 5, p. 142*

Hi Burak!

Hooray! We have a week's holiday!
I think I'll stay at home today. Maybe I'll be good and tidy my room. But tomorrow I'll go into town with some friends, and in the evening we'll watch the new Sherlock Holmes film. I hope it won't be too American!

And next Friday I'll start my new job. I'll get up early and do my first paper round. I hope it won't rain!

I'd really like to come and see you in Germany this week, but I won't have the money. But I'm sure I'll have more money in summer, so maybe I could visit you in August. When will your summer holidays begin?
Do you have plans for this weekend? Will you stay at home, or will you visit your grandma again?

Best wishes, Andy

2 100 weekend activities

a) ◯ What will you do next weekend?
Write ten sentences with the words from the table.

> Hier sammelst du Ideen für Wortschatz, den du in ex. 4 benutzen kannst.

Maybe I'll	buy • do • go • make • meet • start • travel • tidy • visit • watch	to Berlin • my grandparents • some new clothes • into town • my new job • a special dinner • a film • my friends • my homework • my room

b) Think: Write sentences with the same verbs, but with different endings.
Write as many as you can.

1 *Maybe I'll buy a new laptop / tickets for a concert / …*
2 *I think I'll make a cake / a birthday card / …*
3 *I'm sure we'll go to the water park.*

c) 👥 Pair: Compare with a partner.

d) Share: Write your ideas on the board.

Do you have a **100** ideas for weekend activities?

3 The weather

Andy lives in Leeds, in the north of England.
On Monday you look on the internet and find the five day weather forecast for Leeds.

Today: Mon	Tues	Wed	Thurs	Fri
🌧️ 10° C	☁️ 15° C	☀️ 18° C	🌧️ 12° C	☀️ 18° C
🎏 5	🎏 6	🎏 1	🎏 15	🎏 14

a)  Look at the online information. What will the weather be like in Leeds this week?

1 It will be sunny / cloudy tomorrow in Leeds,
   but it will / won't rain.
2 Tomorrow will be warmer / colder than today.
3 On Wednesday it will be sunny / cloudy.
4 And it won't be windy / sunny on Wednesday.
5 On Thursday it will be rainy / foggy and
   it will / won't be very windy.
6 Thursday will be warmer / colder than Wednesday.

b) Andy will do his paper round on Friday.
What can you say about the weather on Friday?

Friday will …
It will …
It won't …
I think it will be a good / bad day for Andy's paper round because …

4 NOW YOU

a) Read Andy's email in exercise 1 again. What questions does he ask you?

b) Write to Andy and answer his questions. Write at least six sentences.

Hi Andy
Thanks … I hope we'll meet …
My holidays start …, so maybe you could come …
You ask for my plans …
On Saturday I'll…
On Sunday …
How is your new job?
I hope …
…

> Say what you will do or what you won't do.
> You can find ideas in Andy's letter and in exercise 2.

🔵 Maybe you can also write what you did yesterday (1–2 sentences). Then you'll need the *simple past*. Look at pages 26–27 for help.
Example:
I didn't read your email yesterday because I went to a party. It was good fun, but it was late when I got home.

c) 👥 Partner check: Show your email to a partner and check your partner's email.
Check especially the verbs with *will* and *won't*.

🎧 1 About Liverpool

a) Listen to six sound files. Match them with **six** of the pictures of Liverpool (A–H).

b) Listen again and pick the right answer.

1 When was the Titanic disaster? **A** 1900 **B** 1912 **C** 1932.
2 What's the colour of Liverpool FC? **A** white **B** blue **C** red.
3 When did people start to come from China to Liverpool? In the **A** 1850s **B** 1900s **C** 1950s.
4 Ships from Liverpool took slaves from Africa to **A** Europe **B** China **C** America.
5 What can you find in Liverpool ONE? **A** a harbour **B** a museum **C** shops and cafes.
6 Lots of people from Liverpool went to America and **A** Turkey **B** Australia **C** Germany.

E

F

H

G

The ferry across the river Mersey

2 PEOPLE AND PLACES   The Beatles

Watch the film and find out:

a) **What are the names of the four Beatles?**

... Lennon   ... Mc Cartney

... Harrison   ... Starr

b) **When did the Beatles sing together?**

– In the 1960s.
– In the 1980s.
– In the 1990s.

c) **What are the full song titles?**

– She ... you, yeah, yeah, yeah!
– Eight days a ...
– Let it ...
– Baby, you can drive my ...

▶ Workbook 2–3, p. 29

Ben is in trouble

🎧 1 **Trouble at school**

a) 👥 Talk to a partner about the pictures.
What's the right order of the pictures?   **More help** p.103

> I think picture ... is first.

> Yes, and then it's picture ...

> Really? I don't agree. I think picture ... comes before picture ...

b) Now listen to the story and check.

c) 🔘 Read sentences 1–4. Match them with pictures A–D. You can listen again and check your answers.

1 "You aren't allowed to sell junk food."
2 "A packet of crisps, please."
3 "Hey, what are you kids doing?"
4 It was a very heavy school bag today.

d) 🔘 Listen again and finish these sentences.   **// ●** p.104

1 Ben does not want to meet   **A** his friends   **B** the teachers   **C** the principal.
2 He tries to sell   **A** sausages   **B** chicken   **C** crisps.
3 **One** packet of crisps costs   **A** 50p   **B** 55p   **C** £1.
4 When the teacher comes Ben puts his bag behind   **A** his bicycle   **B** his friend   **C** his back.
5 Ms Hall takes Ben to   **A** the classroom   **A** the principal's office   **C** his father.
6 At this school you aren't allowed to   **A** sell   **B** bring   **C** buy   crisps and chocolate bars.

2 A letter from school

a) The principal asks Ben's dad to do two things. What are they?

b) Find these words in the letter. Then pick the right meaning from the box.

1 sell
2 healthy food
3 junk food
4 less
5 school rules
6 yours sincerely

A best wishes
B opposite of *more*
C sweets, crisps, burgers, etc.
D what the school says you must do
E opposite of *buy*
F food that is good for you

South Liverpool High School

Monday, 10th January

Dear Mr Chung

We only sell healthy food here at school. This is very important because young people are eating more and more junk food. We want them to eat less junk food and as much healthy food as possible.

Today your son, Ben, brought junk food to school and sold it to other students. This is against our school rules. Please talk to Ben about this. If he sells junk food in school again, I will send him home for a week.

Please come to the school, and we will of course give you Ben's junk food.

Yours sincerely

Roger Bell

3 Trouble at home

Read what Ben's father said. Then put Ben's answers in the right order and act the dialogue.

Dad

Ben, what happened at school?
What sort of food?
Why did you sell junk food?
But it's against the school rules!
You must never do this again, Ben!

Ben

– Oh, Dad. It was nothing.
  I sold some food at school.
– I know! I'm really sorry, Dad.
– Er ... crisps.
– OK, Dad.
– I wanted to make some money.

4 WORDS

a) Match the pictures with words in the box. Example: *A – cereal bars   B – ...*

- biscuits
- cereal bars
- chocolate bars
- chips
- energy drinks
- fruit
- hot dogs
- sweets

More practice 1 p. 104

b) 👥 **Walk around:** Talk to other students about food at your school. What do *you* think? And what do *they* think? ▶ *Wordbank 3, p. 148*

We can't buy ice cream at school. I think that's bad.

Really? I think ...

More practice 2 p. 105

Good at selling things

1   **What's wrong?**

a) 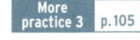 How does Ben feel? And can Mrs Fox, his business studies teacher, help him?
Read the dialogue and find out.

Mrs Fox — Oh, Ben, I'd like to talk to you, please.

Ben — Yes, Miss?

Mrs Fox — You aren't as active in class as you were last term. What's wrong?

Ben — Well, Miss, I'm not doing very well at school this term.

Mrs Fox — But everybody is good at something. I hear that you're the best salesperson in the school!

Ben — Ha, ha, ha, Miss. Very funny!

Mrs Fox — Seriously, Ben. I think you could be good at business.

Ben — If I sell things at school, I'll be in trouble again.

Mrs Fox — You shouldn't sell junk food. Look … I've heard of a competition. It's for people who are interested in business. Perfect for you!

Ben — It sounds good, Miss. But I don't know what I can sell.

Mrs Fox — If you take part in the competition, I'll help you as much as I can.

Ben — I'll think about it, Miss.

Mrs Fox — You'll find more information if you look in the school newsletter.

b) Which sentences of Mrs Fox tell you …
1 that she wants to chat with Ben?
2 that Ben isn't taking part in her lessons very much this term?
3 that she knows Ben has tried to sell junk food?
4 that she wants to help Ben?
5 where he can read about the competition?   More practice 3   p.105

c) WORDS

Look again at the dialogue in 1a) and find the missing words.
Each word has only **two** letters.
1 Ben, I'd like to talk … you, please.
2 Ben isn't … active in class … he was last term.
3 Mrs Fox says that Ben could be good … business.
4 … Ben sells things at school, he'll be … trouble.
5 But if Ben takes part in the competition, Mrs Fox will help him … much … she can.
6 Ben will find more information … he looks … the school newsletter.

2 A competition

a) Read about the competition. What must students do?

SOUTH LIVERPOOL HIGH SCHOOL
NEWSLETTER

BIZ 4 KIDZ – a school competition

The competition:
· Work in teams. Teams begin with £75.
· Try to make as much money as you can.
· Teams who make the most money win.

On TV: The TV programme BIZ 4 KIDZ will film you at school. So if you take part, you'll be on TV.

The prize: If you win the competition, your team will visit London for a weekend!

Talk to Mrs Fox today about your ideas for a business!

b) Sentences 1–6 are wrong. Read the newsletter again and correct the sentences.

1 You take part alone.
2 You try to make £75.
3 Teams who make £75 win the competition.
4 If you take part, you'll go to London.
5 If you win, your team will go to the USA.
6 Phone the TV people if you want to take part.

3 YOUR TASK Are you good at business?

Make teams of three or four. Each team has to think of a good business idea and present it on a poster.

Step 1 Ideas
Decide what you can make or sell.
Find a name for your business.
Decide where you can sell.

Step 2 Money
Decide these things in your team:

We need:	Cost?	We can sell:	Price?	Profit:
50 balloons	4 €	50 balloons	1 € per balloon	50 €
pens	5 €			– 9 €
	Total: 9 €			Total: 41 €

Step 3 Present your business plan More help p.105
Make a poster with your business plan. Then present it to the class. Vote for the best idea.
Here are some ideas for your presentation:

BIZ 4 KIDZ
Our business plan:
Make and sell animal balloons
What do we need?
Balloons, pens
How much will they cost?
50 balloons cost 4 euros.

Here's our business plan. It's for animal balloons.

We think that we can sell …

We must buy …

1 Before you read

Match the captions with pictures 1–5.

a) Not many people want to buy cakes.   b) Show me the photo!
c) A good talk with dad   d) A messy kitchen   e) At the market

🎧 Something special

1   Ben looked around the kitchen. There was flour everywhere.
And there was a broken egg on the table.
"If Dad comes home now, I'll be in trouble," Ben thought.
Then Ben's dad came home. He was earlier than usual.
5   "What has happened to this kitchen?" he asked. He looked
angry.
"Take it easy, Dad," Ben said. "I made these cupcakes with my
friends. It's for a business competition at school. If we win, …"

But Ben's father wasn't impressed.
10   "Forget the competition," he said. "You have to work hard at
school. If you work hard at school, you'll get a good job."
"But Dad, I want to leave school as soon as I can – at 16.
I want to work in the shop with you," Ben answered.
Ben's father sat down. "Listen, Ben," he said. "Your grandfather

15   left China when he was a boy. He came to Liverpool and worked
hard. And I left school when I was 16. Now I have to work seven
days a week in the shop!"
"Dad," Ben said. "I don't want to hear these boring old stories!"
"But you can learn from them!" his dad answered. He was
20   angry now. "You aren't going to leave school at 16. You're going
to work hard at school and get a better job!"
Ben and his dad didn't talk again that evening.

The next day Ben and his friends brought the cupcakes to
school. But in an hour they only sold six cakes. What a disaster!
25   Ben was very fed up at home that evening. His dad felt it.
"I'm sorry that I was so negative last night," he said.
"Thanks, Dad," Ben said. Then he told his father about the
disaster.

"Please try a cupcake, Dad," he said. "I have 44 cakes here!"
30   Ben's dad laughed. He took a cake and tried it.
"Hmmm, it's good," he said. "But it isn't good enough!"
"What do you mean, Dad?" he asked.
"Well, I mean it's as good as the cupcakes in my shop. But if you
want to sell your cakes, they'll have to be something special!"
35   "You're right, Dad. I'll think about that," Ben said.

The next day Ben took the bus to school. He remembered his father's words. How could the cupcakes be 'something special'? Then the bus stopped outside a music
40 club, and Ben saw a poster. "Maybe this is an idea for our business," he thought. He took a photo. When the other kids saw the photo,
45 they were very excited.
"We can do something with this," they all agreed.

BEATLES PARTY

• at the Cavern Club, Liverpool
• wear Beatles clothes
• dance to Beatles music

On the day of the competition, lots of schools from Liverpool sent a team to a market in the city centre. They tried to sell as much as they could. The team with the
50 biggest profit could stay in the competition and represent Liverpool. Ben was very excited about his team's new idea. What was their idea? And could they win the competition?

If you want to find out, listen to the radio programme in 3.

2 ⭕ What's the right answer? // ⬤ p.106

Copy the sentences and complete them correctly – Ⓐ, Ⓑ, Ⓒ or Ⓓ.
1 Ben's dad was unhappy at first because Ⓐ Ben ate the cakes. Ⓑ Ben had no friends. Ⓒ the kitchen was messy. Ⓓ the cakes were bad.
2 Ben's dad thinks school is Ⓐ important. Ⓑ not important. Ⓒ a waste of time. Ⓓ easy.
3 Ben's dad thought the cakes were Ⓐ fantastic. Ⓑ better than the cakes in his shop. Ⓒ terrible. Ⓓ OK, but could be better.
4 Ben got his new idea from Ⓐ his friends. Ⓑ Mrs Fox. Ⓒ a poster. Ⓓ a text message.

More practice 4 p.106

🎧 3 The end of the story

a) ⭕ Listen to the radio programme. Who won the Liverpool competition?
b) Listen to the programme again. Put pictures A–D in the right order.

A Woodlands High School

B King Richard High School

C South Liverpool High School

c) Listen again. **More help** p.106
Note what the three teams sold and what profit they made.

D BIZ 4 KIDZ - Liverpool Second prize

Beatlemania cakes £1!
Healthy!
made with organic eggs and flour

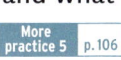
More practice 5 p.106

1 Natasha Jonas

a) First read the notes.

<u>Natasha Jonas</u>
Where she is from: _____
Sports: _____ and _____
In 2012: _____
Why she is special now: _____
What's bad about boxing: _____
What's good about boxing: _____

> When you read a text, it's useful to take notes. They help you to find out the most important information.

b) Now read the article about Natasha Jonas. Work with a partner and find out: Is the underlined information useful for the notes above or not? *1 not useful   2 …*

Liverpool girls want to be like Tasha!

1 Natasha Jonas, who was <u>born in 1984,</u> is from
2 <u>Toxteth in Liverpool</u> and she's a top British
3 sportswoman. She started as a <u>footballer,</u> but
4 then she changed to <u>boxing.</u>

Female boxers weren't allowed to fight in the
5 Olympics <u>before 2012.</u> But at the <u>London</u>
6 <u>Olympics</u> in 2012, Tasha was one of three British
7 women boxers <u>in the British Olympic team.</u>

8 Natasha is a <u>great role model for young people</u>
<u>in Liverpool.</u> Her motto is: 'Respect your talent.'
In other words, find what you're good at and be
the best you can. For her it was boxing.

9 Of course, some people think <u>people shouldn't box.</u>
10 They say that <u>boxers can get hurt.</u> That's true, but
11 footballers and <u>rugby players can get hurt too.</u>

Lots of girls watched Natasha and the other female
boxers at the Olympics and they saw that <u>boxing</u>
12 <u>makes you fit and strong.</u> And now they want to
be like Tasha!

c) Copy and complete the notes about Natasha.

d) ◉ Use your notes and give a short talk about Natasha.

▶ *Skills file 10, p. 136*

> To find out the most important information in a text:
> – Read the text.
> – Underline **important** facts for your task.
> – Write **short** notes.

▶ *Skills file 4, p. 127*

Giving opinions – for or against

1 **Two comments about Natasha and boxing**

a) Read the two comments about the article on page 56 and answer the questions:

1 Who doesn't like boxing?
2 Who thinks Natasha is a great person?

> I think that the article about Natasha is very interesting for lots of reasons.
>
> In my opinion Tasha is an amazing woman. She is a really good role model for young people. I also think that Natasha looks good.
>
> In a word, I would like to be like Tasha!
>
> Hannah, Liverpool

> When you write a comment, follow these three steps:
> • Give your opinion.
> • Then give reasons.
> • Think of a good ending.

> I really don't like boxing. I don't think that it should be an Olympic sport.
>
> The first thing is that boxing is dangerous. Even Natasha says that. And the second thing is that it's violent. In my opinion people shouldn't fight!
>
> I really hope that young people will prefer different sports.
>
> Sam, London

b) Read Hannah's and Sam's comments again. Find the English phrases for:

1 Ich denke, dass …
2 Meiner Meinung nach ist Tasha …
3 Ich denke auch, dass …

4 Kurz gefasst möchte ich …
5 Und zweitens ist es …
6 Ich hoffe sehr, dass …

2 **NOW YOU**

○ Write your own comment on Natasha and boxing.
● Choose your own sport and write a comment about it.   More help p.107

a) Write a first draft. Follow the three steps *(opinion – reasons – ending).*

I think	boxing is a great / stupid sport for women.
In my opinion	it's a violent sport and women shouldn't fight.
	it makes you fit and strong.
	women can do the same sports as men.
I also think that	other sports are more interesting.
	other sports make you fit.
	boxing is very popular with men and women.
I really hope that	more women will start boxing.
	all boxing will stop.
	boxing for women will stop.

> **Remember:**
> • Use sentences from the comments in exercise 1, but change some words:
> *She is a really good role model.*
> *=> She is a terrible role model.*
> • Use linkers:
> *I think boxing is a great sport. It's exciting.*
> *=> I think boxing is a great sport because it's exciting.*

b) Partner check: **Read your partner's comment and check:**

1 Did your partner follow the three steps *(opinion – reasons– ending)*?
2 Did he / she use phrases from exercise 1 *(In my opinion, I think, …)*?
3 Did he / she use linkers *(because / and / so …)*?

c) Now correct and rewrite your comment. Then put it in your DOSSIER.

▶ *Skills file 8, pp. 132–134*

1   At the tourist office

Two German tourists are at a tourist office in Liverpool.
The boy doesn't speak English well.

a) Look at the poster and read the boy's questions in German.

b) Now read questions 1–4. There is often more than one way of asking the same question.
With a partner, decide which **two** ways are correct.

GREAT FERRIES
Take a tour across the
the River Mersey today.

Adults: £8.00   Family: £20.50

1   Excuse me, please,
-   **A** are there cheaper tickets for students?
-   **B** we're students. Can we get less expensive tickets?
-   **C** can students buy tickets?

2   And can you tell me:
-   **A** how long is the tour, please?
-   **B** how is the tour, please?
-   **C** how long is the trip on the ferry?

3   And can you also tell me, please,
-   **A** is there a cafe on the ferry?
-   **B** do you sit inside or outside on the ferry?
-   **C** can we sit inside on the boat?

4   And one more question, please.
-   **A** We only have euros. Is that OK?
-   **B** Where can we get euros?
-   **C** Can we pay in euros?

> Und frage bitte auch, wie lange die Tour dauert.

> Kannst du herausfinden, ob es für Schüler billigere Karten gibt?

> Ich möchte auch noch wissen, ob man auf der Fähre drinnen oder draußen sitzt.

> Oh, und frage, ob wir in Euros bezahlen können.

c) Now listen to the dialogue.
Which questions do you hear –
A, **B** or **C**?   [More practice 6   p.108]

> Es ist wichtig, höflich zu sein! Sage z.B.:
> *Excuse me, please, ...*
> *Can you tell me, please, ...*
> *And one more question, please, ...*
> Und sage immer *please* und *thank you*!

2   ▢ The man in the tourist office   [// ● p.108]

a) Listen to the dialogue again.
This time, listen to the man in the tourist office. What are the right answers?
1   If you're under 15, a ticket is only   **A** £2.50   **B** £4.50   **C** £4.75.
2   The next ferry leaves at   **A** 10.00   **B** 11.00   **C** 11.30.
3   You can sit inside **or** outside. Outside you   **A** pay more   **B** pay less   **C** see more.
4   There's a bank near here, in   **A** Water Street   **B** Walton Street   **C** Warbury Street.

b) Now give your partner the information – in German. Then listen and check.
Der Mann sagt, dass die Karten nur ..., wenn wir ...
Die nächste Fähre ...   Wir können ...   Es gibt eine Bank ...

▶ *Skills file 11, p. 137*

1   The 'SW6 Olympics'

a) Before you watch: Look at the photos of Sam, Tally, Ruby and Alfie.
Who is in which photo? And what will you see in this film?

A A football match in the park.   **B** A sports competition.   **C** A sports lesson at school.

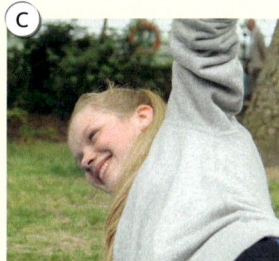

b) Now watch the film and check your answers in a).

2   Who said what?

a) Work with a partner. Who said sentences A–F? Write the names.

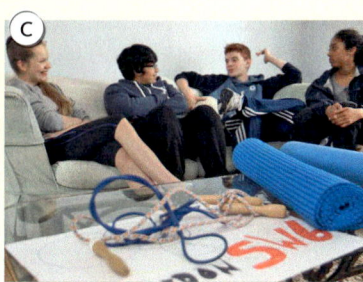

Scene 1
A We want to go to town.
B We all know that you're the football champion.

Scene 2
C You can do it!
D Get ready. Steady. Go!

Scene 3
E That was fun today.
F Yeah, I guess you're right.

b) Now watch the film again and check your answers.    More practice 7   p. 109

3   The message of the story

a) What do you think is the message in this story?

Some sports are better than others.

The most important thing is to have fun.

Sport is a waste of time.

It's most important to be good at sport.

All sports are good.

b) Compare with two partners. Do they agree with you?

I think the message is …

Really? I think …

I agree. I think …

1 Good business ideas!

Mrs Fox is talking to a different group of students about their ideas.

○ First look at the picture and make a list of the five business ideas.

> Let's make fruit ice cream! If it's sunny, lots of people will buy it.

> I know! If we sell football flags, they'll be really popular!

> What about vegetable soup? If it's cold, people will want hot soup.

> But people won't buy it if it's cold.

> Everybody loves cupcakes. We'll make lots of money if we make cupcakes.

> We can make T-shirts. If we put cool pictures on them, kids will love them!

BIZ 4 KIDZ BUSINESS IDEAS
(1.) fruit ice cream
(2.)
(3.)

2 If …

a) Read the FOCUS-box.

FOCUS

Mit *if*-Sätzen sagst du, was unter bestimmten Bedingungen passieren wird:
If it's cold, people will want hot soup.

Der Satz besteht aus zwei Teilen:
Einem Nebensatz mit *if* im *simple present* + einem Hauptsatz mit *will (Kurzform 'll)* oder *won't.*

If it's cold, *people will want hot soup.*

Der Nebensatz mit *if* kann vorne oder hinten stehen:
People won't buy it if it's cold.

b) Now look again at the sentences in exercise 1. Write the six sentences with *if*.

1 If it's sunny, …
2 But people won't …
3 … 4 … 5 …

▶ *Language file 11, p. 145*

3 ⭕ Ben's plans for Saturday

Put the sentence parts together.

1 If the weather is nice, I'll …
2 But if the weather is bad, I'll …
3 If I have enough money, I'll …
4 If my friends are free, I'll …
5 But if I have lots of homework, I won't …

… meet them in town.
… ride my bike in the park.
… go out. I'll stay at home and work.
… stay at home and watch a DVD.
… go bowling. Bowling isn't cheap!

4 ⭕ What are Ben's ideas for Sunday? // ● p. 109

Finish the sentences.

1 If it … (rain) on Sunday, Ben will stay
  at home.   *If it rains, …*
2 But if Ben … (stay) at home,
  he'll be bored.
3 If Ben's friends … (come) to
  his house, they'll have fun.
4 If Ben … (have) some milk,
  eggs and flour, they'll make
  more cupcakes.
5 And if the cupcakes … (look)
  nice, Ben's friends will eat them.
  They don't need any cakes for
  the competition now!   **More practice 8** p. 109

5 ● What will happen if …?

a) Think: Write as many sentences about the picture as you can.

If the cat jumps, the baby will be surprised.
If the baby is surprised, the ice cream will fall.
If the ice cream …, the dog will jump.
If the dog …, …

b) 👥 Pair: Compare
your sentences
with a partner.

c) Share: Read
your sentences to
the class. Who has
the best sentences?

STOP! CHECK! GO!

Ein Lösungsblatt für die Aufgaben 1–4 kannst du von deiner Lehrerin/deinem Lehrer erhalte Die Audio-Datei für Aufgabe 7 findest du onlir bei den Dateien zum Workbook.

1 **WORDS** **A quiz about countries**

a) ⃝ Look at the flags. Write the country for each flag.

Australia • China • Britain • Denmark • France • Spain • Turkey • the USA

b) 👥 Now compare with a partner.

> I think number 1 is France.

> Really? I think you're wrong. I think it's ...

> Yes, I think you're right!

c) ⬤ Which two countries do you want to visit? Why? Write two sentences.

I'd like to visit ... because there are good beaches/they have great food/it's always sunny/...

---

2 **WORDS** **Business words**

a) Match the words on the left with the phrases on the right: *take part in a competition*

take part in	as much money as you can
be good	your bike to a friend
advertise	your business online
make	a good idea
have	*a competition*
sell	at business

b) ⬤ Choose verbs from a) and make your own sentences – as many as you can.

1 I make money with my Saturday job.
I work in a garden center and I ...
2 I took part in a competition last summer. I went to ...

---

3 **REVISION** **An interview with a footballer**

Ben writes for a football magazine. He interviewed footballer Tarik in Liverpool. Complete the interview. Use the *simple past*.

Blue verbs are regular (+ -ed).
Red verbs have a special form. You can check them on page 200.

Reporter — Hi Tarik. Great to meet you! You ... (come) to Liverpool last year from Germany. Are you German?

Tarik — Yes, I am. I was born in Germany and I ... (start) to play football in Germany. But later I ... (play) for a Turkish club.

Reporter — When ... you ... (leave) your Turkish club? And why?

Tarik — I ... (leave) them in September 2012 because I ... (want) to go back to Germany. First I ... (miss) my old club, but soon I ... (find) new friends and ... (feel) at home in my new club.

Reporter — And when ... you ... (start) in Liverpool?

Tarik — I ... (arrive) in the last week of August 2013. My first match ... (be) in September.

Reporter — You ... (make) people happy with your two goals last Saturday.

Tarik — Yes, lots of Liverpool fans ... (write) to me after that. I'm glad they're happy because I like Liverpool a lot!

▶ *Language file 3, p. 140*

4 LANGUAGE Comparing

a) Compare these things.
Write like this:

Ferry A is bigger than ferry B.
Ferry C is the biggest.

1 Plymouth (258.700 people) – Liverpool (445.200 people) – Manchester (503.100 people) *big*
2 Beatles Museum (£ 15.95) – River trip (£ 4.70) – Liverpool bus tour (£ 10) *cheap*
3 the River Mersey (112 km) – the River Weser (452 km) – the River Thames (246 km) *short*
4 skiing – swimming – football *easy*

b) Expressions with *as … as …* can make texts more interesting. Match some of the expressions in the box with the pictures (1–7).

as big as a house
as green as grass
as strong as a lion
as hungry as a bear
as cold as ice
as quiet as a mouse

▶ *Language file 10, p. 144*

c) Make up your own comparisons.
1 Our cat is as black as …
2 He ran as fast as …
3 I was as tired as …
4 The film was as boring as …
5 The river was as deep as …
6 The house was as big as …

5 LANGUAGE Your plans for next weekend

a) Use the ideas below and make a questionnaire. Choose at least four questions.
What will you do if …
… friends suddenly arrive at your house?
… it rains all weekend?
… you get lots of homework on Friday?
… you're not well and have to stay in bed?
… you're not allowed to watch TV?
… you're alone at home on Saturday evening?

What will you do if …	me	Partner 1: …	Partner 2: …	Partner 3: …
… you get lots of homework on Friday?	I'll be very angry			
…	…			

b) 👥 Answer the questions for yourself. Then talk to three partners. Ask them your questions and answer their questions.

c) 🔘 Write about your partners. Write as many sentences as you can.
If we get lots of homework on Friday, three of us will … and one will …

6 👥 **SPEAKING** Making plans in Liverpool

Partner B: Look at page 91.

Partner A: You want to spend the day with a friend in Liverpool. You want to go to the places below. Your friend has different ideas.

a) Tell your partner
- where you want to go,
- what you want to do there,
- what it costs.

Partner A — I'd like to ...
Partner B — Oh? Why?
Partner A — Because I like ... / it's ...

The Beatles story tells you the exciting story of the Beatles. Hear and see everything about the greatest band of all time.

- Prices: Adult £15.95
          Child (5–16 years) £7
- Britannia Vaults, Albert Docks.

Enjoy a 50-minute trip on a Mersey ferry.
See Liverpool from the river. Sit inside or outside.
Departure: 10 am–3 pm every hour
River Explorer Cruise: Adult £8
                          Child (5–15 years) £4.50

b) Listen to your partner's ideas and take notes.

c) Talk to your partner and choose two things that you want to visit together.

Partner A — In my opinion we should ...
Partner B — Really? I disagree. I think ...
Partner A — Oh, ..., OK. I agree. Let's go to ...

🎧 **7** **LISTENING** and **MEDIATION** *City Explorer Bus Tour*

a) Du bist mit deiner Familie in Liverpool. Ihr plant eine Bustour. Höre dir die Ansage an und mache Notizen. Deine Familie möchte wissen:
- wie lange die Tour dauert,
- wann die erste Tour am Morgen startet,
- wie viel die Karten für Erwachsene und Kinder kosten,
- ob es auch ein Familienticket gibt und wie viel das kostet.

b) Überprüfe deine Notizen beim zweiten Hören.

8 READING and WRITING More sport at school?

a) Read these online comments. Who likes more sport at school and who doesn't?

In my opinion everybody should have two sport lessons a day. Sport makes you active and strong.
And at school you can try different sorts of sport like rugby, basketball, or hockey. Students like sport because it makes them feel great!
I really hope all the students will have as much sport as possible. **(Kelly, 14)**

I believe sport lessons are as important as maths and English. We need sport to stay healthy. Most of our sports are team sports. You don't have to be good at the sports, you do your best for your team. So I say: more sport, please! **(Jordan, 13)**

You can do sport outside school if you want to be fit. I like ice skating and canoeing – so I don't need sport at school. Sport lessons are boring because there aren't enough really good sports like zumba or yoga.
I really think we should have less school sport. **(Evie, 14)**

b) Copy the table. Then read the comments in a) again and complete it. Make your notes as short as possible!

More help p.110

reasons for more sport	reasons against more sport	linkers
makes you active and ...	boring	In my opinion ...

c) ⬤ Write your own comment about more school sport. Remember the three steps: Give your opinion – give reasons – find a good ending.

d) Put all the comments up on the wall. Who has the best arguments?

9 My learner log

Copy and complete your learner log. Then put it in your DOSSIER.

My learner log for Unit 3

Now I can ...
– present a business idea: 😄 😐 😟
– find important facts from a text and take notes: 😄 😐 😟
– give my opinion when I agree or disagree: ...
– talk about things if something happens: ...

After Unit 3
– I know some facts about LIverpool.
– I know more food words.
– These pages were interesting: ...
– These pages were difficult: ...

After Unit 3 my English is: GREAT! 👍 / OK 👊 / NOT VERY GOOD 👎

Writing about you or your family – using the simple present

You met a nice boy last week. His name is Angelo and he's Italian.
Angelo doesn't speak German and you don't speak Italian – so you write in English.

[MK] 1 Angelo's first email

a) Read the email. What does Angelo write about?

1 his family   2 his parents   3 his sister   4 his brother   5 his pet   6 his school   7 his hobbies

Hi,

Thanks for your email and your photos. I like the photo of your funny hamster!
I don't live in a house – we live in a flat. My parents work in the city
of Bologna. My dad helps in a home for old people and my mum works
in the big post office in the centre of town. I have an older brother, Luigi.
He doesn't have a job, but he sometimes helps in a garden centre.
My school isn't too far from our flat. School is OK, but we get homework
every day. Does your school give you lots of homework too?
After school I chat with my friends and we sometimes go bowling or
swimming together. When I'm at home, I listen to music. I really like
music. Do you have a favourite singer?
That's all for now. Please write soon!
Angelo

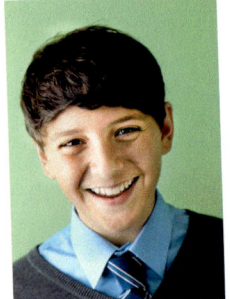

b) The simple present

Verben nach *I, you, we, they*

1 Copy eight verbs in the simple present
from the email: *I …   we …   my parents …*

Verben nach *he, she, it* enden auf -*s*.

2 Copy three examples from the email:
my dad …   my mum …   he …

Verneinungen bildest du mit *don't* oder *doesn't*.

3 Copy two examples from the email:
I …   he …

Fragen beginnen mit *Do …?* oder *Does …?*

4 Copy two examples from the email.
Does …?   Do …?

▶ *Language file 1, p. 138*

[MK] 2 [O] Angelo's second email

Read the email and pick the right form of the verb.

Hi,
I want/wants (1) to send you a photo of our dog,
Mona. She's so cute! Mona like/likes (2) running in
our park. Luigi take/takes (3) her there every
morning and I go/goes (4) with her in the evening.
Mona often dive/dives (5) into the water there
because she love/loves (6) swimming.
We all love/loves (7) Mona!
Angelo

Mona sleeps in the kitchen.

3 ● **Angelo and his family**

Your brother tries to tell your parents about Angelo. But he gets everything wrong! Look at the correct information in exercises 1 and 2 and write correct sentences with *doesn't* or *don't*.

> **Remember:**
> I / you / we / they + don't
> he / she / it + doesn't

> Angelo and his parents live in a house.

> Angelo's parents work in a village.

> Angelo's brother Luigi has a job.

1 No, they don't live in a house! They live in a flat.

2 No, they … in a village! They work …

3 No, he … a job! He helps …

> Angelo gets home-work once a week.

> Angelo and his friends always go home after school.

> Mona, Angelo's dog, sleeps in his room.

4 No, he …! He …

5 No, they …! They …

6 No, she …! She …

4 **A video chat with Angelo**

You have some questions for Angelo.
What are the missing words?

> Bei Interviews brauchst du meist Fragewörter und das *simple present*. Achtung:
> Where? = Wo?
> Who? = Wer?

> How • What • When • Where • Who • Why

You:
1 … does your school begin?
2 … do you go to school?
3 … is your favourite lesson?
4 … do you like this lesson?
5 … do you have lunch?
6 … are your best friends at school?

Angelo:
– At 8.30 am.
– I walk.
– Art.
– Because the teacher is nice.
– I have lunch at school.
– Luciano and Carlo. They're fun!

5 **NOW YOU**

a) Look again at Angelo's email in exercise 1.
Then write an email to Angelo. Answer his questions and write about your family, your school and your hobbies. Write as many sentences as you can.
● Ask a question. Look at exercise 4 for ideas.

> Use some sentences in ex. 1, 2 or 3 and change them for your text. Example:
> My mum works in the big post office.
> => My dad works in a hospital.
> We live in a flat.
> => We live in a flat too.

Hi Angelo!
Thanks for your two emails and for the photo of Mona. She's cute!
I have … brothers and sisters. My dad works in … and my mum …
I go to school …   After school I … and I sometimes …

b) 👥 **Partner check:** Show your email to a partner and check your partner's email:
Is there information about family, school and hobbies?
Should there be more information? If so, what sort of information: about brother / sister, …?

Scotland is different

Welcome to Scotland

Inverness

Aberdeen

HIGHLANDS

Glasgow

Edinburgh

A Scotland is famous for its castles.

B Glasgow

BEWARE OF THE MONSTER

C The Scottish word for *lake* is *loch*. Here is Loch Ness.

D A 82
Inbhir Nis
Inverness 14

E

F

Shinty is a Scottish game, a bit like hockey.

G

How far can he throw it?

H

1 Talk about the photos

What can you see in photo A? — I can see …

a bridge • a castle • a lake • people • a grey sky • flags • modern buildings • hills • woods •…

What are the people doing? — I think they're …

dancing • playing a game • jumping • taking part in … • throwing … • …

2 YOUR TASK   Find out about Scotland

a) 👥 Work in groups of three. Read all the question cards together. Write down any answers that you know.

A Scottish geography
1 What's the capital of Scotland?
2 What's the biggest city in Scotland?
3 Which Scottish lake has a monster?

B Scottish history
1 Does Scotland have its own a) football team b) parliament c) money?
2 What are the colours of the Scottish flag?

C Scottish life
   Give Scottish examples: a) clothes b) sport
   c) a language d) a musical instrument

b) Each student in the group takes one question card (A–C). Go to pages 122–123. Find the answers to your questions and write them down.

c) 👥 Sit in a new group with three students who worked on the same questions (all three A, all three B, etc). Compare your answers.

d) 👥 Go back to your first group. Tell your group the answers to your questions.

▶ Text file 4, pp. 122–123

Time for a change

🎧 **1** **News for the MacDonalds**

The MacDonald family lives in Scotland.

a) ⊙ Listen and pick two answers:

Do the parents and children sound   **A** happy?   **B** sad?   **C** surprised?

b) Listen again and find out:

1 What are the names of the family (A–D?) Match the names from the box with the photos.

 A

 B

Kate
Jamie
Alec
Kara

 C

 D

2 Where do they live?
3 Does the dad have a job?
4 Does the mum have a job?

A 828   Glasgow   170 miles

DORES

2 **Bad news for Inverness**

a) ⊙ Read the article. Find out: Is it good or bad news for the MacDonalds?

INVERNESS NEWS

Another Inverness shop closes

Today the doors of MacBean's in Church Street in Inverness closed for the last time. MacBean's was the number one shop in Inverness for sports clothes and equipment.

"Now most of our customers like to go to big shopping centres or shop online," Alec MacDonald, the manager of MacBean's, said to *Inverness News*.

CLOSING DOWN EVERYTHING MUST GO!

"Eight people including me are un-employed now and there are no jobs here."

Two other shops closed in Inverness centre last month – a hairdresser's and a toy shop. This is bad news for the town centre and bad news for Inverness.

b) Read the article again and take notes:

1 Name of shop: ...
2 Address: ...
3 What you can buy there: ...
4 Why it is closing: ...
5 How many people worked there: ...

c) WORDS

Find these words in the article:

1 you open them when you go into shops
2 things that you wear
3 people who buy things in a shop
4 the person who is the boss in a shop
5 when somebody has no work
6 a person who cuts your hair

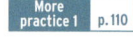
More practice 1   p. 110

3 Hard times

a) 👥 Talk to a partner. What do you think the MacDonalds should do?

A Mr MacDonald should take a job in Glasgow.   **B** The family should go to Glasgow.

C Mr and Mrs MacDonald should look for work nearer home.

b) Now read and find out what their ideas are.

The next evening, the MacDonalds had dinner in the kitchen. But it wasn't a very happy meal!

Kara — Dad, we know you're fed up about your job. But don't blame yourself.

Dad — Maybe I'll have to go to Glasgow. I can be a manager in MacBean's Glasgow shop.

Jamie — No, Dad. It's too far away.

Kara — Yeah, we should stay together in hard times. We're the MacDonalds. And the MacDonalds always look after themselves!

Dad — Your mum and I talked about things and we asked ourselves – how can we all stay here in our home? And mum had an idea …

Mum — Well, first I told myself – we live in a beautiful place. And lots of tourists come here to visit Loch Ness and the Highlands. And they need places to stay where they can enjoy themselves …

Jamie — Like hotels …

Mum — And bed and breakfast places.

Kara — Yes … and …?

Mum — That's my answer! We have a big old house with lots of rooms. We can start a B&B!

Jamie — But we don't know anything about B&Bs!

Kara — We can learn. We can teach ourselves!

Dad — Let's think about it. Now the soup is getting cold, so help yourselves!

c) True, false or not in the text?

1 The kids think their dad should go to Glasgow.
2 Mum and dad had a new idea.
3 Tourists think Loch Ness is more beautiful than Glasgow.
4 Tourists only stay in hotels.
5 The MacDonalds are thinking about starting a B&B.
6 Jamie loves the new idea.

d) Find all the words with *-self* and *-selves* in the text. Example: *yourself, …*

e) Copy and complete this table.

I tell	…
you blame	…
he helps	himself
she enjoys	herself
we ask	…
you help	…
they look after	…

▶ *Language file 8, p. 143*    **More practice 2** p. 111

The MacDonalds are open for business

1 The new website

a) ⊙ Look at the website for the new B&B.

1 Does it give   Ⓐ the phone number?   Ⓑ prices?   Ⓒ the number of rooms?

2 Does it tell you about   Ⓐ the family?   Ⓑ activities for tourists?   Ⓒ equipment in the rooms?

Bed and breakfast next to Loch Ness

Welcome to our family-friendly bed and breakfast near Dores, next to Loch Ness!

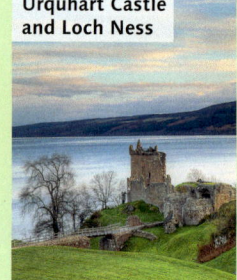
Urquhart Castle and Loch Ness

It's a great place for water sports and there are lots of places to visit: the Loch Ness monster exhibition, beautiful Urquhart Castle, the RockNess music festival, etc.

We have a family room (for four guests), a twin room and a single room. The rooms have TV, DVD player, hairdryer, kettle to make tea or coffee and Wi-fi. There's also a room where you can dry your coats and boots.

£25 per person per night. (Children: under 10 free, 10–16 years old £10, 16–18 £20.)

Email: macdonaldfamily@lochside.com   Telephone: 01463 751878

RockNess

Lochside B&B

The twin room

b) Details about the B&B.

1 How many guests can stay in the B&B?

2 What equipment is there in the rooms?

3 How do you know that families are welcome?

4 What activities are there for tourists near the B&B?

5 What does one night cost for two parents and a child under 10?

6 How do you know that the weather can often be wet?

2 Canadian guests

a) Listen to this Canadian family.

1 Who finds the MacDonalds' website?

2 Is there a room free for the Grants?

b) Listen again and note the missing information A–G.

c) Now write the full email.

From: Abigail Grant	To: Lochside B&B

Hi!
We're a family of … (A) people – two adults and … (B) teenage kids (… (C) and … (D) years old). We'd like to book your … (E) room for … (F) nights from … (G)
Will the room be free? Thanks a lot.
The Grant family

3   Our first guests!

a)  Read the dialogue. How will the Grants find their B&B?

Mrs Grant	Hello, is that *Lochside B&B?*
Jamie	Yes, that's right. This is Jamie MacDonald.
Mrs Grant	Hi, Jamie. This is Michelle Grant. I'm phoning to confirm our reservation for 22nd July.
Jamie	Oh right, great. That was the family room for two nights, right?
Mrs Grant	Yes, that's right. Two nights from tomorrow.
Jamie	OK. What time will you arrive?
Mrs Grant	I'm not sure. Maybe about 7 pm tomorrow.
Jamie	Do you need directions?
Mrs Grant	I think we'll be OK. We have a GPS.
Jamie	OK, well just take the road to Loch Ness and Dores. Phone us if you have a problem.
Mrs Grant	Great. See you tomorrow evening then.
Jamie	OK, bye!

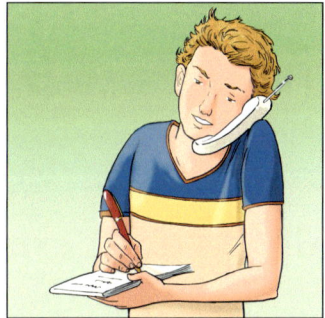

b) Copy and complete the telephone message.

More practice 3 p. 111

Telephone messages

Who rang? _____

How many nights? _____

Will arrive on: _____ at: _____

Room: single ☐   twin ☐
family ☐

4   👥 ROLE-PLAY   Phoning *Lochside B&B*

a) Partner B: Go to page 92.
Partner A: You phone *Lochside B&B*
to confirm your reservation:
– a single room for 2 nights
– you'll arrive 2nd August between 6 and 7 pm

– Hi. This is ... I'm phoning
  to confirm my ... for ....
– That's right, a ... room.
– I'd like to stay ...
– I'll arrive between ...

*If you don't understand,
say: Sorry, can you say
that again, please?*

b) Now you're Jamie. Copy the
telephone message above. Then
answer the phone and write the
message.

– Let me see. That was the twin
  room, right?
– How many nights?
– Yes, that's fine. What time will ...?
– No problem. Thank you.

5   PEOPLE AND PLACES   Welcome to Scotland

a) Before you watch: What things could you see in a film about Scotland?
Look again at pages 68 and 69 and make a list. Then compare with a partner.

b) Now watch the film. How many of the things on your list were in the film?

c) Read these questions, then watch the film again and try to answer them.
1 Where does Mehdy start his trip?   A In Glasgow B In Edinburgh C In Inverness.
2 You can wear a knife with a kilt. You put it in   A your sock B your shoe C your hat.
3 How much do Mehdy's Scottish clothes cost?   A Less than £500 B £500 C More than £500.
4 What didn't you see in the DVD?   A Food B Cycling C Dancing D Shinty E Bagpipes.

1 JIGSAW A story in four parts

Your teacher will put you in groups of four. Each student in your group reads a **different** part of the story (A, B, C, D). Try to answer these questions and take notes.

1 **Who** was in the text?	2 **When** did it happen?	3 **Where** did it happen?	4 **What** happened?
…	…	…	…

Ghosts don't exist (Careful! Parts A, B, C and D are not in the right order!)

A

The Grant family came into the big old house. The old man took them upstairs to a room with four beds. "Make yourselves comfortable," he said.
Duncan and Abi were very excited. "This is a real Scottish castle," Duncan said.
"Maybe there are ghosts!" Abi said and laughed.
"Ghosts don't exist," her mum answered.

Later in the evening the family went down to a kitchen with a warm fire and big table that had lots of food on it. Some people played music and some people danced. The Grants chatted, enjoyed the food and danced too.
"Our family left Scotland more than 200 years ago," Mr Grant said.
"Then you're welcome home," the old man said.

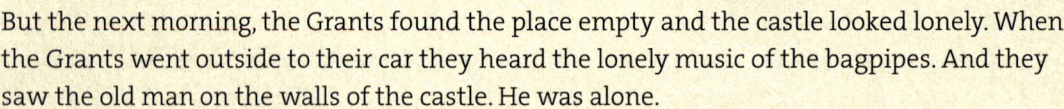

But the next morning, the Grants found the place empty and the castle looked lonely. When the Grants went outside to their car they heard the lonely music of the bagpipes. And they saw the old man on the walls of the castle. He was alone.
The Grants waved and shouted "Thanks!" But the old man just played his bagpipes.

B

It was the Grant family's first night in Scotland. But their plane was late and the sky was dark grey when they landed at Inverness. Then one of their bags was missing. And when they wanted to hire a car, Mrs Grant couldn't find her driving licence.
"It's OK," Mr Grant said. "I have mine."
But, when he began to drive, the other cars all hooted.
"Dad, you have to drive on the left!" the kids shouted.
Mr Grant stopped quickly and luckily nothing happened.

The Grants drove to Inverness and looked for the road to Dores, the village where their B&B was. But it wasn't so easy because it was dark. Mrs Grant looked for the map of Scotland – but it was in the missing bag, with the GPS!
"Dores is near Loch Ness, so let's find the road that goes to the lake," Duncan said. And that's what they did.
They soon saw a sign to Loch Ness. "Ah! Things are looking better," Mr Grant thought to himself.

C

The Grants found the right road to Dores and arrived at *Lochside Bed and Breakfast* at about 11 am. They told the MacDonalds about the old man and the castle. Then they looked at a map and Mrs Grant put her finger on Urquhart Castle.

"I think that's the place that we visited last night," she said.

"It can't be – it's a ruin!" Kate MacDonald said. "But … the last family who lived at Urquhart Castle was the Grant family!"

The Grants from Canada were very excited. "Let's go there!" Abi said.

So in the afternoon the Grants parked at Urquhart Castle. Was it the car park from the night before? They weren't sure. Then they walked around the ruins. It really was a beautiful old castle – about 1500 years old.

"So maybe our family came from here a long time ago," Mr Grant said.

"Yes, I can feel the ghosts of the Grants here," Duncan smiled.

"But ghosts don't exist," the others answered and laughed.

D

The rain started at about 10 pm. The sky was black now and the road was narrow. So it was very difficult for Mr Grant to drive. After 20 minutes the Grants began to worry. Dores is only about 10 miles from Inverness. But they didn't find a village – only woods and fields.

"I'll stop at this car park," Mr Grant said. "We have to find someone who can help us."

"Let's phone the MacDonalds," Mrs Grant said. "But my mobile doesn't work. Can we try yours, Abi?" "Sorry, mine doesn't work either", Abi said.

"It must be the mountains," Mrs Grant thought to herself.

It was after 11 o'clock and everybody was tired.

Then Mrs Grant said, "Look! There's a light over there!"

She and Mr Grant ran in the rain to the end of the car park and came to a building. An old man was at the door. The Grants told him about their problems.

"Och, come in. You can stay here for the night," he said in a Scottish accent.

---

2 👥 **What's the story?**

a) Find three other students who read the same text as you. Talk about the questions in exercise 1.

1 The people in the story were …
2 It was in the morning at …
3 They were in a castle / in …
4 They went / met / drove / saw / thought / couldn't find …

b) Go back to your first group. Tell your group about your text. Listen to the others. What's the right order of the texts A, B, C, D?

> I think that text C is first because …

> I don't agree. I think that text B is first because …

🎧 **c)** Now close your books and listen to the whole story. Enjoy it!

More practice 4+5 p. 112

Writing a story

1 An amazing day

Back in Canada, Duncan writes about his holiday for *Hi guys* magazine which has prizes for short stories.

a) Read the first part of his story.

b) 👥 What's good in Duncan's text? Work with a partner and find the answers for 1, 2 and 3 in Duncan's text.

> **An amazing day**
>
> Last July I flew to Scotland with my parents and my sister. We landed at Inverness late in the evening, so it was dark on the roads. Then we couldn't find our B&B because we had no map. We felt tired and scared.
>
> Suddenly there was a light. And then we saw a man. Mum and dad talked with him and he said we could stay in his house. We felt so happy!

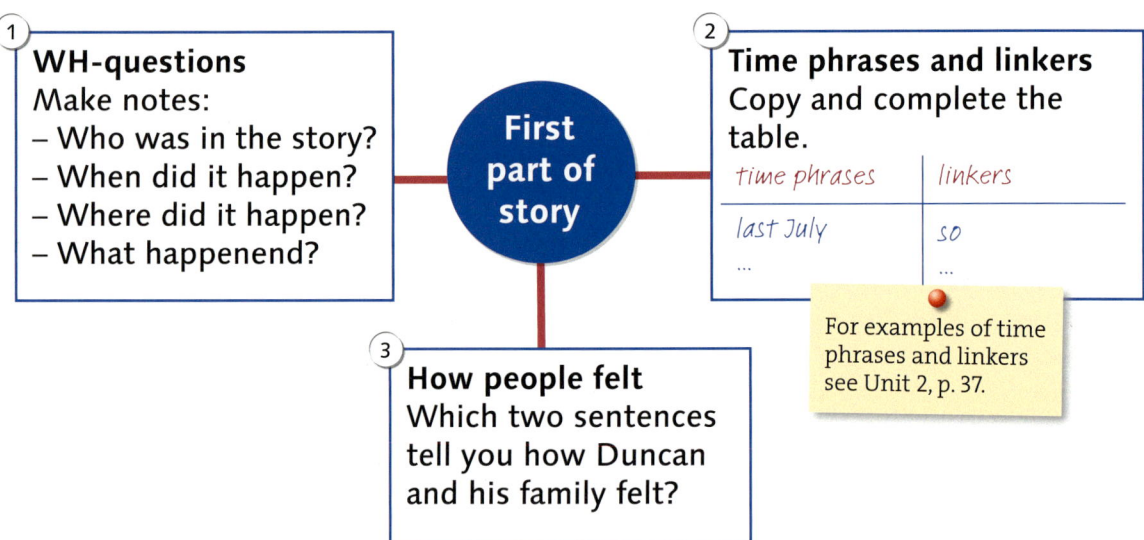

1 WH-questions
Make notes:
– Who was in the story?
– When did it happen?
– Where did it happen?
– What happenend?

First part of story

2 Time phrases and linkers
Copy and complete the table.

time phrases	linkers
last July	so
...	...

For examples of time phrases and linkers see Unit 2, p. 37.

3 How people felt
Which two sentences tell you how Duncan and his family felt?

2 NOW YOU

Finish Duncan's story. [More help p.113]

a) Look again at the story on pages 74–75. Write notes for the next parts of the story. Example:

At the castle
– Who?
– When?
– Where?
– What?

b) Use your notes and write your story.

c) 👥 Partner check: Swap your story with a partner. Check your partner's story. Then write a good version of your story and put it in your DOSSIER.

OR ● Write your own story for *Hi guys*.
1 Think of an amazing day in your life
2 What are the parts of your story?
3 Write ideas for each part.
Example:

A great birthday
– Who?
– When?
– Where?
– What?

> Check:
> 1 Are there answers to the *wh*-questions?
> 2 Are there time phrases and linkers?
> 3 Does the text say how people felt?

▶ *Skills file 8, pp. 132–134*

1   Who is Amy Macdonald?

a) Listen to the radio programme about Amy Macdonald.
Choose the best answers.

1 Amy Macdonald   **A** plays football for Scotland
   B is in the British Olympic team   **C** is a Scottish singer.
2 Amy's biggest hobby is   **A** music   **B** football   **C** cars.
3 Amy is very proud when   **A** she sings at football matches
   B she meets famous bands   **C** she sings in big cities.
4 Amy's song *Pride* is about   **A** Glasgow   **B** her first teachers
   C singing for Scotland's football team.

b) ● Listen again. Make notes about Amy Macdonald:
her work?   born in …?   big hits?   instrument?   hobbies?

More help p.113

2   Pride

a) Listen to the song and look at the text.

1 Is it a happy or a sad song?
2 What instruments do you hear?

the drums

the guitar

the bass guitar

the piano

b) ● Listen again and look at the text.
What words or phrases tell you that …

1 this song is about a football game?
2 the singer is nervous at first?
3 she then feels proud?
4 this song is about
   Scotland?

More practice 6   p.113

Verse 1
I never felt like this before
Try to hold it back and I feel it even more
Sweat drips down my spine
And my knees are weak
I cannot move, I cannot speak.

Verse 2
But then you came
And I held it together again
I managed to stumble through
Fifty thousand voices singing in the rain
There's nothing that I wouldn't do.

Chorus
'Cause I'd move mountains
If you asked me to
I'd swim the seven seas
I'll be the one to hold your torch again
I'll do anything you ask of me.

Verse 3
I never knew how proud I would feel
Just standing in the rain
These three words mean everything to me
And I'll sing them again and again.

Verse 4
Well the blue and the white
Of the flag shines bright
And it's blowing there for me
With my hand on my heart,
The honest truth
There's nowhere I'd rather be.

(Text by Amy Elizabeth Macdonald)

1 Loch Ness brochures

a) First read these three tourist profiles.

b) Then skim the two brochures and find out:
- Which brochure is useful for which tourist (A, B, C)?
- Which tourist has no brochure?

> **When you skim a text:**
> – Look at headings, pictures and captions.
> – Don't read every word – you don't need to understand everything.

Tourist A
You're on holiday and want to spend two or three days near Loch Ness with a friend. You don't have a lot of money, you need a cheap place.

Tourist B
You're staying in Inverness with your family. You love Nessie stories, so you would like to visit a good Nessie museum.

Tourist C
You've just arrived in Scotland with some friends. You'd like to visit the Loch Ness region – quickly. You only have one day!

1

Sightseeing tours through the Highlands
Around Loch Ness
Your complete Loch Ness experience

Tour around Loch Ness
We offer a fully guided day tour around Loch Ness with castle visit and a boat trip on Loch Ness.

Highland Highlights
This is a fully guided day tour of the Highlands including Clava Cairns, Culloden, Inverness, Loch Ness with options for a castle visit and a boat trip on Loch Ness.

2

MAGGIE'S LODGE
LOCH NESS

Comfortable rooms

Outdoor sports

The perfect place to stay in the Highlands.

Rooms
Double rooms, twin rooms or less expensive beds in four- and six-bed dormitories.

Food
Self-catering kitchen, or we can provide breakfast, packed lunches and evening meals.

We have bikes for hire.

c) 👥 Talk to a partner. What helped you to pick the right brochures?
Headings? Examples: …   Pictures? Examples: …

| More practice 7 | p. 114 |

▶ Skills file 6, p. 130

2 WORDS

Now look for details. What words in the *Maggie's Lodge* brochure tell you that …

1 you can cook your own food.
2 you can buy picnic food.
3 you can have dinner.
4 you can borrow bikes.
5 they have some cheaper rooms.
6 they have rooms with one bed for two people.

LONDON
SW6

4

1 Tally's video diary

a) Before you watch:
Which of these things do you think are
different between Scotland and England?

accents • dancing • food • houses •
shopping • money • music • sport

b) Watch the film. Which of these things do we learn about?

2 Four scenes

a) Think: Look at the four pictures and read the questions. Can you answer some questions?

A

1 What meal is Tally making?
2 Will Hamish like it?
3 Does Tally use salt or sugar?

B

4 What's Ruby's problem?
5 What does the Scottish word *wee* mean?
6 Who helps Ruby to understand Hamish?

C

7 Why does Alfie need money?
8 Why is Alfie surprised?
9 Can you use Scottish money in England?

D

10 Does Hamish play the bagpipes?
11 What are the kids doing in this picture?
12 Who do you think will fall?

b) Pair: Watch the film again. When you see the four scenes above, stop the film and
answer all the questions with a partner.

c) Share: Compare your answers with another pair. Then compare your answers in class.

1 Tourist questions

Read the tourist questions. What words do they need?
Look at the pictures and write the words. *1–kettle, 2 …*

1 What's the thing that we use to make hot water for tea?

2 Do you have the thing that you use to dry yourself after a shower?

3 What's the thing that you use to look at yourself in the bathroom?

4 What do you call the person who is the boss in a hotel?

5 I need somebody who can help me with my car.

6 What do you call the man or woman who brings the food in a restaurant?

A a waiter/waitress

B a manager

C a mechanic

D a mirror

E a towel

F a kettle

2 Who/That

a) Work with a partner. Look at the speech bubbles above. What's the difference between the sentences on the left (1–3) and on the right (4–6)?

b) Now copy and complete these rules.
You'll find example sentences in exercise 1.

FOCUS

Mit Relativsätzen beschreibst du eine Sache oder eine Person noch genauer,
z. B.: *Wie nennt man das Ding, das …?   Wie heißt der Mann, der …?*
Auf Englisch benutzt du *that* oder *who*.
Wenn du über **Dinge** redest, benutzt du …
Beispielsatz: …
Wenn du über **Menschen** redest, benutzt du meistens …
Beispielsatz: …

▶ *Language file 12, p. 145*

3 ⭕ More questions // ● p.114

Pick the answers to these questions.

1 What do you call visitors who spend the night in your house?
2 What's the white stuff that you use to make bread or cake?
3 What do you call the thing that you use to cut food?
4 What do you call a person who wins a sports competition?
5 What do you call a person who sells things like cars?
6 What's the thing that you wear when you go outside and it's cold?

A — a coat
B — guests
C — a champion
D — a knife
E — flour
F — a salesperson

4 👥 ROLE-PLAY What is it?

a) **Partner B:** Go to page 92.
Partner A: Listen to your partner. What words does he/she mean?

> Oh, you mean a waiter/the sky/ a bus driver/a diswasher/a B&B.

b) Now ask your partner the words for these people and things.

 1
 2
 3
 4
 5

What do you call	the small animal	who that	eats cheese?
	somebody		works on a farm?
	the machine		makes hot water in the kitchen?
	the big animal		gives milk?
	somebody		buys things in a shop?

5 WORDS

a) Copy and complete the network with words from these two pages.

b) 👥 ● Work with a partner. Can you add more words to the network? ▸ *Wordbank 4, p. 149*

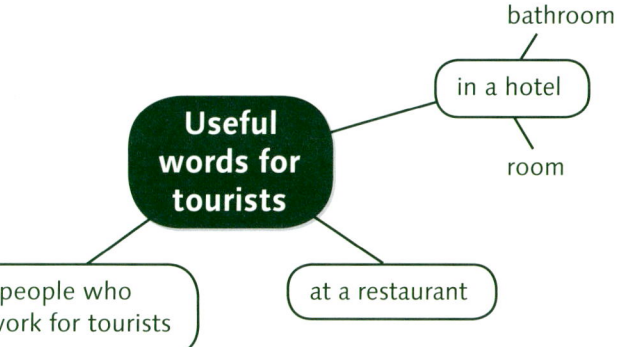

Useful words for tourists
— bathroom
— in a hotel
— room
— people who work for tourists
— at a restaurant

STOP! CHECK! GO!

Ein Lösungsblatt für die Aufgaben 1–5 kannst du von deiner Lehrerin / deinem Lehrer erhalten.

1 **REVISION** **If the weather is good, …**

The Grant family are telling Kara MacDonald about their plans for tomorrow. Copy and complete the sentences.

Mrs Grant — If the weather … (be) good, we … (stay) here two
more days. *If the weather is good, …*

Kara ——— That's great! If you stay here longer, what … (you, do)?

Duncan ——— If it isn't too expensive, we … (hire) a canoe for
a tour of Loch Ness.

Abi ——— Perhaps we … (see) Nessie if we go out early enough!

Mr Grant — But if the weather isn't good, we … (not stay).

Duncan ——— Yes, if the weather is bad, we … (go) to Edinburgh.

Mrs Grant — And if we visit Edinburgh, we … (go) to the castle.

Abi ——— If we find a nice kilt shop, we … (look for) a kilt for
dad's birthday.

Kara ——— Are you sure he … (wear) a kilt if you find one for him?

Duncan ——— You're right. If we buy a kilt, he … (not wear) it!

2 **O** **LANGUAGE** **What do you call …?** **// ●** p.115

Eight tourists can't think of the word in English. Copy and complete what they say or ask.

① "I need a paper *that shows where places are.*"

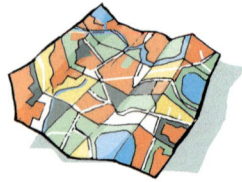

"It's a map."

② "What do you call a person …"

"You mean an adult."

③ "What's the boat …"

"It's a ferry."

④ "What do you call the people …"

"Firefighters."

⑤ "What's the name of the person …

"A hairdresser."

⑥ "What's the white stuff …"

"Oh, you mean salt."

⑦ "What do you call the things …"

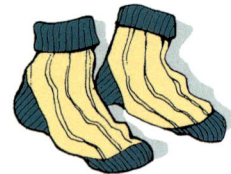

"You mean socks."

⑧ "Can you tell me the word for the person …"

"It's a mechanic."

… who fight against fire?	… that you wear on your feet under your shoes?
… who helps when your car is broken?	… that you put on rice or potatoes or eggs?
… who is not a child?	… *that shows where places are.*
… who cuts or styles your hair?	… that takes people across a river?

3 ◯ **LANGUAGE** **Enjoy yourselves!** `// ● p.115`

Jamie and Kara want to go camping. They are talking to their parents.
Pick the right word: *myself, yourself, herself, …*

> If you need help, look at
> ▸ *Language file 8, p. 143*.

Jamie ___ Mum, Kara and I want to go camping.

Mum ___ Camping? Is that a good idea? That's what I ask myself / herself.

Dad ___ Oh, I'm sure the kids can look after himself / themselves, Kate.

Jamie ___ Of course we can look after ourselves / yourselves!

Kara ___ Don't forget Jamie has taught myself / himself to cook!

Dad ___ Ah yes, I hear you're good at cooking soup for myself / yourself, Jamie!

Mum ___ Well, OK then. You two go camping and enjoy themselves / yourselves.
But I won't blame myself / herself if you come back hungry!

4 **WRITING and SPEAKING** **Booking a B&B**

Dolby B&B

Our beautiful B&B is located in beautiful country near Aberdeen. We have single rooms, double rooms and a family room with four beds. **>>> More details**

To book online click here

> From £35
> price per room
> per night

a) You want to stay eight nights in this B&B from 14th July to 22nd July. There are four of you in your family. You'd like the family room. Write the email to the B&B.

> Hi!
> We are a … of four: two … and two …
> We'd like to book …
> Will the room be …? Many thanks.
> Simon Koch

b) You phone the B&B to confirm the reservation. Write your sentences.

You ___ Hi. is / Simon Koch / This phoning / our reservation / I'm / to confirm

B&B ___ Thanks for phoning. I'm sorry, but our family room isn't free. But we can give you two double rooms for the same price.

You ___ OK / double / Two / rooms / are

B&B ___ Great. Two double rooms from 14th to 22nd July.

You ___ pay / we / euros / Can / in / ?

B&B ___ Yes, no problem. It's a total price of 610 euros.

You ___ with / breakfast / Is / that / ?

B&B ___ Yes, including breakfast. What time will you arrive?

You ___ arrive / evening / We'll / the / in

B&B ___ In the evening is fine.

You ___ very / you / Thank / much

B&B ___ No problem. Bye.

> Zwei Doppel-zimmer sind OK.

> Wir zahlen in Euros.

> Wir werden am Abend dort sein.

> Frage, ob das Früh-stück mit drin ist.

5 READING Brochures

Read statements 1–7. Then skim the brochures A–E and choose the best brochure for each statement. Be careful: There are more statements than brochures – so you can use some brochures more than once.

1 You are a big Harry Potter fan and you want to see places that you know from the films.
2 You like going on organised group bike tours.
3 You are a good mountain biker and you want to try riding in more difficult country.
4 You like trips in old trains.
5 You are interested in Scottish history.
6 You like all kinds of water sports, but you have never tried rafting.
7 You want to buy presents for your friends and family.

A

Fancy a ride?
Bike hire ...
and so much more

Discover one of the most spectacular parts of the Scottish Highlands by bike – with one of our expert guides.

B

Experience the fun
Outdoor activities in Scotland

Quad biking
Experience riding a quad bike in some of the most beautiful settings in Scotland.

Canyoning
Canyoning is an adrenaline-filled adventure – jump from cliffs and abseil from waterfalls.

White-water rafting
Experience the best white-water rafting trip in Scotland.

C

Edinburgh – explore the jewel of Scottish cities
Edinburgh has something for everybody!

Discover Scotland's past
Visit Edinburgh Castle, The Royal Scottish Museum or Old Town with its narrow streets and learn something about Scotland's history.

A dream for shoppers
Shopping in Edinburgh is a fantastic experience as you can browse the shops of several great spots including Princes Street, George Street and the St James Centre.

D

Jacobite Steam Train

Follow in the footsteps of Harry Potter along the route used by the Hogwarts Express.

- See the carriages that were used in the Harry Potter films.
- Travel to Mallaig along the line used in the films.
- Cross the famous Glenfinnan Viaduct, a unique landmark for all Harry Potter fans.

It's a great day out for all the family.

E

Wolftrax Trails and Activities
Located in one of the most beautiful parts of Cairngorms National Park, Laggan:

- Our exciting, off-road mountain bike park. There are trails for all abilities.

- The Haflinger Pony-Trekking Centre with various lovely trekking trails.

Booking:
Mountain Bikes: 01528 544756
Pony-Trekking: 07926 178529

6 WRITING A story about Slains Castle

a) Look at the pictures of Slains Castle. Imagine you and your family went there for a trip. Write your story:

Last August I travelled to … with …
We stayed in a hotel / … near …
One day we visited …
It was a sunny / foggy / … day. The sky was …
Suddenly I saw something white / …
I heard a noise / something / …
I felt nervous / excited / scared / …
Was it a ghost? No, of course not! It was only …
Silly me! We all laughed when I told my family about it!

> – Answer the questions *Who? When? Where? What?*
> – Use time phrases and linkers *(so, but, because, …)*
> – Write how you felt. If you need help, see page 76.

b) 👥 Work with one or two partners. Compare your ideas.
Maybe a partner has a good idea for you?

c) Put the new ideas in your story. Then put your story in your DOSSIER.

7 My learner log

Copy and complete your learner log. Then put it in your DOSSIER.

My learner log for Unit 4

Now I can …
– understand words in a B&B advert: 😄 🙂 🙁
– write an email to book a room: 😄 🙂 🙁
– phone a B&B to confirm a reservation: 😄 🙂 🙁
– use some tips to write a good story: 😄 🙂 🙁
– ask for things even if I don't know the word: …

After Unit 4
– I know some things about Scotland.
– I understand a Scottish accent.
– I have listened to a Scottish song.
– My favourite part of this unit was …

After Unit 4 my English is: GREAT! 👍 */ OK* 👊 */ NOT VERY GOOD* 👎

A German student in Dublin

In May, Maike Hoffmann travelled from Berlin to Dublin to spend one week with the O'Briens. She wanted to practise her English – but she also learned lots of things about living in another country.

1 **Part 1 Maike arrives at the O'Briens**
Mrs O'Brien, her son Dara and her daughter Ciara met Maike at the airport. They then drove her to their house – a small, cute

5 house, in a line of other houses. Inside, Maike met two younger

10 boys. They looked shy[1].
"I'm Maike," the visitor said and she put out her hand. But the boys didn't take her hand. They

15 only looked at her and smiled shyly.
"That's Liam and Sammy," Mrs O'Brien said.
"Say hello to Maike, boys."
The boys said hello, then a small girl and a dog came out of a room.

20 "And that's Tess – with Milo the dog," Mrs O'Brien said.
Maike smiled at Tess but she didn't put out her hand this time.

"I'll make some tea," said Dara. "Milk and
25 sugar, Maike?"
"No, thanks – just black, please," Maike answered.
Dara was surprised. And Maike was surprised when she tried the tea. It was

30 very, very strong.
"Oh, I will some sugar, please," she said.
"You mean I'd like some sugar, please," Mrs O'Brien said. "Is it OK if I correct your English?"

35 "Yes, please, Mrs O'Brien," Maike said.
"That's good for me."

"OK, Maike. But don't call me 'Mrs O'Brien'. My name is Nora, so please call me Nora."
"OK, Mrs O'Brien … erm, I mean Nora."

40 Maike was surprised. She liked Nora O'Brien already.

Maike had some presents – marzipan sweets for the kids and a *Black Forest* ham[2] for Mrs O'Brien.

45 "Oh, thanks very much," Mrs O'Brien said and put the ham in the fridge[3].

Maike's Blog (1)

Endlich in Irland angekommen … es ist schon irgendwie alles anders und neu hier!
50 Aber die Familie ist echt nett, besonders Nora, die Mutter.
Morgen gehe ich mit Dara in die Schule und bin schon sehr gespannt!
Einiges habe ich hier schon gelernt, z.B. …

---

55 **Part 2 Maike's first day at school**
Peep – peep – peep … Ciara woke up[4] with a shock. "What's that?" she thought. "It's only 7 o'clock." It was Maike's alarm clock on her mobile.

60 "Oh, Maike, it's too early! School starts at 9 o'clock," Ciara said and went back to sleep.

But Maike got up. She was excited because this was her
65 first day at school in Dublin. She was in Dara's class, because Maike and Dara were both 16.

---

[1] shy *schüchtern*   [2] Black Forest ham *Schwarzwälder Schinken*   [3] fridge *Kühlschrank*   [4] she woke up *sie wachte auf*

At 8 o'clock Maike was in the bathroom.
70 Three O'Brien kids were outside the bathroom. They wanted to go to the toilet – it wasn't funny! When Maike came out at last, she understood the problem.
"Oh I'm sorry," she said. "I forgot that there
75 was only one toilet in the house."

Nora had a school uniform for Maike. Maike looked great in it.

80 It was a new experience[5] for her and Dara had to help her with the school tie.
85 Maike was really excited and a bit nervous.

When they got to school, some of Dara's friends looked at Maike and smiled.
"Is this your new girlfriend, Dara?" they asked.
90 "I'm not his girlfriend!" Maike said. Dara went a bit red[6].
After that, the day at school was OK. Lots of kids asked Maike about Germany, her school, her family. She didn't
95 understand everything, but it was fun.

Maike's Blog (2)

Heute war ich in der Schule. Alle haben gedacht, dass ich Daras Freundin bin ☺. Auch heute habe ich ein paar Sachen
100 gelernt, z. B. dass man in der Schule …

Part 3 **After school**

It was a long day at school. Lessons finished at 4 pm, and they got home at 5 pm.
"Hi, Maike," called Nora. "It's tea time."
105 "Tea time?" Maike asked Ciara. "I'm tired – but I'm very hungry!"
Ciara smiled. "Don't worry. We say 'tea', but we mean dinner."

Maike found Dara in the kitchen.
110 "Guess what's for tea," he said to Maike with a smile. "It's your *Black Forest* ham." He showed Maike a big pot on the cooker. The ham
115 was in hot water. "Oh no!" Maike said. "You don't cook this ham. You eat it cold!"

120 Ciara looked at Dara. Dara looked at his mum. And Nora looked at Maike. Then they all laughed.
So they didn't have *Black Forest* ham that evening. (Milo, the dog, had a very nice
125 surprise for his dinner!)
Dara cooked sausages, eggs, tomatoes,
130 beans and potatoes. "Good appetite,"

Maike said – and Dara's brother Liam
135 laughed.
"Did I say something wrong?" Maike asked.
"No," Nora answered. "We understood you, but we don't say 'Good appetite'. We say 'Enjoy your meal'."
140 "Oh, OK. Enjoy your meal," Maike said.

After tea, Dara had a question for Maike. He was a bit shy, but in the end he asked her.
"Hey Maike, there's a disco on Friday. My
145 friends want to go. It's for kids under 18. There's no alcohol and it's over[7] before 12 pm. Would you like to come?" Dara asked.
"Yes, OK," Maike said. "But I don't have the right clothes."
150 "That's no problem," said Ciara. "I'll phone some friends."

---

[5]experience *Erfahrung*   [6]go red *rot werden*   [7]it's over *es ist vorbei*

On Friday after school three girls brought some disco clothes and other things to the house. Maike had lots of fun with the girls.
155 She tried different clothes and shoes. They did her hair too. She soon looked very different.

At the disco Maike met more of Dara's friends. They were very nice and they all
160 had lots of fun that evening.

Maike's Blog (3)

Mittwoch abend hat Nora den Schwarzwälder Schinken gekocht ... das war lustig. Wenigstens hat sich Milo darüber
165 gefreut ☺. Heute war ich mit Dara in der Disco, das war voll genial. Ein paar Mädels haben mir Anziehsachen geliehen und Schminke – das war richtig cool! Ich habe wieder was dazu gelernt, z.B. ...

170 **Part 4 The last day**
The day before Maike left, she and Dara went into Dublin centre on the bus. They walked along the busy Dublin streets and went into some shops. Maike bought
175 presents for her family and friends at home. She bought a silly hat for her sister.
Then they saw some street musicians and they listened to some good Irish music.

At lunchtime Maike said she was hungry.
180 "Can we eat something Irish?" Maike asked.
"OK," Dara said. "I have an idea!"
So Dara took Maike to the old part of Dublin, with narrow streets and old buildings.

There they found a place called Leo
185 Burdock.
"It's the best fish and chip shop in Dublin!" Dara said.
They waited, and then Dara asked for two fish and chips.
190 "Do you want salt and vinegar[8] on the chips, love[9]?" the friendly woman asked them.
"Vinegar on my chips?" Maike said, shocked. "No thanks!"

195 They took their food to St Patrick's Park. It was nice there. The fish and chips were fresh, hot and very good.
"Try my chips with vinegar," Dara said to Maike. She tried one ... and she liked it!
200 "What do you put on chips in Germany?" Dara asked.
"Tomato ketchup or mayonnaise," Maike answered.
"Mayonnaise on chips? Yuck![10]" Dara said,
205 shocked.
"When you come to Germany you can try it. It's great!" Maike answered and smiled.
"You learn a lot when you travel," she thought, "things that you can't learn at
210 school."

1 Maike's blogs
a) Pick one of Maike's blogs (1–3). Find examples of things that she learned.

b) You're Maike. Write a blog for Part 4 of the story – in English or in German.

---

[8] vinegar *Essig*   [9] love *hier: meine Liebe (freundliche Anrede)*   [10] Yuck! *Igitt!*

1   People and places   Welcome to Dublin, the capital of Ireland

a) Before you watch, look at these places in Dublin.

1 Where can you – buy fruit?   – take a bus?   – listen to street musicians?
– go shopping?   – relax?   – see the river?   – look at the sea?

2 What's the name of a famous old ship?

b) Then watch the film. Make a list of the places in the brochure in the right order.

A TOUR OF DUBLIN – in three hours

Grafton Street

O'Connell Street

The Jeanie Johnston

Moore Street

Temple Bar

Molly Malone

Stephen's Green

The Ha'penny Bridge

Dublin Bay

c) Match these sentences with your list of places from b). Watch the film again and check.

A This is a quiet place in the city centre.

B It's very important in Dublin's history.

C It goes across the River Liffey.

D It's the oldest part of Dublin.

E Poor people travelled on it to the USA.

F It's Dublin's most popular shopping street.

d) Imagine you're in Dublin with a partner. Agree on three places to visit. Say why.

I'd like to visit … because I like …

I don't really want to go to …

So we want to visit …

… looks fun / quiet / exciting / nice / …

I think you can go shopping in …

Unit 2

3 👥 **ROLE-PLAY** **Talking on the phone** ▸ *Unit 2, p.33*

b) Partner B: You are the babysitter for the Smiths, a family in England. First copy the notepad. Then answer the phone and listen to your partner.
– Say Mrs Smith can't answer the phone right now.
– Ask if you can take a message.
– Make notes on your notepad.

c) Swap roles. You are staying in England with your host family, the Smiths. Now you want to phone and tell Mr Smith that you'll be outside school at 6 o'clock. Ask if Mr Smith can meet you there, at the big gate.
– First practise what you want to say.
– Then make the phone call.

📞 **Messages**

Who phoned? _____

Wanted to
speak to: _____

Message: _____
_____
_____

> Hello. This is ... Can I ... Mr Smith, please?

> Can Mr Smith ... me there?

> I'll be ... at 6 o'clock.

2 **WORDS** **How many differences can you find?** ▸ *Unit 2, p.42*
Partner B

a) 🔘 Make a list of eight things in the picture and write where they are: *in the foreground/ background, in the middle, on the left/right, behind, in front of, next to, near, ...*

Things in the picture	Where in my picture?	In my partner's picture
a wood	in the background, on the right	
	...	

b) 👥 Now talk to your partner about your pictures.
Find at least five differences. Make notes in the third column of your table.

> There's a ... in the background on the left.

> In my picture it's on the right.

6 👥 **SPEAKING**   **Making plans in Liverpool** ▸ *Unit 3, p. 64*

Partner B: You want to spend the day with a friend in Liverpool.

a) Find out
- what your partner wants to do,
- why,
- what it costs.

Listen to the answers and take notes.

Partner B __ What would you like to do?
Partner A __ I'd like ...
Partner B __ Oh? Why?
Partner A __ Because I like ... / it's ...
Partner B __ What does it cost?
Partner A __ ...

b) But you have different ideas. You want to go to the places below. Tell your partner where you want to go, why and what it costs.

What about 170 shops, cafes and restaurants?

LIVERPOOL ONE

Liverpool ONE is the biggest shopping centre in the city. Here you'll find the ODEON cinema and two hotels. The ODEON cinema is open until late.

Entry to the shopping centre is free.

Merseyside Maritime Museum

Everything about Liverpool's seafaring history. Real boats, ship models, pictures and films bring Liverpool's shipping stories to life. And of yourse you can learn everything about the story of the Titanic.

Free entry!

c) Talk to your partner and choose two things that you want to visit together.

Partner A __ In my opinion we should ...
Partner B __ Really? I disagree. I think ...
Partner A __ Oh, ..., OK. I agree. Let's go to ...

4 👥 ROLE-PLAY **Phoning** *Lochside B&B* ▶ *Unit 4, p. 73*

a) Partner B: You work in the B&B. Your partner is a tourist. Copy the telephone message. When your partner phones, talk to him or her and note the information.

Partner A — Hi. This is ... I'm phoning to confirm my reservation for ...
You _____ Let me see. That was the single room, right?
Partner A — ...
You _____ How many nights?
Partner A — ...
You _____ Yes, that's fine. What time will you arrive?
Partner A — ...
You _____ No problem. Thank you.

b) Now you ring Lochside B&B to confirm your reservation:
– a twin room for one night
– you'll arrive 1st September late in the evening (about 9 pm)

You _____ Hi. This is ... I'm phoning to confirm our ... for ...
Partner A — Let me see. That was the twin room, right?
You _____ ...
Partner A — How many nights?
You _____ We'd like to stay for ... night.
Partner A — Yes, that's fine. What time will you arrive?
You _____ We'll arrive ...
You _____ No problem. Thank you.

☎ **Telephone messages**

Who rang? _____
How many nights? _____
Will arrive on: _____ at: _____
Room: single ☐ twin ☐
       family ☐

If you don't understand, say: *Sorry, can you say that again, please?*

---

4 👥 ROLE-PLAY **What is it?** ▶ *Unit 4, p. 81*

a) Partner B: Ask your partner the words for these people and things.

What do you call	the blue	who that	is over us?
	the machine		washes cups and glasses?
	somebody		brings food to people in a restaurant?
	a small house		has rooms for guests?
	somebody		drives a bus?

b) Now listen to your partner. What words does he / she mean?

> Oh, do you mean a cow / customer / farmer / mouse / kettle?

Unit 1

More practice 1   **Which advert is best?**   ▶ *Unit 1, p. 12*

Read the sentences below. Then pick the best advert (A–G) on page 12 for each sentence.

1 You love music, especially pop music. And you're free this evening!

2 You watched the 2012 Olympic Games on TV. Now you want to see where they happened.

3 You like clothes and you love interesting food. But you don't want to spend lots of money.

4 You want to travel around London for a day and you want the cheapest ticket.

5 You love the theatre and music. But you don't really like pop music.

6 Your hobby is shopping and you love English shops.

7 You're a football fan and you'd like to visit a famous English stadium.

More help   **2**   👥👥 **ACTIVITY**   **London plans**   ▶ *Unit 1, p. 13*

Step 2: Agree with partners in a group.

Work in a group. Talk to your partners and agree on three (or more) ideas. Write them down. Write why you want to go there. You can use some of these ideas:

You should	visit go to see	…	because	it's	cheap • free • interesting good • fun • very popular amazing • famous great for football / sport fans
				you can	buy presents / do some shopping there. see a great show there. see the hottest fashion there. listen to cool music.

More practice 2   **About the story**   ▶ *Unit 1, p. 15*

a) Which sentences give the main points of the story?

About me   **A** Sherlock is different from his friends.   **B** Sherlock likes books.

Disaster on the Tube   **A** The friends ran to the train.   **B** Alfie didn't get on the train.

Shopping disaster   **A** The kids had to leave Harrods.   **B** Things are expensive in Harrods.

Disaster in Hyde Park   **A** Alfie kicked a ball.   **B** The friends had trouble with some teenagers.

In the museum, at last   **A** Everybody liked the museum.   **B** The museum has dinosaurs.

b) 👥 What do you think was Sherlock's best idea? Talk to other students – do they agree?

> I think Sherlock's best idea was … on the Tube / in Harrods / in Hyde Park / the Natural History Museum.

> Yes, I agree.

> I don't agree. I think his best idea was …

Unit 1

More help **4** **Why and what?** ▶ *Unit 1, p. 15*

Complete the sentences with the right endings A–F.

1 Sam's friends call him *geek* because …
2 His friends said BORING! when …
3 Alfie missed the Tube train because …
4 They had a problem at Harrods because …
5 The teens in the park ran away when …
6 They went to the museum because …

A they heard a noise like a police car.

B they had no money and the museum was free.

C Alfie had a rucksack and they weren't with an adult.

D he likes things like books, history and museums.

E he was too slow.

F Sherlock wanted to go to the Natural History Museum.

More practice 3 **Alfie's story** ▶ *Unit 1, p. 15*

● You're Alfie. Read the paragraph *Disaster on the Tube* again.
Then write about your experience in about six sentences. The sentences below will help you.

> Denk daran: Du bist Alfie und erzählst die Geschichte aus Alfies Sicht:
>
> Wo warst du?
> Was hast du gemacht?
> Wie hast du dich gefühlt?
> Was kannst du nicht wissen?

Sherlock's story	Alfie's story
We went to the Tube station in Fulham.	Hier bleibt alles gleich.
We ran to our train but ~~Alfie~~ was too slow.	Hier musst du die Person ändern: → … I was too slow.
The train left and ~~poor Alfie~~ was still on the platform.	Hier musst du wieder die Person ändern: → … I was still on the platform.
~~We tried to phone, but our mobiles didn't work on the Tube. Then I had an idea.~~	Du kannst das alles nicht wissen, also weglassen!
We'll get out at the next station and wait for the next train.	Hier musst du Person und Zeit ändern: → My friends got out … and waited …
~~And that's what we did.~~	Das gehört nicht zu deiner Geschichte, also weglassen.
Ten minutes later the next train came and ~~Alfie was~~ on it.	→ I got on.
~~He~~ was happy to see ~~us.~~	→ I was happy to see my friends.
~~"Very clever, Sherlock," Tally said. So I was happy too.~~	Auch das gehört nicht zu deiner Geschichte, also weglassen.

More practice 4 **Find the right order** ▸ *Unit 1, p. 15*

Here's a short version of the story. What's the right order of the sentences?

A After Harrods they went to Hyde Park.
B Sam, Tally and Ruby got the Tube train, but Alfie was too slow.
C On Saturday Sam met his friends Ruby, Alfie and Tally.
D Then they went to the Natural History Museum.
E They went to Fulham Tube station.
F They all really liked the museum, especially the earthquake room.
G When they got out of the Tube they went to Harrods.
H They had trouble with some teenagers because Alfie kicked a ball into their picnic.
I They had trouble with a security man because Alfie had a rucksack.

More help **1b** **Ideas for a text about your neighbourhood** ▸ *Unit 1, p. 16*

Add 20 of these words to your list or network about your neighbourhood.

> bank • bike shop • bus station • bus stop • cake shop • cinema • farm • fields • flats • gardens •
> hairdresser's • harbour • houses • museum • park • post office • restaurant • school •
> second-hand shop • sports centre • stadium • supermarket • swimming pool • taxis • theatre •
> traffic lights • train station • video shop

More help **2** **NOW YOU** ▸ *Unit 1, p. 16*

a) First read this example text.

> I live in Wimbledon. It's not far from London.
> The best thing about Wimbledon is the tennis.
> There are lots of great shops here.
> And there's a train station near our house.
> But there aren't any swimming pools near us.
> I think Wimbledon is great.

b) Now tell Ruby or Darren about your neighbourhood. Change the words in orange.
Write about 40 words.

> I live in Lüneburg. It's not far from Hamburg.
> The best thing about Lüneburg is ...

Unit 1

More practice 5   **Two articles**   ▶ *Unit 1, p. 17*

There are some new words in these articles. Can you guess what the red words mean
in German? Think of English words that you already know or German words. Pick a) or b).

a)

> Everybody was very muddy after the five
> kilometre fun run in the park this weekend.
> The winner was May Keating. She is a bus
> driver in Wimbledon.
> There were no losers in this fun run, but there
> was a bag of prizes at the finish for everybody.

b) ●

German footballers surprised

The well-known German team Borussia Dortmund got a surprise last night when they
played against a little-known team from Dublin – Shamrock Rovers. More than one
hundred Irish fans travelled to Dortmund and sang noisily in the half-full German
stadium. It was a rainy day and the field was very muddy.

The Dortmund players didn't start well. They all looked sleepy and played
like sleepwalkers. Shamrock Rovers looked dangerous, and after 11 minutes one
of the Shannon Rovers players put the ball in the back of the Borussia net.
1-0 to Shamrock Rovers! That was a wake-up call for Dortmund.

After that they played much better and they won 2-1. So it was a good win for the
German team, but the Irish fans were good losers – they sang all through the match!

More help   **1a**   **Is fashion important?**   ▶ *Unit 1, p. 18*

Serena and Andy are talking about shopping and fashion. Listen to them and read
the dialogue. Do you agree with Andy or Serena?

Andy — Hey, Serena. I'm going shopping. Do you want to come?
Serena — No thanks, Andy. I'm not interested in fashion.
Andy — Why not?
Serena — Because fashion is a waste of money.
Andy — That's rubbish! Fashion is so important!
Serena — Why is fashion so important for you, Andy?
Andy — If you look good, you feel good!
Serena — I don't agree. You don't need expensive clothes to feel good!
Andy — OK, Serena, but you don't have to spend a lot of money on fashion.
Serena — You're right. But **you** spend all your pocket money on clothes!
Andy — You're wrong! I always buy cheap clothes. Erm, ... Serena, can I borrow some money?
Serena — Oh!!! Not again!

More practice 6   **Emma and Habib are good friends**   ▶ *Unit 1, p. 18*

Copy and complete the dialogue with words from the box.

> have • if • expensive • interested • rubbish • waste • wrong

Emma   Oh, Habib! I'm going to the new shopping centre in town. Do you want to come too?

Habib   No thanks. I'm not ... (1) in fashion.

Emma   Why not?

Habib   Because it's a ... (2) of money.

Emma   You're ... (3)! Fashion is really important! ... (4) you look good, you feel good!

Habib   That's rubbish! You don't need ... (5) clothes to feel good!

Emma   But you don't ... (6) to spend a lot of money on fashion.

Habib   That's true. But you always spend a lot of money, Emma!

Emma   That's ... (7)! I always buy cheap clothes. But, Habib, can I borrow some money?

Habib   Oh, Emma!!! Not again!

// ●   **4a**   **A letter to buzz**   ▶ *Unit 1, p. 21*

Complete the letter with *has to / have to / don't have to*.

Dear buzz

My friend often visits me in the evening, but then she ... (1) walk home alone. Her mum and dad can't pick her up because they ... (2) work in the evenings. The problem is that she ... (3) walk along dark streets. She says that I ...(4) worry about her, but I worry a lot. I ... (5) be sure that she's OK, so I phone her on her mobile.

A nervous friend

More practice 7   **Tips for visitors in your town**   ▶ *Unit 1, p.21*

Write tips for British visitors in your town. Use the ideas from exercises 1 and 5 and your own ideas. Put the text in your DOSSIER. Think about these questions:

– What's famous / interesting / fun / popular in your town?

– Do you have to travel by car?

– Where can you watch or do sports / go shopping?

– What do you have to wear in winter?

– What parts of the town aren't interesting for tourists?

– What food or drink should tourists try?

Unit 2

More practice 1 **WORDS** **Teen talk** ▶ *Unit 2, p. 30*

When teenagers talk together, they often use special phrases.

a) Copy each phrase onto a piece of card.

| All's good. | Cool! | That's good. | It sucks! |

| Oh, come on! | You're joking! | Sounds good. | What a pain! |

Pick the correct German phrase from the box and write it on the back of the card.

> Spitzenwitz! • Na, komm schon! • Das ist gut. • Voll blöd! •
> Klingt gut. • Das nervt! • Alles ist gut. • Cool!

b) Pick good answers from your cards for these sentences:

1 I met a really nice boy at the youth club yesterday.   ?

2 How's life?   ?

3 You have to help your dad in the kitchen.   ?

4 What's your new school like?   ?

5 Do you have 50 euros for me?   ?

c) 👥 **Walk around:**

Half the class **(partners A):**
– Walk around with your English book.
– Say one of the sentences in b).
– Then go on to another partner.

The other half of the class **(partners B):**
– Walk around with your *Teen Talk*-cards.
– Listen and answer with a phrase on one of your cards. Show the card too.
– Then go on to another partner.

After a few minutes, partners A and B swap roles.

More help **2d** **This isn't a park!** ► *Unit 2, p. 31*

Find the right answers for the five questions.
Be careful! You won't need two answers.

Because I like sheep.

1 Is that your car?
2 How old are you?
3 Can you drive?
4 Where are you from?
5 Do you like it here in Mickleton?

With my dog.   Yes, it is.   No, not really.

Yes, I can.   I'm from London.   I'm 14.

More practice 2 **The story** ► *Unit 2, p. 32*

a) What are the missing words in sentences 1–9?

father • Police officer Butler • daughter

Who did what?
1 Molly, the ... of farmer John Taylor, saved three sheep.
2 John Taylor, Molly's ... was proud of her.
3 ... spoke to the newspaper.

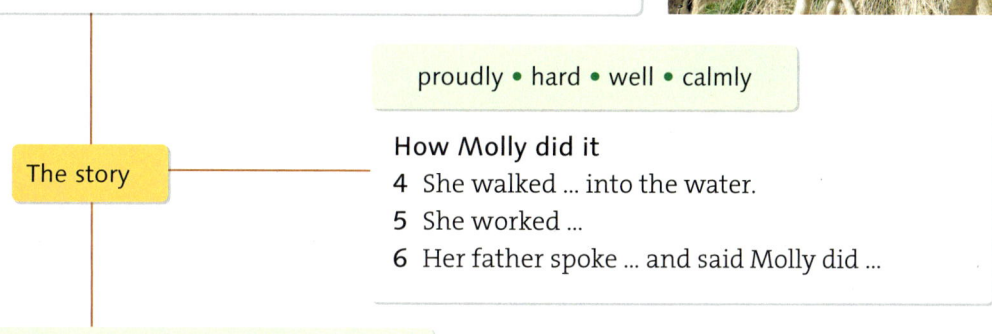

proudly • hard • well • calmly

The story

How Molly did it
4 She walked ... into the water.
5 She worked ...
6 Her father spoke ... and said Molly did ...

deep • dangerous • heavy • wet • brave

How things were
7 Molly was ... when she walked into the water.
8 The water wasn't too ... or ... for Molly.
9 The sheep were ... because they were ...

b) Now look back at page 32 and check your answers.

c) 👥 Look again at your sentences and tell a partner the story of Molly and the sheep:
Molly, the daughter of farmer John Taylor, saved three sheep.
She walked ...
...

Unit 2

More practice 3   **NOW YOU** ▶ *Unit 2, p. 32*

What can *you* do well? Write as many sentences as you can.

I can cook well.
I can play the guitar well.
I can …

2   You're a reporter ▶ *Unit 2, p. 35*

a) **Finish the sentences with the right words.**

> car • dog • farm • home • idea • night • Rob • rubbish

A   Rob ran to Molly's field with his …

B   Molly phoned …

C   The two police officers couldn't drive …

D   The police said the CCTV was a good …

E   Rob wrote the number of the …

F   Rob and Molly saw lights of a car at …

G   Rob's dad put CCTV cameras on the …

H   Rob's dog, Wally, found some …

b) **Now put sentences A–H in the right order and tell the story for a newspaper.**

More practice 4   **Who was it?** ▶ *Unit 2, p. 35*

a) **Copy the sentences and write the missing name(s).**

> The fox • Missy • Molly (3x) • Molly's dad • Molly's mum •
> police officers (2x) • Rob (3x) • Robs's father • Wally

1   … wasn't well and had to stay in bed.

2   … and … ran along the track to Molly's farm.

3   The sheep ran into the next field and … and … came behind them.

4   … and … put up CCTV cameras on the Taylors' farm.

5   … and … saw the fox.

6   … had a chicken in its mouth.

7   Much later … went to the door.

8   Two … spoke with her.

9   The … couldn't go home because …'s car was at the end of the track.

b) **Look back at the story and check your answers.**

More practice 5 **An exciting night!** ► *Unit 2, p. 35*

Imagine that you're Rob or Molly. Write your diary about the night at the Taylors' farm.
- Before you write, first decide if you're Rob or Molly.
- Then write like this:

Rob's story
Saturday night was very exciting!
I watched a DVD with Molly and then
we checked the CCTV monitor.
Suddenly we saw ...
We ran to the chickens and suddenly
we saw ...
Molly parked the car at the end of ...,
so the big black car couldn't ...
I wrote down ...
Then I went back to ... and waited
for Molly.
Later two ... came to the door.
They spoke with ...
They couldn't go home because ...

Molly's story
Saturday night was very exciting!
I watched a DVD with Rob and then
we checked the CCTV monitor.
Suddenly we saw ...
We ran to the chickens and suddenly
we saw ...
I parked the car at the end of ...,
so the big black car couldn't ...
Rob wrote down ...
Then Rob went back to ... and waited
for me.
Later two ... came to the door.
They spoke with ...
They couldn't go home because ...

More help **3**  **NOW YOU** ► *Unit 2, p. 37*

Now write your comment (40–60 words) for the internet forum *My ideal place*.
Put your text in your DOSSIER.
Copy the sentences from the Düsseldorf text, but change the words in red and write about
your ideal town.

Düsseldorf is a big city in the west
of Germany. My uncle and aunt live
there, and I think it's a great place
to live.
I like the shops.
Also, you can go everywhere by bus.
That's great when I want to visit my
friends.
So Düsseldorf is my ideal place to
live.

Do you remember the *Writing Course* from
Unit 1?

You can use sentences from your English
book and change them.

For example from Alfies's text on page 37:

You can go everywhere by bus.

=> You can go to town / to the beach / to the
park / to the shops ... by bus.

Unit 2

3b Molly and Rob ▸ *Unit 2, p. 41*

NOW YOU   What about you? Write six sentences about yourself.
I've … once / a few times / lots of times.   I've never …

(ride) a horse

(speak) to a star

(be) to a beach

(have) a disaster

(find) money in the street

(work) on a farm

More practice 6   **Chores**   ▸ *Unit 2, p. 41*

The table shows you how often Molly,
Rob and his sister Jodie have helped
at home over the last few days.

a) Look at the table. Then copy and
complete the sentences.
1 … has helped a lot.
2 … and … haven't helped a lot.

b) Now copy and complete the sentences.
1 Molly has … (hoover) the house.
2 And she has … (fill) the dishwasher.
3 She has … (wash) the car too.
4 Molly and Rob have … (clean) the kitchen.
5 And they've … (cook) lunch.
6 And what about Jodie – has she … (help) at home? – No, she hasn't. Not once!

	Molly	Rob	Jodie
hoover house	I	never	never
fill dishwasher	IIII	never	never
wash car	I	never	never
clean kitchen	II	I	never
cook lunch	II	I	never

Diese Verbens sind
alle regelmäßig.
Endung also: *-ed.*

Unit 3

More help | **1a** **Trouble at school** ▶ *Unit 3, p. 50*

Talk to a partner about the pictures. What's the right order of the pictures?

1 First talk about these questions:

Who is in each photo? Where are they? What is happening?

A

B

C

D

> In picture A there are some kids. They're at school. One boy has money. Maybe he's buying something?

> In picture B there are two teachers. One teacher is talking to the boy from picture A. Maybe he is the principal and the boy is in trouble.

> In picture C a … is coming to school. He has a big …. His bag is … than the other students' bags. What's … his bag?

> In picture D there are some … and a …. She's talking to the students. Maybe they have done something wrong?

2 Then talk about the order of the pictures.

> I think picture … is first.

> Yes, and then it's picture …

> Really? I don't agree. I think picture … comes before picture …

1d Trouble at school ▸ *Unit 3, p. 50*

Listen again and finish these sentences.

1 Ben does not want to meet the …
2 He tries to sell …
3 **One** packet of crisps costs …p.
4 When the teacher comes Ben puts his bag behind his …
5 Ms Hall takes Ben to the … office.
6 At this school you aren't allowed to … crisps and chocolate bars.

More practice 1 **WORDS** ▸ *Unit 3, p. 51*

a) Copy the network. Then write food and drink words
for the five blue boxes. Write as many words as you can.

> Use the words in the
> green box and use
> your own ideas too.

> biscuits • bread • cake • cereal bars • cheese • chicken • chips • chocolate bars • crisps •
> fruit • hot dogs • ice cream • jam • juice • lasagne • milk • potatoes • salad • sausages •
> energy drinks • soup • tea • toast • vegetables • water

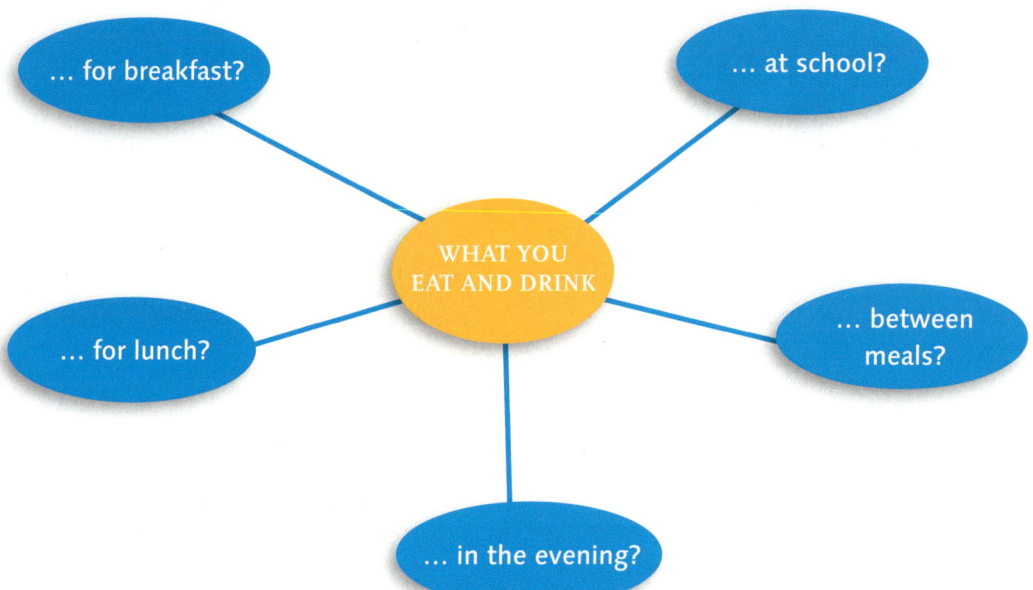

b) Now complete these sentences. Give as many examples as you can in each sentence.

1 I should eat less …
2 I should drink less …
3 I should eat more …
4 I should drink more …

More practice 2 **Food at your school** ▶ *Unit 3, p. 51*

What did you learn in your walk around? Report to the class:

I talked to four / six / … people.

Two people said we can / can't buy …

Two people think this is good / bad.

Three others think …

More practice 3 **Ben and Mrs Fox** ▶ *Unit 3, p. 52*

Read these sentences. Are they true, false or not in the dialogue?

1 Ben was better at school last term.

2 Mrs Fox says Ben isn't a good salesperson.

3 Ben is the best at maths.

4 Ben wants to sell things at school again.

5 Mrs Fox heard about the new competition on the internet.

6 There's information about the competition in the school newsletter.

More help **3** 👥 YOUR TASK **Are you good at business?** ▶ *Unit 3, p. 53*

Here are some ideas for your poster: And here are some ideas for your presentation:

BIZ 4 KIDZ

Our business plan:
make and sell animal balloons

What do we need?
balloons, pens

How much will they cost?
50 balloons cost 4 euros.
4 pens cost 5 euros.

How much money do we need?
only 9 euros

How many balloons can we sell?
maybe 50

How much can we get for the balloons?
1 euro

How much profit can we make?
41 euros

> Here's our business plan. It's for animal balloons.

> We must buy the balloons and some pens – about 9 euros.

> We think that we can sell about 50 balloons. People have to pay 1 euro for each balloon.

> If we sell 50 balloons, we'll make 50 euros. That's a profit of 41 euros.

> That's our business plan. Thank you for listening.

3 DIFF BANK

//● 2 What's the right answer? ▶ Unit 3, p. 55

Copy and complete the sentences about the story.
1 Ben's dad was unhappy at first because the kitchen ....
2 Ben's dad thinks school is ...
3 Ben's dad thought the cakes were OK, but ...
4 Ben got his new idea from a ...

More practice 4 Tell the story ▶ Unit 3, p. 55

Put the sentences in the right order and tell the story.
A Ben's dad tried a cupcake and said it was OK – but it had to be something special.
B Ben and his friends made cupcakes in Ben's kitchen.
C Ben got an idea for his business on the way to school – from a Beatles poster.
D Ben and his friends didn't sell many cupcakes at school, so Ben was fed up.
E Ben told his dad about the competition, but his dad wasn't impressed.
F The kitchen was messy and Ben's dad was angry.

More help 3c The end of the story ▶ Unit 3, p. 55

Copy the table into your exercise book. Then listen again to the radio programme and complete your table.

	King Richard	Woodlands	South Liverpool
What are they selling?	...	...	cupcakes
What's their profit?	£...	£153	£...

More practice 5 Tell the end of the story ▶ Unit 3, p. 55

● Finish the sentences to tell the end of the story.

First Kiera Patel, the TV reporter, talked to the kids from ...
They had different sorts of milkshakes, for example ...
Kiera tried a milkshake and it was ...

Next Kiera talked to the team from ...
They had lots of ...
The books weren't expensive because ...

Then Kiera talked to the kids from South Liverpool High School. They looked like ...
Their cupcakes were ...
And they looked good too because ...

In the end, Ben and his friends didn't win the competition. They got ...

More help **2** **NOW YOU** ▸ *Unit 3, p. 57*

| I think | diving   dancing   football
gymnastics   hang gliding
hiking   ice hockey   judo
skateboarding   skiing
swimming   street surfing
tae kwon do   table tennis | is | a
an | amazing
great
terrible
boring
exciting
dangerous
stupid | sport | for everybody.
for women.
for men.
for young people. |

| In my opinion | its too dangerous.
it's too violent.
it's expensive.
it's a waste of time.
it makes you fit and strong.
it's a great team sport. |

| I think | women
men
young people | can do the same sport as | men.
women.
older people. |

| I also think that | it's a very popular sport.
other sports are more popular.
… |

| I really hope that | (more) women
(more) young people
everybody | will | do this sport.
stop doing this sport. |

More practice 6 **Mediation** ▸ *Unit 3, p. 58*

Du sollst dolmetschen, aber weißt das Wort nicht?

a) Versuche es mit dem Gegenteil. Beispiel:

Mein Haus ist klein. => *My house isn't big.*

> Wenn du für jemanden dolmetschen sollst, brauchst du nicht jedes Wort zu übersetzen. Es reicht, wenn du den Sinn wieder gibst.

1 Das Wasser ist heiß. (Du weißt *hot* nicht.)
  => *The water isn't c...*
2 Mein Freund ist traurig. (Du weißt *sad* nicht.)
  => *My friend isn't h...*
3 Deine Tasse ist leer. (Du weißt *empty* nicht.)
  => *Your cup isn't f...*
4 Ich glaube, Arsenal wird verlieren.
  (Du weißt *lose* nicht.)
  => *I think Arsenal won't w...*

5 Das war ein spannender Film!
  (Du weißt *exciting* nicht.)
  => *The film was not b...*
6 Ich bin anderer Meinung.
  (Du weißt *disagree* nicht.)
  => *I don't a...*

b) Versuche, dich anders auszudrücken. Verwende Wörter aus dem grünen Kasten, die dasselbe bedeuten.

> Vielleicht kennst du ein Wort mit ähnlicher Bedeutung? Beispiel:
> *on the ferry* => *on the boat*
> Oder du kannst dasselbe mit anderen Worten sagen? Beispiel:
> *Can we pay with euros?* => *We only have euros. Is that OK?*

an apple, banana or orange • hard • mother's sister • quickly • sells things • who aren't children

1 Meine Hausaufgaben sind schwierig.
  (Du weißt *difficult* nicht.) => *My homework is ...*
2 Meine Tante hat angerufen.
  (Du weißt *aunt* nicht.) => *My ... phoned.*
3 Du schreibst schnell.
  (Du weißt *fast* nicht.) =>*You write ...*
4 Möchtest du etwas Obst?
  (Du weißt *fruit* nicht.) => *Would you like ...?*
5 Was zahlen Erwachsene?
  (Du weißt *adults* nicht.) => *How much is it for people ...*
6 Meine Schwester ist Verkäuferin.
  (Du weißt *salesperson* nicht.) => *My sister ...*

//● 2 **The man in the tourist office** ▸ *Unit 3, p. 58*

a) Listen to the dialogue again.

This time, listen to the man in the tourist office. What are the right answers?

1 If you're under 15, a ticket is only ...
2 The next ferry leaves at ...
3 You can sit inside or outside. Outside you ... more.
4 There's a bank near here, in ... Street.

b) 👥 Now give your partner the information – in German. Then listen and check.

> Der Mann sagt, dass ...

More practice 7   **A summary – with mistakes!**   ▸ *Unit 3, p. 59*

a) Read the summary. Then correct the mistakes in red.

The three friends meet in North Park. Alfie plays basketball there.
Then they have a competition, and Sam wins.
The next week they meet again in the street.
They play three games – skipping, pilates and jogging.
Tally is very good at jogging. Sam is very good at pilates. And Ruby is good at skipping. Alfie is good at all three sports.
In the end they all play tennis together.

b) Now watch the film again and check your answers.

4   **What are Ben's ideas for Sunday?**   ▸ *Unit 3, p. 61*

Finish the sentences.

1 If it … (rain) on Sunday, Ben … (stay) at home.
2 But if Ben … (stay) at home, he … (be) bored.
3 If Ben's friends … (come) to his house,
   they … (have fun).
4 If Ben … (have) some milk, eggs and flour,
   they … (make) more cupcakes.
5 And if the cupcakes … (look) nice,
   Ben's friends … (eat) them. They don't
   need any cakes for the competition now!

> Im *if*-Satz: *simple present*
> Im Hauptsatz: *will-future*

More practice 8   **NOW YOU**   ▸ *Unit 3, p. 61*

What can you say about next weekend? Complete the sentences.
Use your own ideas if you can.

1 I'll be very happy if … I have no homework / there's a good show on TV / …
2 But mum and dad won't be very happy if … my music is too loud / dad can't find work / …
3 I'll stay in bed late if … we don't go on a trip / I'm tired / …
4 But I'll get up early if … we visit my uncle and aunt / I go swimming with my sister / …
5 I'll go to town if …
6 I'll be a bit sad if …

Unit 3 ▶ **Stop! Check! Go!**

More help **8b** READING and WRITING **More sport at school?** ▶ *Unit 3, p. 65*

Copy the table.

reasons for more sport	reasons against more sport

Now put the phrases from the green box in the correct column.

> makes you active and strong • need sport to stay healthy • lots of sports are boring •
> do your best for your team • not enough really good sports • as important as maths •
> can try different sorts of sport • don't need sport at school • feel great •
> can do sport outside school

reasons for more sport	reasons against more sport
makes you active and ...	boring

Unit 4

More practice 1 **Sports clothes and equipment** ▶ *Unit 4, p. 70*

What things did MacBean's sell?

a) Match the photos (A–H) with the right words. Example: *A: first aid kits*

Trainers only **£9.99**

Rain jackets from **£12.99**

Walking boots from **£39.99**

Sunglasses from **£4.99**

First aid kits **£4.99**

Sleeping bags from **£8.99**

Tents from **£29.99**

Rain trousers from **£8.99**

b) 👥 Work with a partner. Pick **A** or **B**.

A	Cover the words in the yellow bubbles. Partner A draws one of the things A–H on paper.  Partner B writes the word for each thing next to the picture.
B	Cover the words in the yellow bubbles. Partner A spells one of the things A–H. 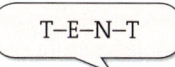 Partner B writes the word(s) on paper.

Now look at the words and check that Partner B has written them correctly.
Then change roles.

More practice 2   **How to run a B&B**   ▶ *Unit 4, p. 71*

Read Kara's comments about their new *bed and breakfast*. Write the correct sentences.

1 "We must teach ourselves / themselves business," said mum.
2 And mum bought herself / himself a book – *How to run a B&B*.
3 "You'll have to look after themselves / yourselves in the morning," mum said to Jamie and me, "because we'll be busy."
4 Jamie said, "I want to help, so I'll teach myself / yourself how to cook nice meals."
5 Jamie put tea and coffee in the visitors' rooms, so they can help themselves / ourselves.
6 And dad has stopped blaming herself / himself for what happened at MacBean's!

🎧 **More practice 3**   **More visitors for *Lochside B&B***   ▶ *Unit 4, p. 73*

Write the names of the visitors. Then listen and write the correct date next to each name.
🔘 Write the times too.

1 Perry
2 Brown
3 Johnson
4 Taylor
5 Jones
6 Schmidt

27th July	31st July	1st August
15th August	16th August	27th August

More practice 4 **Tell the story** ▶ *Unit 4, p. 75*

⭕ Copy and complete the network with the right adjectives.

1
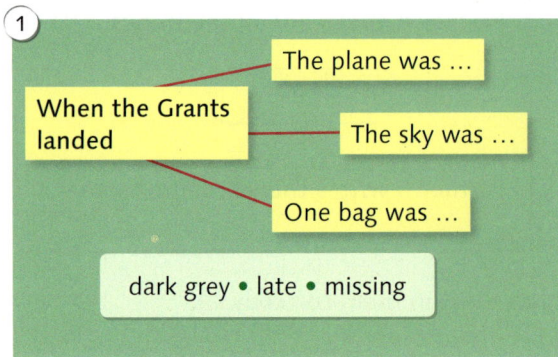

When the Grants landed
- The plane was …
- The sky was …
- One bag was …

dark grey • late • missing

2
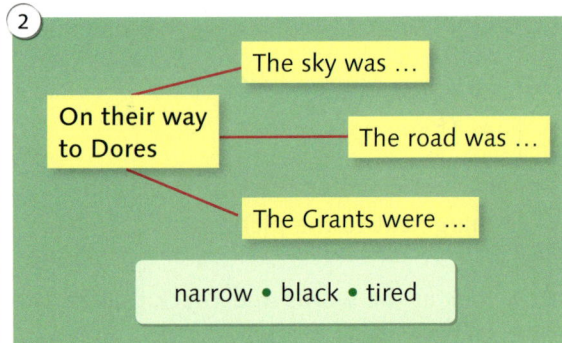

On their way to Dores
- The sky was …
- The road was …
- The Grants were …

narrow • black • tired

3
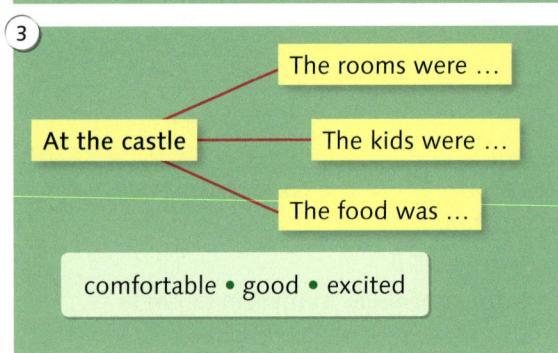

At the castle
- The rooms were …
- The kids were …
- The food was …

comfortable • good • excited

4
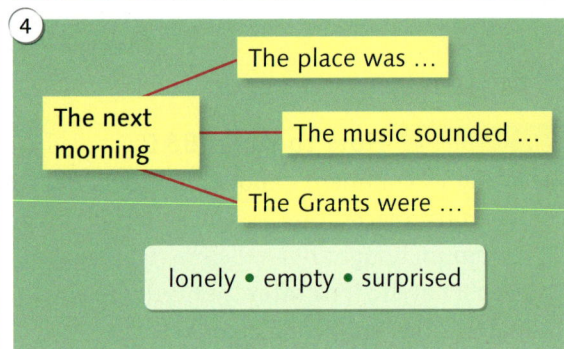

The next morning
- The place was …
- The music sounded …
- The Grants were …

lonely • empty • surprised

More practice 5 **WORDS** ▶ *Unit 4, p. 75*

Be careful: The verbs are in the wrong sentences!
Write the sentences with the six verbs in the right sentences.

1

The plane ~~laughed~~.

2

She ~~waved~~ a warning.

3

They all ~~hired~~ happily.

4

The old man ~~hooted~~.

5

The car isn't mine. I ~~landed~~ it.

6

The young man ~~chatted~~ goodbye.

More help **2** **NOW YOU** ▸ *Unit 4, p. 76*

You're Duncan.

a) Read the story *Ghosts don't exist!* again (pages 74/75).

b) Then write your story. The sentences below will help you.

We came into a big old …
My sister and I were very excited because …
First we went upstairs to our room. Then we went …
Some people played music and some people danced.
We … too.

But the next morning, the castle was …
When we went outside, we heard …
We saw … But he was alone.

At about 11 am we arrived at our …
Then we found the castle on a ….
It was … castle.

In the afternoon we visited …
It was a ruin. But the last family who lived
at Urquhart Castle was … !
So maybe we saw the ghosts of the Grants?

 More help **1b** **Who is Amy Macdonald?** ▸ *Unit 4, p. 77*

Listen again. Make notes about Amy MacDonald.

– First copy the headings on the right
  in your exercise book.
– Then listen and make short notes
  (1–4 words per answer).

Amy Macdonald
Her work: She's a …
Born: (year) …
Country: …
First hit: …
Instrument: …
Hobbies: …
Favourite groups:

 **More practice 6** **A famous Scottish person** ▸ *Unit 4, p. 77*

a) Find information about a famous Scottish person: age, hobbies, where he/she lives, why he/she is famous, what he/she does or did, etc. Here are some ideas:

Alexander Bell – scientist   Sean Connery – actor   Arthur Conan Doyle – writer
Robert Burns – poet   Kenny Dalglish – footballer   Amy Macdonald – singer

b) Now write a text about him or her for an online magazine.
Write as many sentences as you can.

My famous Scottish person is …
He/She was born on [date] in …
He/She is/was a famous singer/actor/
football player/film star/writer/…
He/She is famous because he/she …
He/She also likes/liked …
He/She is/was good at …

Alexander Bell

Robert Burns

Unit 4

More practice 7 **Holidays in Scotland** ▸ *Unit 4, p. 78*

a) Read these statements. Then pick the best brochure from page 78
(*Around Loch Ness* or *Maggie's Lodge*) for each statement.
1 You'd love to visit a Scottish castle.
2 You're a big mountain biking fan.
3 You want to go for a walk in the Highlands, but you don't have any food.
4 You want to see as much of Loch Ness and the Highlands as possible.
5 You enjoy trips on lakes.
6 You need accommodation, but you don't have enough money for your own room.

b)  Read the three tourist profiles below again and complete these sentences.
1 Tourist A will choose Maggie's Lodge because …
2 Tourist B won't be very happy because …
3 I think that tourist C will take the … tour because …

Tourist A
You're on holiday and want to spend two or three days near Loch Ness with a friend. You don't have a lot of money, you need a cheap place.

Tourist B
You're staying in Inverness with your family. You love Nessie stories, so you would like to visit a good Nessie museum.

Tourist C
You've just arrived in Scotland with some friends. You'd like to visit the Loch Ness region – quickly. You only have one day!

3 **More questions** ▸ *Unit 4, p. 81*
Pick the answers to these questions.
You won't need two words.
1 What do you call visitors who spend the night in your house?
2 What's the white stuff that you use to make bread or cake?
3 What do you call the thing that you use to cut food?
4 What do you call a person who wins a sports competition?
5 What do you call a person who sells things like cars?
6 What's the thing that you wear when you go outside and it's cold?

champion • coat •
cook • guests • flour •
knife • mirror •
salesperson

Unit 4 ▸ **Stop! Check! Go!**

2 LANGUAGE What do you call …? ▸ *Unit 4, p. 82*

a) Eight tourists can't think of the word in English. What do they say or ask?
Write the correct sentences.

1 I need a paper that / who shows where places are.
2 What do you call a person that / who is not a child?
3 What's the boat that / who takes people across a river?
4 What do you call the people that / who fight against fire?
5 What's the name of the person that / who cuts or styles your hair?
6 What's the white stuff that / who you put on rice or potatoes or eggs?
7 What do you call the things that / who you wear on your feet under your shoes?
8 Can you tell me the word for the person that / who helps when your car is broken?

b) Now look at the pictures below. Write the right word after each sentence in a).

salt   mechanic   hairdresser   firefighters

socks   map   ferry   adult

3 LANGUAGE Enjoy yourselves! ▸ *Unit 4, p. 83*

Jamie and Kara want to go camping. They are talking to their parents.
Pick the right words from the box
and complete the dialogue.
– You won't need all the words.
– You'll need one word twice.

myself • yourself • herself • himself
ourselves • yourselves • themselves

Jamie Mum, Kara and I want to go camping.
Mum Camping? Is that a good idea? That's what I ask … (1).
Dad Oh, I'm sure the kids can look after … (2), Kate.
Jamie Of course we can look after … (3)!
Kara Don't forget Jamie has taught … (4) to cook!
Dad Ah yes, I hear you're good at cooking soup for … (5), Jamie!
Mum Well, OK then. You go camping and enjoy … (6).
But I won't blame … (7) if you come back hungry!

TF 1 London facts

Travel …

… by Tube	… by a London bus	… or by taxi

The Tube is the popular name for London Underground trains. It's the oldest underground train system in the world – it opened in 1863! Today there are 270 stations and 11 lines. Over 3 million people go on the Tube every day.

London's red double-decker buses are famous. The city has more than 700 bus routes and most Londoners live only 400 metres away from one of the 19,500 bus stops. Teens from 11–15 travel free – but they need a special photo card.

Taxi drivers must take a very difficult test. To pass the test[1] they must know 25,000 streets in London. Drivers learn for the test for two to four years.

Buckingham Palace

The king or queen lives and works here. When the Queen is at home, you see her flag on top of[2] the palace.

You can see the guards change in front of the palace at 11.30 am every day in summer, or every second day for the rest of the year. It's free to watch the guard ceremony.

The palace has 240 bedrooms, 78 bathrooms and 775 rooms in all. About 800 people work in or for the palace: cooks, cleaners[3], gardeners, drivers, etc.

Buckingham Palace is **open** from July to the end of September. **Travel** by bus, or take the tube to St James' Park, or walk! It's only 15 minutes on foot from Big Ben.

Guards[4] (soldiers[5]) with black and red uniforms and big, black hats stand outside the palace.

---

[1] pass a test *eine Prüfung bestehen*   [2] on top of *oben*   [3] cleaner *Reinigungskraft*   [4] guard *Wache*   [5] soldier *Soldat/in*

Wembley Stadium

Wembley Stadium, the home of the England national football team, opened in 2007. With space for 90 000 fans and 310 fans in wheelchairs, it's the second largest stadium in Europe. It has 688 places where fans can buy food and drink, and 2,618 toilets.

Wembley is a stadium for lots of different sports, especially American football, rugby and athletics. It's also a famous place for music concerts.
It's open every day, but not over Christmas and on 1st January, or when there is a game or concert. **Travel** by tube or bus. It's 12 kilometres from the centre of London to Wembley!

London Eye

About 3.5 million people ride the London Eye every year. It's 135 metres tall and a tour takes 30 minutes. The Eye moves[6] so slowly that it doesn't stop when people get on. **It's open** every day (but not on Christmas Day). **Travel** by tube to Waterloo. Or walk over the river from the Houses of Parliament.

Harry Potter

There are lots of Harry Potter film places in London. The way into the Leaky Cauldron is at Leadenhall Market, Harry speaks to a snake in London Zoo, and the train to Hogwarts goes from platform 9¾ at Kings Cross Station.

Big Ben

Dong, dong, dong, dong! For many people Big Ben is the most famous sound of London. When Londoners say "Big Ben" they

usually mean the clock tower – but Big Ben is really the name of the very large bell. You can hear Big Ben very well if you stand next to the Houses of Parliament.

Sherlock Holmes

Sherlock Holmes lived at 221B Baker Street ... No! That's not true! Sherlock Holmes wasn't a real person. He was a famous detective in books by Arthur Conan Doyle. The first Sherlock Holmes story came out in 1887.
But today, 221B Baker Street is a great museum about Sherlock Holmes. **It's open** from 9.30 am to 5.30 pm. **Travel** by tube to Baker Street, and see the statue of Sherlock Holmes outside the station!

---

[6] move *sich bewegen*

TF 2 Dick Whittington – a Christmas pantomime

What is a pantomime?

In Britain a pantomime (or 'panto') is a funny show. The characters[1] in a panto talk, shout and sing. Pantos are in every theatre at Christmas time and also in small villages, schools and clubs. And they are very, very popular.

The stories are traditional children's stories, but pantos aren't just for kids – everybody loves them!

Pantomimes have some very special rules:

- A big man in colourful clothes plays a woman. This character is always very funny. He (or she?!) makes lots of silly jokes and sings a silly song.

- The audience[2] laughs and shouts a lot! For example, the people shout "Boo!" when they see the bad guy.

- There's always a bad guy who tries to make trouble. But everything is always OK in the end.

The audience at a pantomime

Everything is OK in the end.

1 It's all wrong!

Correct these sentences.

1 In pantomimes the characters don't talk.
2 They're only for children.
3 The people who watch a panto have to be quiet.
4 The ending is sad.

---

[1] character *Figur*   [2] audience *Zuschauer, Publikum*

Scene 1 Welcome!

Narrator[3] —	*(to audience)* Hello everybody!
Audience	Hello!
Narrator	Welcome to our pantomime!
5	It's the story of Dick Whittington. Look! Here he is. Hi Dick! But you look sad … What's wrong?

Dick	I'm sad and tired. You see, I tried to find work in London, but
10	I couldn't find a job. So I'm going home to the Cotswolds!
Cat	*(comes in)* No work in London? You're wrong!
Dick	What? You're a cat, … but you
15	can talk?
Cat	Yes, I'm Tommy the cat. And I know there's work for you in London. Listen to the church bells.
Dick	The bells?
20 Tommy	Yes! Listen!

> Dong! Dong!
> Go back to London, Whittington!
> You'll find a great job!
> Dong! Dong!

Dick	*(to audience)* Hm. Are the bells right? Well, I'll go back to London and I'll look for a job again.
Tommy	And I'll come with you.

25 Scene 2 A London market

(Characters: Dick, Tommy the cat, Alice)

Dick	*(to his cat)* Oh Tommy! I need a job! But nobody at this market can help me.
Tommy	Oh, I'm sure you'll find work 30 soon. Remember the bells. They're never wrong.
Dick	Oh, I don't know …
Alice	Hello. You're beautiful[4], aren't you!
Dick	*(surprised)* Oh, hello. Thank you! 35
Alice	No, not you. I'm talking to your cat! What's his name?
Dick	Ah, the cat. This is Tommy. He's a very intelligent cat. He can talk.
Alice	*(laughs)* Oh no, he can't. 40

(Narrator holds a sign for the audience: Oh yes, he can!)

Audience and Tommy	Oh yes he can!
Alice	*(surprised)*

Oh, you're 45
right! He
can talk!
That's very
clever.
My name 50
is Alice
Fitzwarren. What's your name?

Dick	Dick Whittington. I'm looking for a job.
Alice	Really? My dad needs somebody 55 to help him in his shop. Come on. It's this way. *(They leave.)*

Scene 3 Mr Fitzwarren's shop

(Mr Fitzwarren has a problem with rats in his shop. Sarah, the cook, is running after the rats – 60 but they're not scared of her!)

Sarah	*(sings)* I don't like you rats! You eat my cheese! So run away please!
Sarah	*(to audience)* Can you help me? 65 Maybe if you sing my song, all the rats will run away!
Audience	*(sings)* I don't like you rats! You eat my cheese! So run away please! 70
Sarah	Yes, go away! We don't want you here!

---

[3] narrator *Erzähler/in*   [4] beautiful *schön*

(Dick, Alice and Tommy arrive.)

Dick _____ Oh. That's not very nice!

75 Sarah _____ No, not you. The rats.

Dick _____ Oh, I see. My cat can help you.

Alice _____ Oh yes. Tommy can help you.

Sarah _____ Oh no, he can't.

(Narrator holds a sign for the audience:
80 *Oh yes, he can!)*

Audience _____ Oh yes, he can!

Sarah _____ Oh no, he can't.

Audience _____ Oh yes he can!

Dick _____ Go on, Tommy!

85 *(Tommy runs after the rats and they run*
away. Mr Fitzwarren arrives and sees this.)

Mr Fitzw. _____ That's a good cat. *(to Dick)*
Would you like a job? You and
your cat can live here if you like.

90 Dick _____ Oh, yes please!

Scene 4 King Rat

(Characters: Narrator, King Rat, Rat 2)

Narrator _____ Good! Now Dick has a job and
lives in a nice house. But ... there's
95 a problem. You see, this is a
pantomime, and so there's a bad
guy. And the bad guy is King Rat.
He's very bad. Here he is.

(King Rat and Rat 2 arrive. The narrator holds a
100 *sign for the audience: Boo!)*

Audience _____ Boo!

Narrator _____ Louder!

Audience _____ Booooo!!!

King Rat _____ *(to Rat 2)* I don't like cats! And I
really don't like Tommy the cat! 105

Rat 2 _____ Yes, but what can we do?

King Rat _____ Listen to me! I have a plan.

Rat 2 _____ A plan?

King Rat _____ Yes. Tonight[5] we go to Alice's
room. We take her diamond 110
necklace ...
... and we put
the necklace in
Dick's room.
OK? 115

Rat 2 _____ *(He's not sure)* OK. But ... why?

King Rat _____ You stupid rat! Because Mr
Fitzwarren will find the necklace
in Dick's room. Then he'll be
angry. *(laughs)* Muw-ha-ha-ha- 120
ha-ha-ha! And then Dick and his
cat will have to leave the house!

(Narrator holds a sign for the audience: Boo!)

Audience _____ Boo!

What happens next in the story?

Well, bad King Rat takes Alice's necklace and
puts it in Dick's room. When Mr Fitzwarren
finds it, he calls the police.

Poor Dick! He and Tommy run away. They
go to a country where there are lots of rats
and mice[6] – but no cats. But when Tommy
arrives, all the rats and mice run away! The
people are very happy, and they give Dick lots
of money.

When Dick comes back to London with his cat,
he is very rich[7]. He marries[8] Alice and he is
Lord Mayor[9] of London.

So everything is OK in the end. Hurray!

2 👥 THEATRE TIME

In a group, act out one of the scenes
of the pantomime for your class.

_____

[5] tonight *heute Abend/Nacht*   [6] mice *Mäuse*   [7] rich *reich*   [8] marry *heiraten*   [9] Lord Mayor *etwa: Oberbürgermeister*

TF 3 Liverpool and the Titanic

The Titanic was a Liverpool ship. Liverpool's *White Star Line* owned[1] the Titanic and the Captain, Edward Smith, was a Liverpool man. Some of the 885 people who worked on the
5 Titanic were from Liverpool too.
White Star Line made plans for the Titanic in 1908. They wanted a ship that was bigger and better than all other ships in the world.

People said that the new ship was the
10 strongest and safest ship in history. They thought it couldn't sink.
The Titanic left England for New York on 10th April 1912, but this was its first and last journey[2].
15 On 14th April the ship hit an iceberg. Two hours later, the Titanic sank and more than 1500 people died.

There were three groups of passengers[3] on the Titanic: first-class (325 passengers), second-class (285 passengers) and third-
20 class (706 passengers). The most expensive tickets cost £512 (about €60,000 today) and third-class tickets cost £3 to £8 (about €350 to €950 today). Third-class passengers were not allowed to visit the parts of the ship
25 that were for first-class passengers.

There were not enough lifeboats[4] for everybody. You can see in the plan that third-class passengers were a long way from the lifeboats. When the Titanic sank, 38% of
30 the first-class passengers died, but 75% of the third-class passengers lost their lives. In all, only about 700 people survived[5] and arrived in New York.

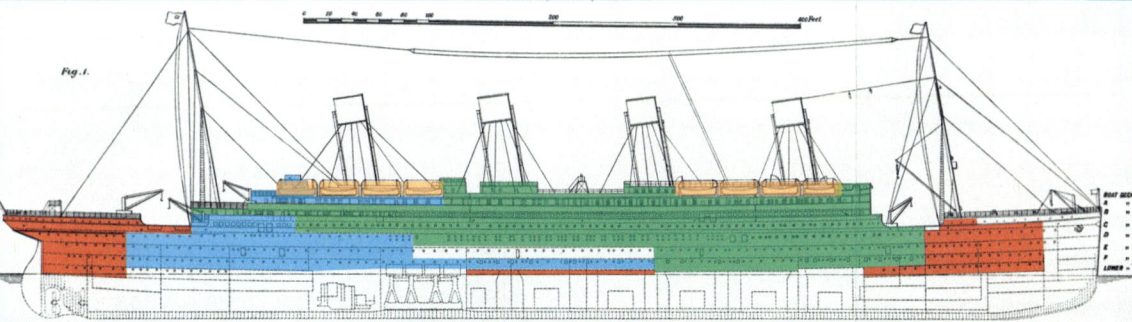

green: first class part of the ship, **blue:** second class part of the ship, **red:** third class part of the ship, **orange:** lifeboats

Erkläre diese Zahlen auf Deutsch: 885 – 1908 – 1912 – 1500 – 706 – 60 000 – 75% – 700
Beispiel: *885 Menschen arbeiteten auf …*

[1] own *besitzen*   [2] journey *Reise*   [3] passenger *Passagier*   [4] lifeboat *Rettungsboot*   [5] survive *überleben*

TF 4 Scotland facts

A Geography

Scotland is the country north of England. It's about half as big as England.

Most people live in the south, in or near the big cities of Edinburgh (the capital) and Glasgow.
Aberdeen is the only big city in the north.

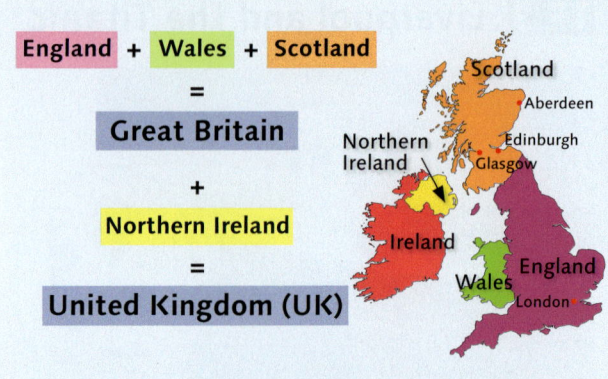

| England + Wales + Scotland = Great Britain + Northern Ireland = United Kingdom (UK) |

Number of people in Scotland's biggest cities:

Glasgow	**598,830**
Edinburgh	**486,120**
Aberdeen	**220,420**

Not many people live in the *Highlands* in the north and west. This is a region of hills and mountains: the highest mountain is Ben Nevis (1344 m).

Oil[1] and gas from the North Sea bring a lot of money and jobs to Aberdeen.

The longest river is the River Tay. There are 790 islands[2] (99 with people) and more than 30,000 freshwater lakes *(lochs)*. The biggest lake in cubic metres is Loch Ness (7,452 million m^3). Loch Ness is the most famous lake because some people think it has a monster.

B History

Scotland is part of the UK. But people from Scotland are proud to be Scottish, so don't call them English!

Older history

For hundreds of years, Scotland and England were two different countries. They often fought each other[3]. Sometimes England won, sometimes Scotland won.

In **1707** Scotland and England joined[4] and became[5] Great Britain. They had one Parliament – in London.

Modern history

Scotland has its own flag and national football team. The Scots have pounds like the English, but Scottish money looks a bit different.

1997: Scotland gets its own parliament again.

2014: The Scottish people vote about independence[6]. They decide to stay in the UK.

---

[1] oil *Öl* [2] island *Insel* [3] they fought each other *sie bekämpften sich* [4] join *sich vereinigen* [5] they became *sie wurden*
[6] vote about independence *über die Unabhängigkeit abstimmen*

C Life

Languages: Everybody in Scotland speaks English. But in the Highlands some people also speak Gaelic[7]. You'll see road signs in English and Gaelic.

Sport: Football is the most popular sport in Scotland. Golf is popular too – it started 600 years ago in St Andrews, near Edinburgh. Golf isn't an expensive sport in Scotland so everybody can play. In the Highlands you can see shinty and other traditional sports like tossing the caber[8].

tossing the caber

Festivals:
In Scotland there is a long tradition of singing and dancing, and Scottish music is very popular.

You'll also see these things at festivals in Scotland:

haggis

bagpipes

a kilt

The Loch Ness Monster

Loch Ness is a big long lake in the north of Scotland.

Is there a monster in Loch Ness? Most people say "no", but every year people take photos of something that looks like a monster.

This photo from 1934 is perhaps the most famous photo. For 60 years, people weren't sure if the photo was real or not. But in 1993 the true story came out.

It was a trick! It was really a toy submarine[9] with a model of a monster.

In 2012, Marcus Atkinson, a tourist boat captain, was on Loch Ness near Urquhart Castle. Something big followed his boat for more than two minutes. Marcus saw it on his sonar equipment, so he took a photo of the sonar picture. It looks like a big snake.

Marcus said: "I was shocked. I showed it to other boat captains and nobody knew what it was."

Experts said it was a photo of plankton (very, very small animals) in the water, but fans of the Loch Ness monster were very excited.

Stories like this explain why thousands of tourists come to Loch Ness every year to look for Nessie. Perhaps you could find Nessie too?

---

[7] Gaelic *Gälisch* [8] tossing the caber *Baumstammwerfen* [9] toy submarine *Spielzeug U-Boot*

SF 1 Vokabeln lernen

- Führe dein Vokabelheft oder deine Vokabel-kartei aus Klasse 6 weiter.

- Lerne nur 5 bis 10 neue Vokabeln auf einmal.

- Versuche, jeden Tag 10 Minuten zu lernen.

- Lerne mit jemandem zusammen. Es macht mehr Spaß, und ihr könnt euch gegenseitig abfragen.

- Finde heraus, wie du am besten lernst: durch Hören oder Nachsprechen, mit Bildern, am Computer oder Handy?

- Schreibe die neuen Wörter auch immer auf.

Weitere Tipps zum besseren Merken:

1 Mache Wortfelder

Ordne die Wörter unter einem Oberbegriff. Du kannst eine Liste machen, ein *network* oder mit Karteikarten arbeiten.

2 Finde Gegensatzpaare

Sammle Gegensatzpaare und schreibe sie z.B. auf die letzte Seite deines Vokabelhefts.

calm ↔ excited

3 Lerne *phrases* oder Beispielsätze statt Einzelwörter

Vor allem schwierige Wörter kannst du dir besser merken, wenn du sie als *phrases* lernst. *Phrases* sind Ausdrücke von zwei Wörtern oder mehr. Lerne z.B. nicht *cup*, sondern *a cup of tea*.

travel	➜	*travel by bus*
spend	➜	*spend money on clothes*
ago	➜	*two years ago*

Oder merke dir kurze Beispielsätze:

especially	➜	*I love sports, especially football.*
have to	➜	*It's late. We have to go now.*

SF 2 Unbekannte Wörter verstehen ▸ *Unit 1, p. 17*

Du kannst englische Texte verstehen – auch wenn du nicht alle Wörter kennst.

1 Schau auf die Bilder

Bilder zeigen dir oft Dinge aus dem Text. Was bedeuten
z.B. *screws, nails* und *screwdriver* im Text rechts?

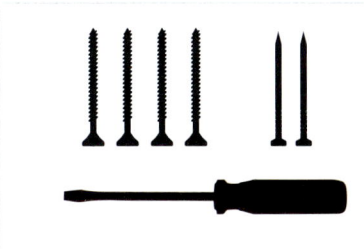

First check if you have all things:
4 screws, **2** long nails and a **screwdriver**.
You also need a **hammer** and some
sandpaper.

2 Denke an ähnliche Wörter im Deutschen

Viele englische Wörter werden ähnlich wie im Deutschen
geschrieben oder klingen ähnlich wie deutsche Wörter:
– *hammer* heißt auf Deutsch „Hammer"
– *sandpaper* bedeutet „Sand- oder Schmirgelpapier"

Was bedeuten die folgenden Wörter auf Deutsch?

> balcony • cable • element • flexible • material •
> optimistic • quality • situation • typical

Hmm, *typical* sieht aus
wie das deutsche Wort
„typisch", oder?

3 Schau auf den ganzen Satz

Du kannst ein unbekanntes Wort auch erschließen.
Lies den ganzen Satz und überlege, welches Wort
Sinn macht. Was könnten z.B. *share* und *population*
bedeuten?

1 *In our hotel my parents had a room and I had to share
a room with my little brother.*
2 *Berlin has a population of about 3 million people.*

Also, es geht um
Hotelzimmer ... ich hab's!

4 Suche Bekanntes in unbekannten Wörtern

Manchmal steckt in einem neuen Wort ein anderes
Wort, das du schon kennst. Wie heißen die folgenden
Wörter auf Deutsch?

> biker • buyer • dreamer • learner • loser •
> fruity • icy • smelly • watery •
> sunlight • haircut • high jumper

Dream kenne ich schon,
das heißt „Traum."
Dann könnte *dreamer*
„Träumer" heißen.

1: screws *Schrauben* nails *Nägel* screwdriver *Schraubendreher*
2: balcony *Balkon* cable *Kabel* element *Element* flexible *flexibel* material *Material* optimistic *optimistisch*
quality *Qualität* situation *Situation* typical *typisch* 3: share *teilen* population *Bevölkerung*
4: biker *Fahrradfahrer/in* buyer *Käufer/in* dreamer *Träumer/in* learner *Lerner* loser *Verlierer/in* fruity *fruchtig*
icy *eisig* smelly *übelriechend* watery *wässrig* sunlight *Sonnenlicht* haircut *Haarschnitt* high jumper *Hochspringer/in*

SF 3 Im Wörterbuch nachschlagen

1 Wörter alphabetisch ordnen

Alles im Wörterbuch ist alphabetisch aufgelistet:
– *U* kommt vor *V*
– *van* kommt vor *vegetables*
– *vegetables* kommt vor *verse*

> **usually** ['juːʒʊəli] meistens, normalerweise III 2 (37)
>
> **V**
>
> **van** [væn] Transporter, Liefer-wagen III 2 (30)
> °**variety (of)** [və'raɪəti] Auswahl (an)
> °**various** ['veərɪəs] (mehrere) ver-schiedene
> **vegetables,** *infml auch* **veg** ['vedʒtəblz], [vedʒ] Gemüse ɪ
> °**verse** [vɜːs] Vers, Strophe *(Lied)*

2 Zusammengesetzte Ausdrücke finden

Der Haupteintrag (z.B. *easy*) steht farbig oder fett am Anfang. Daneben oder darunter findest du oft zusammengesetzte Wörter oder Redewendungen (z.B. *take it easy*).

> **easy** ▶ **take it easy** *(umgs)* sich nicht aufregen
> ▶ **easy-going** ungezwungen, gelassen

3 Unterschiedliche Wortbedeutungen beachten

Die Ziffern 1, 2 usw. bei einem Eintrag zeigen, dass ein Wort mehrere Bedeutungen hat.

> Egal ob du ein englisches oder deutsches Wort suchst: Lies immer **alle** Einträge und entscheide dann, welches die richtige Bedeutung ist.

a) Englisch-Deutsch
Das Wort *enter* heißt am Computer *eingeben*. Was aber heißt *enter* in diesen Sätzen?

1 *When did you enter the USA? – Two weeks ago.*
2 *Please use the door on the right to enter the building.*
3 *Please enter your name here at the top of the list.*
4 *Lots of people were seasick, so they were happy when the ferry entered the harbour.*

> **enter** *Verb*
> 1 *(Zimmer)* eintreten
> 2 *(Gebäude)* betreten, hineinkommen
> 3 *(Land)* einreisen
> 4 *(Hafen)* einlaufen
> 5 *(in Liste)* eintragen
> 6 *(Computer)* eingeben

b) Deutsch-Englisch
Welches sind die richtigen englischen Wörter für *anmachen* in diesen Sätzen?

1 *Kannst du den Salat anmachen?*
2 *Wieso machst du mich an? Ich habe nichts getan.*
3 *Bitte mach das Licht an.*
4 *Er machte einen Spiegel im Bad an.*

> **anmachen** *Verb (umgs)*
> 1 *(anbringen)* put up
> 2 *(einschalten)* put on
> 3 *(anzünden)* light
> 4 *(Salat)* dress
> 5 *(kritisieren)* have a go at someone *(infml)*

3a): 1 einreisen; 2 hineinkommen; 3 eintragen; 4 einlaufen; 3b): 1 dress; 2 have a go at someone; 3 put on; 4 put up

SF 4 **Texte markieren** ▸ *Unit 3, p. 56*

1 **Wie kannst du markieren?**

Wenn du Aufgaben zu einem Text bearbeiten sollst,
solltest du wichtige Textstellen im Text markieren.
Du kannst die Stellen

– (umkreisen),

– unterstreichen,

– oder mit Textmarker hervorheben.

Aber das geht nur auf Fotokopien, nicht im geliehenen Schülerbuch.

2 **Wie gehst du vor?**

a) Lies zuerst die Aufgabe.
Rechts ist ein Beispiel.

*Read the text. Then tick the correct answers
(a, b or c).*

1 *In the 1980s Liverpool FC*
   a) won two League Championships. ☐
   b) won three FA Cups. ☐
   c) won the "Double" in 1986. ☐

2 *The Hillsborough disaster happened*
   a) in 1991. ☐
   b) in the FA Cup final. ☐
   *c) because too many people were
     in the stadium.* ☐

b) **Dann lies den Text.**
– Markiere nur die Informationen,
  die du brauchst.
– Die Textstellen für Frage 1 sind schon
  markiert. Welche Stellen würdest du
  für Frage 2 unterstreichen?

c) Jetzt ist die Lösung leicht:
Welche Kästchen musst du bei Aufgabe 1
und 2 oben rechts ankreuzen?

The Hillsborough Disaster

In the 1980s Liverpool FC had a great time.
The club won another three League
Championships and two FA Cups. In 1986
they won the "Double", which is FA Cup and
League Championship in the same year. But
the club's great time ended with the Hillsborough disaster. It was a very sad day for
Liverpool. In the FA Cup semi-final against
Nottingham Forest on 15 April 1989 there
was a panic in the stadium and hundreds of
Liverpool fans were thrown against the
fences. Ninety-four fans died that day; two
people died some time later. A report later
said that too many people were in the
stadium.

2b: FA Cup semi-final; 1989; too many
people were in the stadium.
2c; 1c; 2c.

SF 5 Prüfungen und Klassenarbeiten

1 Was musst du immer beachten?

Do Lies <u>alle</u> Arbeitsanweisungen.

better Unterstreiche wichtige Punkte.

in tests Überprüfe am Ende, ob du alle Punkte abhaken kannst.

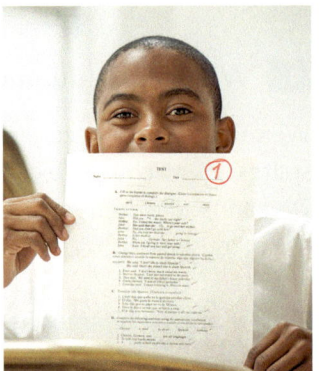

2 READING

First read the text.
Then do tasks 1–9.
Decide if the statements are true or false and tick the correct box.
Then finish the sentences. You can quote from the text.

I've lived in London since January. At first I didn't like the city, because it is very loud and noisy. After some time I really enjoyed it here and I think it's an amazing place for lots of reasons.
Firstly, you can go to many interesting places like the National History Museum where you can see dinosaurs. The best thing is: You don't have to pay to get in.
Secondly, you have nice parks, where you can have a break …

1. *He came to London at the beginning of the year. This statement is*
   a) ☐ *true*
   b) ☐ *false*
   because the text says

   _____

2. *Now he likes life in the city. This statement is*
   a) ☐ *true*
   b) ☐ *false*
   because the text says

   _____

3. *...*

Hier ist ein Beispiel für eine Leseaufgabe.

a) Lies zuerst die Arbeitsanweisung. Unterstreiche, was du tun oder beachten sollst. Hier ein Beispiel:

First <u>read</u> the text.
Then do tasks 1–9.
Decide if the statements are true or false and <u>tick</u> the correct box.
Then <u>finish</u> the sentences. You can <u>quote from the text</u>.

b) Was musst du bei dieser Aufgabe tun?
– eine Tabelle vervollständigen?
– Kästchen ankreuzen?
– Textstellen suchen?
– aus dem Text zitieren?
– falsche Aussagen korrigieren?

Du musst Kästchen ankreuzen, Textstellen suchen und aus dem Text zitieren.

3 LISTENING

Lies auch bei Höraufgaben die Arbeitsanweisung genau und unterstreiche das Wichtigste.

First read the tasks 1–6.	Was sollst du zuallererst tun?
Then listen to the discussion.	Was wirst du hören?
<u>Tick</u> the correct box or <u>complete</u>	Musst du bei jeder Aufgabe Kästchen ankreuzen?
the sentences while you are listening.	
Tick <u>only one box</u>.	Kannst du mehrere Kästchen ankreuzen?
At the end you will <u>hear the discussion again</u>.	Wie oft wirst du den Text hören?
Now read the tasks 1–6. You have 1 minute.	Wie viel Zeit hast du, um die Augaben zu lesen?

4 WRITING

Hier ist ein Beispiel für eine Schreibaufgabe.

Write an email to your English penfriend Steve. Tell him about your last class trip (two things or more).

Ask him two questions about his class trip.

Write 60 words or more.

1 Lies zuerst die Arbeitsanweisungen. Welche würdest du unterstreichen?

Dear Steve

How are you?

I feel great. We came back from a class trip last Friday.

It was fantastic. We spent a week in Norderney. It's an island in the North Sea.
We went simming and played beach volleyball.
One night we walked. It was dark and our teacher scared us. It was great fun because all the girls cried.

Where did you go on your last class trip? Tell me about it.

2 Lies Yasins email.
Hat er die Aufgabe richtig gelöst?
– Sind Anfang und Ende wie bei einer Email?
– Hat er mindestens zwei Dinge über seine Klassenfahrt geschrieben?
– Hat er zwei Fragen gestellt?
– Hat er mindestens 60 Wörter geschrieben?

1 <u>Write</u> an <u>email</u> to <u>your English penfriend</u> Steve. Tell him about your <u>last class trip</u> (<u>two things or more</u>). Ask him <u>two questions</u> <u>about his class trip</u>. Write <u>at least 60 words</u>.

2 Yasin hat zwei Dinge nicht befolgt: Er hat die Schlussformel der Email vergessen (Best wishes, Yasin) und er hat nur eine Frage zu Steves Klassenfahrt gestellt.

SF 6 Texte besser verstehen ▸ *Unit 4, p. 78*

1 Skimming

Mit dieser Technik kannst du dir schnell einen Überblick über einen Text verschaffen. Dabei liest du nur ganz kurz und schnell und achtest besonders auf **Überschriften**, **Bilder**, **Bildunterschriften** und **fett gedruckte Wörter**. Du brauchst nicht jedes Detail zu verstehen. Du bereitest z.B. einen Vortrag zum Thema *Shinty* vor und suchst allgemeine Informationen zu diesem schottischen Ballspiel. Welcher der beiden Texte eignet sich besser für dein Thema?

Strathglass Shinty Club

Where
The club is based in the village of Cannich near Loch Ness in the Scottish Highlands.

History and teams
The Shinty club has an amazing history. It started over 125 years ago and today has junior teams, a senior team, a reserve team and a women's team.

Success
The senior team presently plays in North Division 1. The village is very proud of its sports heroes.

Shinty

Game
Shinty is a team game played with sticks and a ball. It's a bit like hockey.

Rules
There are 12 players on each side.
Players can play the ball in the air and are allowed to use both sides of the stick. They mustn't use their hands – only the goalkeeper can do that. The winner is the team that scores the most goals.

League system
At present there are these divisions:

2 Scanning

Mit dieser Technik kannst du einen Text nach ganz bestimmten Informationen durchsuchen.
– Du suchst dabei nur nach wichtigen Wörtern (Schlüsselwörtern) und lässt alles andere beiseite.
– Geh dabei mit den Augen und dem Finger schnell über den Text. Das gesuchte Wort wird dir „ins Auge springen". Lies nur dort weiter, um Näheres zu erfahren. Du möchtest z.B. wissen, wie viele Spieler es bei Shinty gibt. Suche also nach dem Wort *player*.
– Wenn du das Wort nicht findest, suche nach ähnlichen Begriffen.

SF 7 Hören und Notizen machen

1 Vor dem Hören

Lies immer <u>zuerst</u> die Aufgabe. Lies sorgfältig. Hier ein Beispiel:

- *Listen to a phone call. Sarah is phoning a B&B in Glasgow and wants to book a room.*
- *Write down the information that she gives man at the B&B.*
- *There is an example at the beginning.*
- *You will hear the recording twice.*

Überlege vor dem Hören: Was könnte Sarah sagen? (Tag der Ankunft, wie viele Nächte, wie viele Personen etc.)

Merke dir genau, was du tun sollst.

Schau dir das Beispiel an. Es hilft dir.

Es macht nichts, wenn du zuerst nicht alles hast – du hörst den Text zweimal.

Typische Aufgaben sind:
- *multiple choice*-Aufgaben
- *true / false*-Aufgaben
- Bilder nach einer Reihenfolge ordnen
- eine Tabelle oder Lücken in einem Text vervollständigen wie im Beispiel rechts

Example: Name *The Hansen family*
Number of nights: _____
Date of arrival: _____
rooms: _____
number of guests: _____
pets: _____
mobile phone: _____

2 Beim Hören

- Achte beim Hören auf die Wörter, die in der Aufgabe stehen. Achtung! Die Informationen könnten in einer anderen Reihenfolge auftauchen.
- Mache dir Notizen. Verwende Symbole oder Abkürzungen, z.B. *fam r* für *family room*.
- Gib nicht auf, wenn du etwas nicht verstanden hast. Bleib ruhig und höre weiter zu. Vielleicht verstehst du beim zweiten Hören mehr. Oder vielleicht brauchst du diese Information gar nicht.

3 Nach dem Hören

- Vervollständige deine Notizen sofort.
- Konzentriere dich beim zweiten Hören auf das, was du zuerst nicht gut verstanden hast.

SF 8 Eigene Texte schreiben

A Beachte: Welche Art von Text wirst du schreiben?

1 Persönlicher Brief oder Email

– Beginne mit einer persönlichen Anrede,
z.B. *Dear Lily* oder *Hi Alex!*
– Frage, wie es deinem Freund oder deiner Freundin
geht: *How are you?*
– Erzähle, wie es dir geht, und was bei dir Interessantes
geschehen ist: *I'm tired because … Yesterday we went …
Then we had …*
– Frage, was bei deinem Freund oder deiner Freundin
so passiert ist:
What did you do last week / in the holidays / …?
– Schreibe am Ende immer einen freundlichen Gruß,
z.B. *Best wishes* oder *Lots of love* und deinen Namen.

> Hi Alex!
>
> How are you? I'm tired because I was very busy yesterday. I went shopping with my dad. Then I went to the cinema with my friend Charlotte. We saw a funny film and ate lots of crisps. It was great.
> What did you do yesterday? Were you busy too?
>
> Lots of love
> Anne

2 Persönliche Stellungnahme ▶ *Unit 3, p. 57*

Befolge diese drei Schritte:
1 Sage zuerst, was deine Meinung ist *(opinion):*
I think …   In my opinion…
2 Begründe deine Meinung *(reason):*
The first thing is that … And the second thing is …
3 Finde einen guten Schluss *(ending):*
In a word …   I really hope that …

> I think that skiing is the best hobby. The first thing is that you can go really quickly. A bike is too slow for me!
> The second thing is that mountains are really cool. They are better than streets!
> I really hope that I can go skiing in the winter.

3 Story ▶ *Unit 4, p. 76*

Wenn du eine Geschichte schreiben sollst, denke an diese drei Punkte:
1 Mache dir Notizen zu den *wh-questions:*
Who was in the story?
When did it happen?
Where did it happen?
What happened?
2 Verwende *time phrases* und *linkers.*
3 Sage, wie sich die Personen gefühlt haben.

> A great day
> Last week I went to the theme park near our town with my friends. The roller coaster was too expensive so we went on the ghost train. First we felt scared, but then there was …

B Folge diesen vier Schritten beim Schreiben:

Korrigieren
Schreiben
Entwurf machen
Ideen sammeln

1 Ideen sammeln ▶ Unit 1, p. 16

Sammle zuerst wichtige Ideen und Wörter, z.B.
in einem Gedankennetz oder einer Liste.

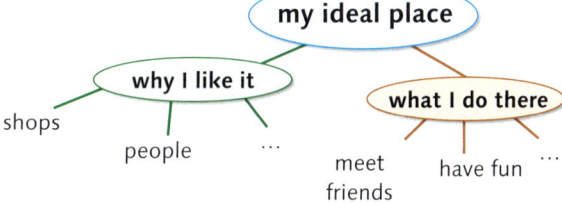

my ideal place

why I like it

shops

people   …

what I do there

meet
friends   have fun   …

2 Textentwurf machen ▶ Unit 4, p. 76

Mache einen Textentwurf auf einem Zettel oder am Computer.

– Schreibst du einen Brief, eine persönliche Stellungnahme
  oder eine Geschichte? Beachte die Hinweise auf S. 132.

– Überlege dir eine sinnvolle Reihenfolge und mache Absätze
  bei neuen Punkten.

– Texte aus dem Buch sind oft ein gutes Muster. Schreibe sie
  aber nicht ab. Ändere sie und ergänze eigene Ideen.

3 Text schreiben ▶ Unit 2, p. 37; Unit 4, p. 76

Nun schreibe deinen Text. So wird dein Text besser:

– Verbinde deine Sätze mit *linking words* (*and, but, so* oder
  because) und *time phrases* (*yesterday, at first, then, …*)

– Wenn du eine Geschichte schreibst, sage, wie sich die
  Menschen fühlten (*happy, disappointed, scared, tired, …*).

Vergleiche z.B. diese beiden Texte. Welcher klingt besser?

Holidays in Scotland
We flew to Scotland. We went
to Loch Ness. We didn't see the
monster. We spent a day in
Inverness. Dad bought a kilt.
We all watched a game of shinty.

Holidays in Scotland
Last July I flew to Scotland with my parents.
We were very excited. On the first day we went
to Loch Ness – but we didn't see the monster
so I was disappointed. Then we spent a day
in Inverness and dad bought a kilt. He felt so
happy with his new kilt! The next day we all
watched a game of shinty. That was fun!

4 Überprüfen und korrigieren

Ein Text ist noch nicht fertig, wenn du ihn zu Ende geschrieben hast! Lies ihn danach noch zweimal durch.

1 Groß- und Kleinschreibung

Im Englischen schreibt man fast alles klein. Prüfe also:
– Hast du Wörter wie *football, cinema, train,* … kleingeschrieben?

In diesen Fällen schreibt man aber groß – prüfe also:
– Hast du alle Satzanfänge großgeschrieben?
  Our school starts at 8 o'clock.
– Hast du das Wort *I* (= ich) immer großgeschrieben?
  I live in Germany.

2 Die richtige Zeitform

– Schreibst du über die Gegenwart? Oder über Dinge, die du regelmäßig machst? (Signalwörter: *today, often, always)* Dann brauchst du das *simple present:*
  I often meet my friends in the park.

– Oder schreibst du über Sachen, die schon passiert sind? (Signalwörter: *yesterday, last Friday)* Dann verwende das *simple past:*
  Last Sunday I went on a bike tour with my family.

– Schreibst du über Dinge, die du vorhast oder für die Zukunft planst? (Signalwörter *tomorrow, next Monday)* Dann brauchst du das *going-to future:*
  Tomorrow I'm going to visit my grandma.

Partner check:
Falls dies möglich ist, suche dir einen Partner oder eine Partnerin und tauscht eure Texte aus.
Versteht ihr die Texte des anderen? Findet ihr noch Fehler?

SF 9 Bilder beschreiben ▸ *Unit 2, p. 36*

Wenn du ein Bild oder ein Foto beschreiben sollst, merke dir folgende Schritte:

1 Beginne allgemein

Sage zunächst in ein oder zwei Sätzen, was du allgemein auf dem Bild siehst:
Welcher Ort ist zu sehen?
Welche Menschen und wie viele?
In the picture I can see a beach with lots of people.

2 Sage, wo sich was befindet

Sage, was du im Vordergrund und im Hintergrund siehst und was links, in der Mitte und rechts auf dem Bild zu sehen ist.

> **In the foreground** I can see a woman with a hat. She's **on the left.**

> **In the middle** I can see two birds.

> **In the background** there are some people in the water.

> **On the right** there's a man with two ice creams.

3 Ordne die Personen und Dinge einander zu

Verwende Präpositionen:
There's a book in front of the woman with the hat. The three children are behind the woman.
There's a ball under the old man's chair. The man with the two ice creams is next to the old woman.
The two birds are between the woman with the hat and the old man and woman.

4 Beschreibe, was die Personen gerade tun

Verwende das *present progressive:*
The woman with the hat is sleeping. The three children behind her are playing in the sand.
The old woman is eating a sandwich.
The man in the water is taking a photo of his family. The woman next to him is surfing.
A boy and a girl are swimming in the sea.
The two birds are looking at the old woman with the sandwich.

SF 10 Einen Kurzvortrag halten ▶ *Unit 3, p. 56*

1 Erarbeitung

– Entscheide dich für ein Thema.

– Sammle Ideen zu deinem Thema und ordne sie:
Was passt zum Thema und was nicht?
Womit fängst du an?
Welche Reihenfolge ist am besten?
Womit hörst du auf?
Schreibe das Wichtigste auf Karteikarten.

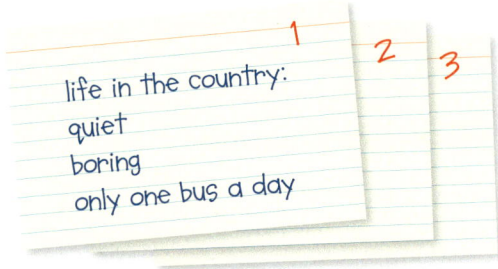

– Überlege dir, welche Bilder du zeigen kannst
und wie du sie präsentieren möchtest –
z. B. als Poster oder am Computer?
Verwende dabei wenig Text.
Schreibe groß und lesbar.

– Übe die Präsentation allein vor einem Spiegel
oder mit einem Partner / einer Partnerin.
Das gibt dir Sicherheit.

2 Durchführung

a) Am Anfang des Vortrags
– Überprüfe, ob alles vorbereitet ist:
Ist das Poster aufgehängt? Ist der Computer bereit? Sind die Vortragskarten sortiert?
– Sage, worüber du sprechen möchtest.

b) Während des Vortrags
– Verwende typische Redewendungen
und sprich langsam und deutlich.
– Schaue deine Zuhörer/innen an.
– Wenn du ein Poster oder Bilder benutzt,
zeige während des Vortrags darauf.

c) Am Ende des Vortrags
– Sage, wann dein Vortrag zu Ende ist.
– Bedanke dich fürs Zuhören und frage deine
Mitschüler/innen, ob sie noch Fragen haben.

SF 11 Mediation ▸ *Unit 2, p. 38; Unit 3, p. 58*

Was hat er gerade gesagt?

1 Worum geht es?

Mediation bedeutet, zwischen zwei Sprachen zu vermitteln, z.B.

– englische Informationen auf Deutsch weitergeben:
Du bist z.B. mit deiner Familie in England. Dein Vater kann nur wenig Englisch und will wissen, was jemand gesagt hat oder was auf einer Broschüre steht.

– deutsche Informationen auf Englisch wiedergeben:
Vielleicht ist bei dir zu Hause ein Austauschschüler zu Gast, der kein Deutsch spricht.

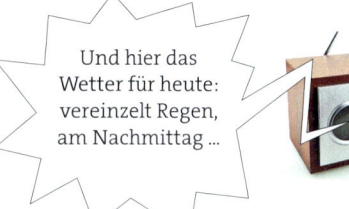

Und hier das Wetter für heute: vereinzelt Regen, am Nachmittag …

2 Worauf musst du achten?

– *Mediation* ist keine wörtliche Übersetzung. Deshalb gib nur das Wesentliche wieder und lasse unwichtige Informationen weg.

– Verwende kurze und einfache Sätze.

Es ist so schön hier. Natur pur. Wir könnten doch länger bleiben. Frag doch mal, ob es in der Nähe ein Hotel gibt.

There is a hotel in the next village. It's nice and cheap. My brother works there.

Is there a hotel nearby?

Im nächsten Dorf gibt es ein Hotel.

– Beachte die Wortstellung – sie ist im Englischen oft anders als im Deutschen.

– Wenn du ein Wort nicht kennst, sage es anders. Beispiele:

außer Dienstags → but not on Tuesdays
ermäßigte Eintrittskarten → cheaper tickets
der Zug hat 10 Minuten Verspätung → the train is 10 minutes late

Wie könntest du folgende Ausdrücke umschreiben?
• *Gibt es hier Übernachtungsmöglichkeiten?*
• *Fußballspielen verboten*
• *Mindestalter 14 Jahre*

When is the shop open?

GEÖFFNET
täglich 9–18 Uhr
außer Dienstags

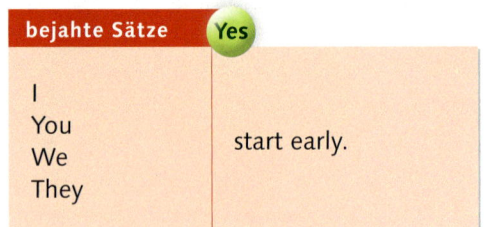
LF 1 REVISION Simple present ▸ p. 66/67

bejahte Sätze Yes

| I You We They | start early. |

Mit dem *simple present* (einfache Gegenwart) sagst du, was oft oder jeden Tag passiert und auch was selten oder nie geschieht:
I often go to the sports club.
We never have lunch at school.

| He She It | start**s** early. |

Mit *he / she / it* musst du immer ein *-s* ans Verb anhängen.
Achtung: bei einigen Verben wird *-es* angehängt:
*do – do**es***
*wash – wash**es***
*watch – watch**es***

verneinte Sätze No

| I You We They | don't start early. |

Wenn du sagen willst, dass etwas <u>nicht</u> passiert oder der Fall ist, setzt du *don't* vor das Verb.

| He She It | **doesn't** start early. |

Mit *he / she / it* verwendest du *doesn't*.

He doesn't like dogs.

Fragen mit do/does ?

| Do I Do you **Does** he / she / it Do we Do they | like crabs? |

Fragen, auf die man mit *ja* oder *nein* antworten kann, beginnen mit *Do* oder *Does*.
Mit *I, you, we* oder *they* verwendest du *Do*.
Mit *he / she / it* verwendest du *Does*.

Fragen mit Fragewörtern ?

Where do I go now?
Why do you do this?
What **does** he / she / it do?
When do we arrive?
How do they run?

Manche Fragen beginnen mit Fragewörtern.
Nach dem Fragewort verwendest du:
do (bei *I/you/we/they*)
oder
does (bei *he / she / it*).

LF 2 REVISION Present progressive

I'm reading a comic.
Ich lese gerade einen Comic.

Dad is cooking dinner.
Papa macht gerade das Abendessen.

What are you doing at the moment?
Was machst du jetzt gerade?

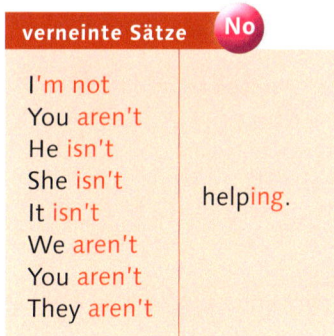

bejahte Sätze Yes	
I'm You're He's She's It's We're You're They're	helping.

verneinte Sätze No	
I'm not You aren't He isn't She isn't It isn't We aren't You aren't They aren't	helping.

Fragen ?	
Am I Are you Is he Is she Is it Are we Are you Are they	helping?

Mit dem *present progressive* (*ing*-Form) sagst du, was gerade jetzt passiert.
Damit beschreibst du auch, was man auf Bildern tut.

Diese Zeitangaben findest du oft in Sätzen im *present progressive:*
now, at the moment, today.

He isn't feeling good today.

Das *present progressive* besteht aus zwei Teilen:

'm *oder*
're *oder*   +   Verb + -*ing*
's

Achtung:
Bei Verben auf -*e* fällt das -*e* bei der *ing*-Form weg:
come – coming
make – making
ride – riding

Bei einigen Verben wird der letzte Buchstabe verdoppelt:
plan – planning
stop – stopping
sit – sitting

LF 3 REVISION Simple past

▶ p.26/27

Yesterday evening I watched TV.
Gestern Abend habe ich ferngesehen/sah ich fern.

Last week I didn't go to football training
Letzte Woche ging ich nicht zum Fußballtraining.

Did you watch the fireworks last night?
Hast du gestern abend das Feuerwerk gesehen?

bejahte Sätze	**Yes**
I You He/She/It We They	help**ed**.

verneinte Sätze	**No**
I You He/She/It We They	**didn't** help.

Fragen mit did		**?**
Did	I you he/she/it we they	help?

Fragen mit Fragewörtern			**?**
What	**did**	she	watch?
When	**did**	it	finish?
Where	**did**	they	go?

What did she **watch**?
– She **watched** the fireworks.

Mit dem *simple past* sprichst du über Dinge, die in der Vergangenheit geschehen sind. Du verwendest es oft mit Zeitangaben wie *yesterday, last week, last year, last summer, in 2010*.
Die Vergangenheitsform ist für alle Personen gleich. Bei regelmäßigen Verben hängst du *-ed* an das Verb:
walk – walked
look – looked

Bei Verben, die auf *-e* enden, wird nur *-d* angehängt:
arrive – arrived

Unregelmäßige Formen musst du lernen:
buy – bought   find – found
go – went   have – had
make – made   meet – met
Du kannst sie in der zweiten Spalte der *List of irregular verbs* auf S. 200 nachschlagen.

Wenn du sagen willst, was nicht geschah, setzt du *didn't* vor das Verb.
Achtung: Das Verb bleibt dann immer in der Grundform:
He didn't watch.
! nicht: *He didn't watched.*

Fragen im *simple past* bildest du mit *did* und der Grundform des Verbs.

Achtung: Das Verb bleibt immer in der Grundform:
Did he watch?
! nicht: *Did he watched?*

Manche Fragen beginnen mit Fragewörtern. Auch hier verwendet man *did* bei allen Personen und das Verb in der Grundform:
How did it go?
! nicht: *How did it went?*

Achtung: Bei Fragen im *simple past* ist das Verb in der Grundform. Bei den Antworten musst du das Verb in die Vergangenheitsform setzen.

LF 4 Present perfect
▶ Unit 2, p. 40

I have moved house three times.
Ich bin schon dreimal umgezogen.

My little sister has never been on a plane.
Meine kleine Schwester ist noch nie geflogen.

Have you ever ridden a pony?
Bist du schon einmal geritten?

bejahte Sätze	Yes
I You We They	have started early. ('ve started)
He She It	has started early.

verneinte Sätze	No
I You We They	haven't started early.
He She It	hasn't started early.

Fragen und Kurzantworten	?
Have you started?	– Yes, I have. – No, I haven't.
Has she started?	– Yes, she has. – No, she hasn't.

Mit dem *present perfect* sagst du, dass du etwas schon einmal, öfter oder noch nie gemacht hast.
Du verwendest es oft mit Zeitangaben wie *ever, never, once, twice, lots of times.*

Das *present perfect* besteht aus zwei Teilen:

have oder *has*   +   einer besonderen
(Kurzformen: Verbform, dem
've oder *'s*)   *past participle*

Wie bildest du das *past participle?*
Bei regelmäßigen Verben hängst du *-ed* an das Verb:
walk – walked   look – looked
Bei Verben die auf *-e* enden, wird nur *-d* angehängt: *arrive – arrived*
Unregelmäßige Verben musst du lernen:
be – been   find – found
go – gone   have – had
make – made   meet – met
Du kannst sie in der dritten Spalte der *List of irregular verbs* auf S. 200 nachschlagen.

Jacob has worked a lot today.

LF 5 REVISION *Will*-future ▸ *p. 46/47*

I think you'll have a great birthday party.
Ich glaube, du wirst eine tolle Geburtstagsparty haben.

Maybe we'll have a barbecue in the garden.
Vielleicht grillen wir im Garten.

I'm sure the weather will be nice.
Ich bin sicher, das Wetter wird schön sein.

Wenn du vermutest, was in der Zukunft geschehen könnte, verwendest du das *will-future.*
Die Sätze beginnen oft mit *I think, maybe, I'm sure* oder *I hope.*

bejahte Sätze	**Yes**	
It	will 'll	be sunny tomorrow.

Du bildest das *will-future*, indem du *will* oder die Kurzform *'ll* vor das Verb setzt.

verneinte Sätze	**No**	
It	will not won't	be sunny tomorrow.

Die Kurzform von *will not* ist *won't.*

Fragen und Kurzantworten	**?**
Will it be sunny tomorrow? – Yes, it will. – No, it won't.	

Will you stop crying?

No, I won't!

LF 6 REVISION *Going to*-future

We're going to have a picnic on Sunday.
Wir haben vor, am Sonntag ein Picknick zu machen.

Oh no, he's going to fall!
Oh nein, er fällt gleich herunter!

Mit *going to* … sagst du
– was du vorhast oder für die Zukunft geplant hast,
– was wahrscheinlich bald passieren wird.

bejahte Sätze	**Yes**	
I'm You're He's/She's We're They're	going to	watch TV.

Du bildest das *going to-future* mit *'m, 're, 's* + *going to* + Verb.

Achtung: Das Verb bleibt immer in der Grundform:
I'm going to watch TV.
❗ nicht: *I'm going to watching TV.*

verneinte Sätze	**No**	
I'm not You're not He's/She's not We're not They're not	going to	watch TV.

Fragen und Kurzantworten:
– *Are you going to leave tomorrow?*
– *Yes, I am./No, I'm not.*

LF 7 *Have to/can/should* ▶ *Unit 1, p. 20*

Can

I can play the guitar.
Tom can't go to school today – he's ill.
Can I open the window?

Mit *can/can't* sagst du, was jemand (nicht) tun kann oder darf.

Should

You should take your pullover – it's cold.
She shouldn't eat so much chocolate.

Mit *should/shouldn't* rätst du jemandem, etwas zu tun, oder nicht zu tun.

You have to be home at 10 o'clock!

Have to

I have to help me in the kitchen now.
He has to look after his sister today.
You don't have to eat this.
She doesn't have to do chores.

Mit *have to* sagst du, was jemand tun muss.
Mit *don't have to* sagst du, was jemand nicht zu tun braucht.

LF 8 Reflexivpronomen ▶ *Unit 4, p. 71*

It was my mistake so I blame myself.
Es war mein Fehler, also gebe ich mir die Schuld.

He has cut himself.
Er hat sich geschnitten.

We can look after ourselves.
Wir können uns um uns selbst kümmern.

Reflexivpronomen enden auf *-self* oder *-selves*.
Du sagst damit, dass jemand etwas selbst tut.
Vergleiche:
She washed the baby.   Sie wusch das Baby.
She washed herself.   Sie wusch sich selbst.

I wash myself.
You wash yourself.
He washes himself.
She washes herself.
We wash ourselves.
You wash yourselves.
They wash themselves.

Merke dir diese Ausdrücke:
Help yourself!   Greif zu! Bediene dich.
Enjoy yourself!   Viel Spaß!

Are you enjoying yourselves?

Yes, I am.

No, I'm not!

LF 9 Adverbien ▸ Unit 2, p. 32

Don't walk so slowly!
Geh nicht so langsam!

She spoke calmly and clearly.
Sie sprach ruhig und klar.

Drive carefully!
Fahr vorsichtig!

clear – clearly	angry – angrily
nervous – nervously	happy – happily
quick – quickly	careful – carefully
slow – slowly	

Adverbien sagen, auf welche Weise etwas geschieht.

Die meisten Adverbien bildet man durch Anfügen von *-ly* an ein Adjektiv. Manchmal gibt es Unregelmäßigkeiten bei der Schreibung.

Es gibt auch Ausnahmen:
! *He worked hard. She did well.*

LF 10 Vergleiche ▸ Unit 3, p. 63

I'm taller than you
Ich bin größer als du.

Mobiles are more expensive than comics.
Handys sind teurer als Comics.

This is the cheapest supermarket in town.
Das ist der billigste Supermarkt in der Stadt.

Today it's as hot as yesterday.
Heute ist es genauso heiß wie gestern.

She's taller than me, but I'm nicer!

Personen und Sachen kann man miteinander vergleichen.

cheap	cheaper	the cheapest
near	nearer	the nearest
tall	taller	the tallest

Bei kurzen Adjektiven hängst du *-er* bzw. *-est* an das Adjektiv, um die Steigerungsformen zu bilden.

! Diese Formen sind unregelmäßig:
good – better – best
bad – worse – worst

big	bigger	the biggest
hot	hotter	the hottest
noisy	noisier	the noisiest
happy	happier	the happiest

Bei einigen Adjektiven musst du bei der Schreibung aufpassen.

expensive	more expensive	the most expensive
exciting	more exciting	the most exciting
popular	more popular	the most popular

Bei langen Adjektiven setzt du *more* bzw. *most* vor das Adjektiv.

Tom is as old as Luca.
The red bike is as expensive as the green bike.

Wenn du sagen willst, dass zwei Personen oder Dinge genau gleich groß, alt, teuer, etc. sind, verwendest du *as ... as*.

LF 11 *If*-Sätze ▸ *Unit 3, p. 60*

If you wash the car, I'll give you 5 euro.
Wenn du das Auto wäscht, gebe ich dir 10 Euro.

If the shop has the computer game, I'll buy it.
Wenn der Laden das Computerspiel hat, kaufe ich es.

if-Satz	Hauptsatz
If you help me,	I'll be faster.
If it rains,	we'll stay at home.

Mit *if*-Sätzen sagst du, was unter bestimmten Bedingungen geschehen wird.

If-Sätze bestehen aus zwei Teilen:
– einem Nebensatz mit *if* im *simple present*
– einem Hauptsatz mit *will* oder *'ll*.

If I don't have a good idea soon, I'll give up.

LF 12 Relativsätze ▸ *Unit 4, p. 80*

He's the boy who lives in our street.
Er ist der Junge, der in unserer Straße wohnt.

It's a shop that sells mobiles and TVs.
Es ist ein Laden, der Handys und Fernseher verkauft.

This is the man who works at the hotel.
Are you the girl who won the first prize?

Mit Relativsätzen kannst du zusätzliche Informationen über eine Person oder eine Sache geben.

Nach Personen verwendest du *who.*

The boy who's playing the guitar is cool.

Nach Sachen benutzt du *that.*

The game that I got for my birthday is great.
The film that we saw yesterday was boring.

Wordbank 1: My neighbourhood ▶ *Unit 1, p. 16*

Transport

airport
bus station
bus stop

garage

harbour

petrol station

traffic lights

tram station

train station
underground

Shopping

baker's

butcher's

bookshop
bike shop

chemist's

dry cleaner's

fruit and veg shop
market

newsagent's

pet shop
phone shop
shopping centre
supermarket
video shop

Sport

bowling centre
football field

ice rink

inline skate track

skate park

tennis court

sports club
sports hall
stadium
swimming pool

Other places

bank
cafe

children's playground

cinema
farm

fast food stand

flats
hairdresser's
hospital
houses
museum
park
post office
restaurant
river
school
second-hand shop
theatre

youth centre

Our nearest ... is ... minutes away. That's good / OK / important / terrible / ...
There aren't any ... near us. That's OK / no problem / a big problem.
We live near ... You can ... there.
There's a big / new / great / good / cool / nice / expensive ... near our house.
There are lots of ... in my neighbourhood. I think that's great / not so good.

Wordbank 2: City and country ▸ *Unit 2, p. 36*

mountains

village

sheep

farm house

trees

hills

track

tractor

cows

farmer

field

farm dog

horses

soil

In the foreground / In the background you can see …
On the left / On the right / In the middle of the picture there's a …
Next to the … there are some … Behind / in front of the … there's a …
Between the … and the … you can see …

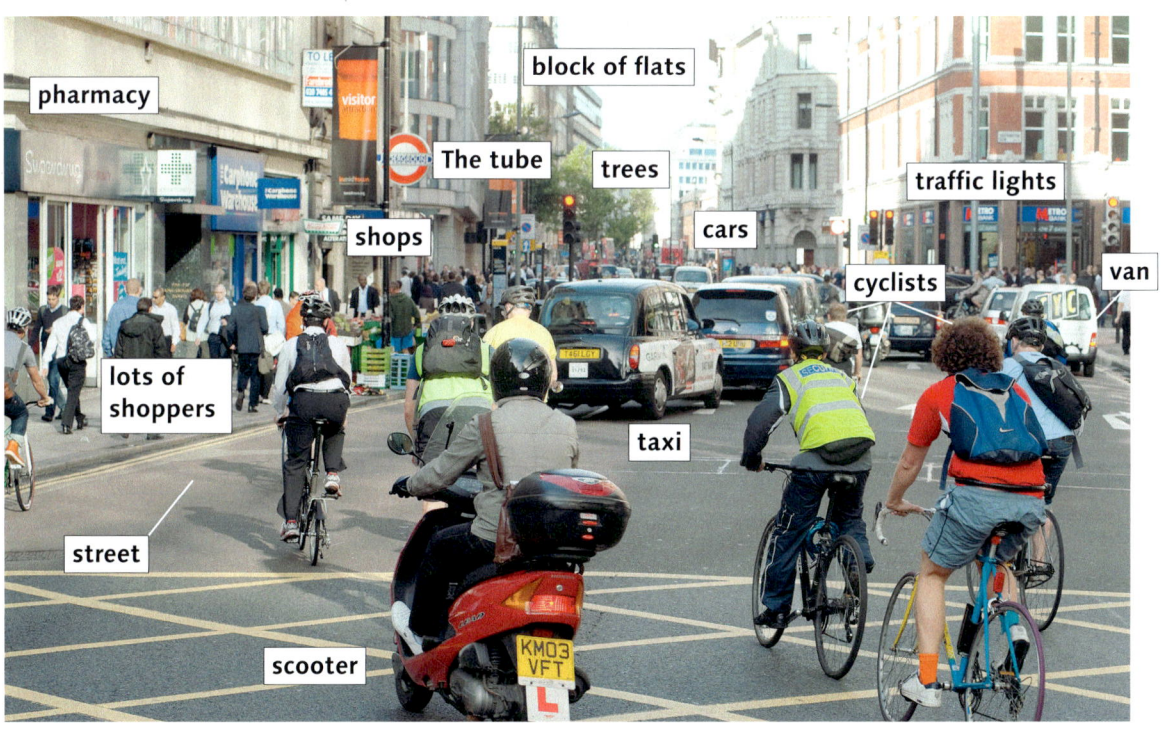

pharmacy

block of flats

The tube

trees

traffic lights

shops

cars

cyclists

van

lots of shoppers

taxi

street

scooter

Wordbank 3: Food ▸ *Unit 3, p. 51*

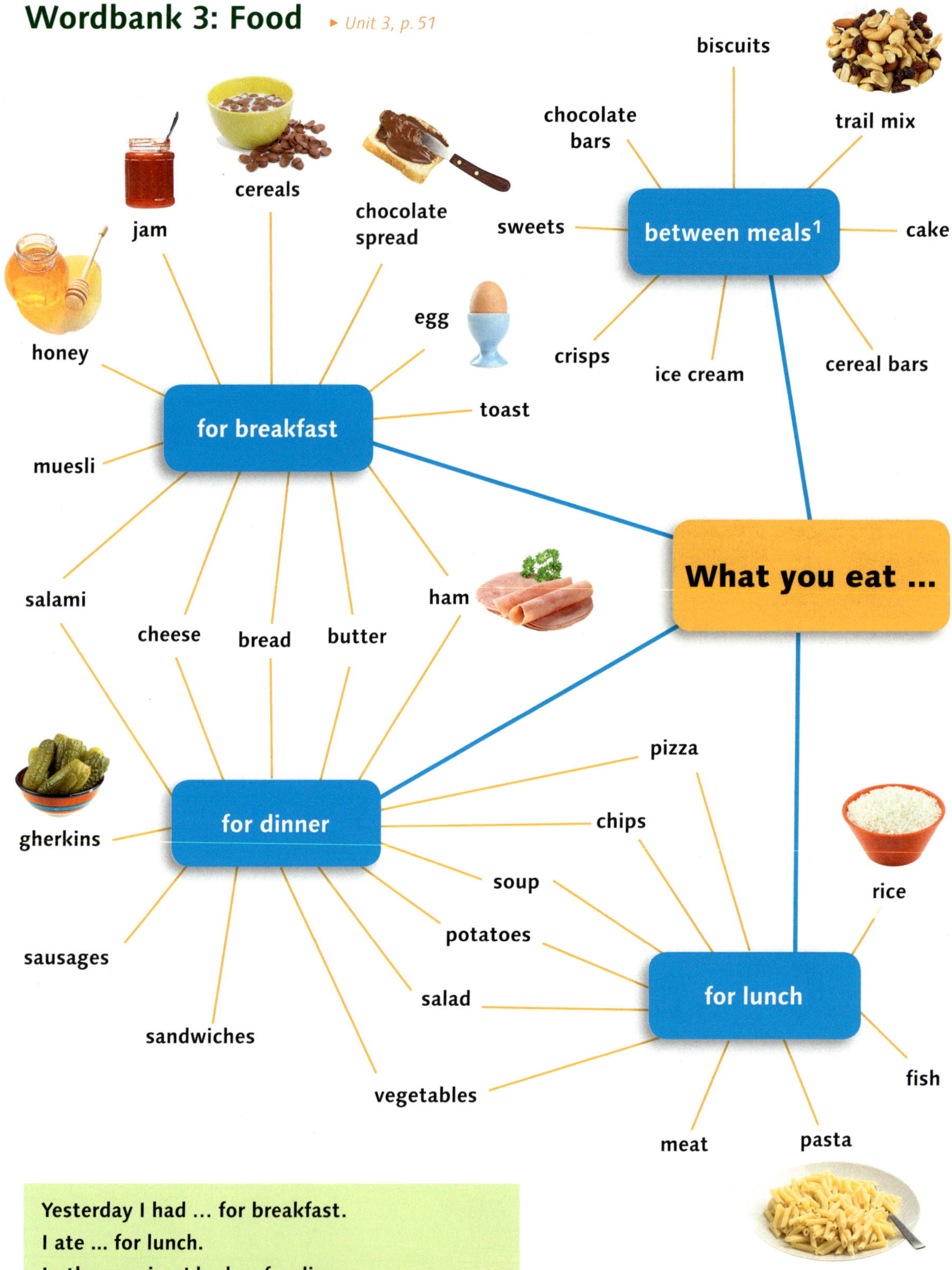

biscuits

trail mix

chocolate bars

sweets

between meals¹

cake

cereals

chocolate spread

jam

crisps

ice cream

cereal bars

honey

egg

toast

for breakfast

muesli

What you eat ...

salami

ham

cheese   bread   butter

pizza

chips

gherkins

for dinner

soup

rice

potatoes

sausages

salad

for lunch

sandwiches

fish

vegetables

meat   pasta

Yesterday I had ... for breakfast.
I ate ... for lunch.
In the evening I had ... for dinner.
Usually we have ... for breakfast/lunch/dinner.

¹between meals *zwischen den Mahlzeiten*

Wordbank 4: Useful words for tourists ▶ Unit 4, p. 81

At a restaurant

In a hotel

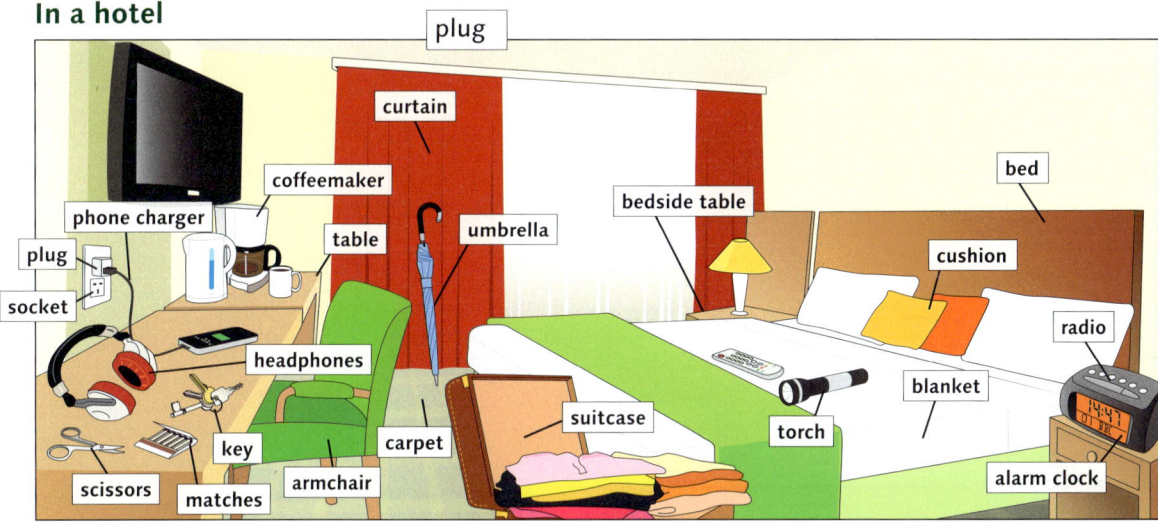

Das **Vocabulary** (S. 150–165) enthält alle neuen Wörter und Wendungen des Buches, die du **lernen** musst. Sie stehen in der Reihenfolge, in der sie im Buch zum ersten Mal vorkommen.

Hier siehst du, wie das **Vocabulary** aufgebaut ist:

Diese Zahl gibt die **Seite** an, auf der die Wörter zum ersten Mal vorkommen.
p. 10 = Seite 10

Die blauen Kästen solltest du dir immer besonders gut ansehen. Dort stehen wichtige Hinweise zu den neuen Wörtern.

mustn't do	nicht tun dürfen	→

must – mustn't
- must = müssen
  You **must** do your homework now.
- **mustn't** = nicht dürfen
  You **mustn't** wear trainers at school.

p.19 **Oh dear!**	oje!	
milkshake	Milchshake	
lose, *simple past:* **lost**	verlieren	

Der blaue Pfeil heißt: Zu diesem Eintrag gibt es in der rechten Spalte einen blauen Kasten.

lose a job ◄► get a job
lose a game ◄► win a game

act	Theater spielen; schauspielern	
surprised	überrascht	

Focus on language

p.20 **aunt**	Tante	
airport	Flughafen	
diner	(AE) Imbissstube, Lokal	**!** (AE) zeigt dir, dass dieses Wort besonders in Amerika gebräuchlich ist.
clothes *(pl)*	Kleidung, Kleidungsstücke	**!** *Deutsch:* Ihre gesamte **Kleidung ist** schwarz. *Englisch:* All her **clothes are** black.
find, *simple past:* **found**	finden	They **found** a house.
p.21 **make friends**, *simple past:* **made**	Freunde finden	
perhaps	vielleicht	I'm not sure, but **perhaps** I can come.

Dies ist das „Gegenteil"- Zeichen.
lose a job ◄► **get** a job bedeutet:
„**lose**" ist das Gegenteil von „**get**".

Das rote Ausrufezeichen bedeutet: Vorsicht, hier macht man leicht Fehler!

Tipps zum Wörterlernen findest du im **Skills file** auf Seite 124.

Im **Vocabulary** werden folgende **Abkürzungen** verwendet:

p.   = page (Seite)
pp.   = pages (Seiten)
sb.   = somebody (jemand)
sth. = something (etwas)
jn.   = jemanden
jm.   = jemandem
pl   = *plural* (Mehrzahl)
infml = *informal* (umgangssprachlich)

Wenn du **nachschlagen** möchtest, was ein englisches Wort bedeutet oder wie man es ausspricht, dann solltest du das **Dictionary English – German** auf den Seiten 166–182 verwenden.

Und wenn du vergessen hast, wie etwas auf Englisch heißt, dann kann dir das **Dictionary German – English** auf den Seiten 183–196 eine erste Hilfe sein.

Unit 1: I love London

p.8	**palace** ['pæləs]	Palast	
	king [kɪŋ]	König	
	queen [kwiːn]	Königin	
	president ['prezɪdənt]	Präsident/in	

queen   palace   king

	the Tube [tjuːb]	die U-Bahn *(in London)*	❗ *English:* **on** the Tube *German:* **in** der U-Bahn
	travel ['trævl]	reisen; fahren, sich fortbewegen	Last year we **travelled** to Italy in the holidays. In big cities we always try to **travel** by bus.
	underground ['ʌndəgraʊnd]	U-Bahn	Another name for the **underground** in London is "the Tube".
	famous (for) ['feɪməs]	berühmt (für, wegen)	London is **famous for** its theatre shows.
	detective [dɪ'tektɪv]	Detektiv/in	
	bell [bel]	Glocke; Klingel	**bells**

Lautschrift

Wie man englische Wörter ausspricht, das zeigt dir die Lautschrift hinter dem Wort.
Sie steht immer in eckigen Klammern. Lautschriftsymbole zeigen dir, wie sich das
Wort anhört. Alle diese Symbole findest du in der Liste English sounds auf S. 182.
Ein Apostroph in der Lautschrift steht vor der Silbe, die du betonen musst.
Zum Beispiel sieht der Name "London" in der Lautschrift so aus: ['lʌndən].

[aɪ]   [uː]   ['haɪlaɪt]   [tjuːb]

---

p.9	**tourist** ['tʊərɪst]	Tourist/in	❗ Betonung auf der 1. Silbe: **tourist** ['tʊərɪst]
	eye [aɪ]	Auge	
	hour [aʊə]	Stunde	
	tower ['taʊə]	Turm	
	high [haɪ]	hoch	What's the **highest** mountain in Germany?
	window ['wɪndəʊ]	Fenster	

window

Theme 1

p.10	**by** Sam Holmes [baɪ]	*(geschrieben)* von Sam Holmes	
	think of/about [θɪŋk], *simple past:* **thought** [θɔːt]	halten von, denken über	
	I've lived here all my life.	Ich wohne hier schon mein ganzes Leben (lang).	
	downside ['daʊnsaɪd]	Kehrseite, Nachteil	
	fashion ['fæʃn]	Mode(trend)	

also ['ɔːlsəʊ]	auch	I like coffee and I like tea too. = I like coffee and I **also** like tea.
be allowed to do sth. [ə'laʊd]	etwas tun dürfen	**Are** you **allowed to** use dictionaries in your English tests?
culture ['kʌltʃə]	Kultur	
Greek [griːk]	griechisch; Griechisch; Grieche/Griechin	
Irish ['aɪrɪʃ]	irisch, aus Irland	
Scottish ['skɒtɪʃ]	schottisch, aus Schottland	
amazing [ə'meɪzɪŋ]	erstaunlich	
p.11 two years **ago** [ə'gəʊ]	vor zwei Jahren	The Bakers moved to Bristol six weeks **ago**. ❗ *English:* **two years/six weeks ago** *German:* **vor** zwei Jahren/sechs Wochen
its football [ɪts]	sein Fußball / ihr Fußball	➔ This is my hamster. **Its** name is Joe. I – **my** name we – **our** names you – **your** name you – **your** names he – **his** name they – **their** names she – **her** name it – **its** name

Theme 2

p.12 **advert** ['ædvɜːt]	Anzeige, Werbung	

Story

p.14 **clever** ['klevə]	schlau, klug	
call [kɔːl]	rufen; nennen; anrufen	Please **call** your dog. It's in our garden. **Call** me tomorrow. Here's my phone number. Her name is Jessica, but we **call** her Jess.
geek [giːk]	*jemand, der sich sehr stark für etwas begeistert (und manchmal von anderen deswegen belächelt wird)*	
museum [mju'ziːəm]	Museum	
natural ['nætʃrəl]	natürlich, Natur-	
natural history [nætʃrəl 'hɪstri]	Naturkunde	
dinosaur ['daɪnəsɔː]	Dinosaurier	❗ Betonung auf der 1. Silbe **dinosaur** ['daɪnəsɔː]
answer ['ɑːnsə]	antworten; beantworten	❗ **answer** = 1. Antwort; 2. anworten; beantworten
disaster [dɪ'zɑːstə]	Katastrophe, Unglück	
begin [bɪ'gɪn], *simple past:* **began** [bɪ'gæn]	beginnen, anfangen	

security [sɪˈkjʊərəti]	Sicherheit	**security men** at the airport

p.15 **next** [nekst] — als Nächstes — First let's eat something. **Next** we can watch a film.

drink [drɪŋk], *simple past:* **drank** [dræŋk]	trinken	❗ **drink** = 1. Getränk; 2. trinken
kick [kɪk]	treten, schießen	
idiot [ˈɪdiət]	Idiot/in	❗ Betonung auf der 1. Silbe: **idiot** [ˈɪdiət]
keep [kiːp], *simple past:* **kept** [kept]	behalten	Thanks for the magazine. Can I **keep** it, or do you want to have it back?
loud [laʊd]	laut	
police *(pl)* [pəˈliːs]	Polizei	→ **police** ist immer Plural: Where **are** the **police**? We have to call **them**. Wo **ist** die **Polizei**? Wir müssen **sie** rufen.
like a million dollars	fantastisch	
at last [ət ˈlɑːst]	schließlich, endlich	
earthquake [ˈɜːθkweɪk]	Erdbeben	
especially [ɪˈspeʃəli]	insbesondere	I love team sports, **especially** basketball.

Skills

p.16 **busy** [ˈbɪzi] — belebt; verkehrsreich — ❗ the road is **busy** = die Straße ist belebt, hektisch / I'm **busy** = ich bin beschäftigt, ich habe (viel) zu tun

far [fɑː]	weit	
plane [pleɪn]	Flugzeug	a **plane**
transport [ˈtrænspɔːt]	Verkehrsmittel; Transport(wesen)	❗ Betonung auf der 1. Silbe: **transport** [ˈtrænspɔːt]

p.17

world [wɜːld]	Welt	
diver [ˈdaɪvə]	Taucher/in	
driver [ˈdraɪvə]	Fahrer/in	
sun [sʌn]	Sonne	**the sun**
postcard [ˈpəʊstkɑːd]	Postkarte	

p.18

waste [weɪst]	Verschwendung	What a **waste** of time!
waste [weɪst]	verschwenden	You're **wasting** so much time!
spend money/time (on) [spend], *simple past:* **spent** [spent]	Geld ausgeben (für); Zeit verbringen (mit)	Do you **spend** a lot of money **on** fashion? I should **spend** more time with my friends.
a lot of [ə ˈlɒt əv]	viel(e)	= lots of I do **a lot of** / **lots of** sport in my free time.

be right	Recht haben	Yes, **you're right**. I agree with you.
be wrong	Unrecht haben	**be right ◄► be wrong**
p.19 **ringtone** [ˈrɪŋtəʊn]	Klingelton *(Handy)*	
a cup of tea [kʌp]	eine Tasse Tee	❗ *English:* a cup **of** coffee *German:* eine Tasse Kaffee

Focus on language

p.20 **safe** [seɪf]	sicher *(gefahrlos)*; in Sicherheit	❗ *German* **sicher**: Be careful and you'll be **safe**. *(sicher, in Sicherheit)* I'm **sure** you'll be OK. *(sicher(lich))*
have to do sth. [ˈhæv tə]	etwas tun müssen	Look, it's late. We **have to** go now. ❗ *German* **müssen** = **1.** have to; **2.** must (**have to** wird häufiger verwendet als **must**)
not have to do sth.	etwas nicht tun müssen / brauchen	❗ You **mustn't** do this. *(darfst nicht)* You **don't need to** do this. *(brauchst nicht)* You **don't have to** do this. *(brauchst nicht unbedingt)*
subway [ˈsʌbweɪ]	Unterführung	
pickpocket [ˈpɪkpɒkɪt]	Taschendieb/in	
escalator [ˈeskəleɪtə]	Rolltreppe	You should stand on the right on British **escalators**.
p.21 **pick** sb. **up** [pɪk ˈʌp]	jn. abholen	He's **picking up** Mr Carter.
dark [dɑːk]	dunkel	It's too **dark** in here. I can't see anything.
worry (about) [ˈwʌri]	sich Sorgen machen (wegen, um)	Mum always **worries about** me when I come home late.

Unit 2: Country life

p.29 **in the country**	auf dem Land	
crossroads, *pl* **crossroads** [ˈkrɒsrəʊdz]	(Straßen-)Kreuzung	
church [tʃɜːtʃ]	Kirche	
block of flats [blɒk əvˈflæts]	Mehrfamilienhaus, Wohnblock	❗ Plural: **blocks** of flats
high street [ˈhaɪ striːt]	Hauptstraße; Einkaufsstraße	

a very busy high street

gate [geɪt]	Tor	
wood [wʊd]	Wald; Holz	
pub [pʌb]	Kneipe	

a pub
a church

Theme 1

p.30 **You're joking!** [ˈdʒəʊkɪŋ]	Du machst wohl Witze! / Spitzenwitz!	
joke [dʒəʊk]	Witze machen, scherzen	

I want to eat more junk food.

Only joking.

Come on! [kʌm ˈɒn]	Komm(t) (schon)! / Ach komm!	
buy: we've **bought** [bɔːt]	kaufen: wir haben gekauft	
CCTV [siː siː tiː ˈviː]	Überwachungssystem; Überwachungskamera(s)	
business [ˈbɪznəs]	Geschäft, Betrieb	My mum's new **business** is on Summer Street.
start a business	ein Geschäft aufmachen, einen Betrieb gründen/eröffnen	
start: he has **started**	anfangen: er hat angefangen ➡	I**'ve** started — I **haven't** started he **has** bought — he **hasn't** bought
van [væn]	Transporter, Lieferwagen	

a **van**

find: she has **found** [faʊnd]	finden: sie hat gefunden	
meet: she has **met** [met]	treffen: sie hat getroffen	
It sucks! *(infml)* [sʌks]	Es nervt/ Es ist Mist!	
believe [bɪˈliːv]	glauben	**Believe** me, he isn't British. He's German.
see: I've **seen** [siːn]	sehen: ich habe gesehen	
speak: I've **spoken** [ˈspəʊkən]	sprechen: ich habe gesprochen	
not … yet [jet]	noch nicht	I need more time. I have**n't** finished my homework **yet**.
What a pain! *(infml)* [peɪn]	So ein Mist! / Es nervt!	
p.31 **close** [kləʊz]	schließen, zumachen	**open the door ◄► close the door**
Take it easy! *(infml)*	Reg dich nicht auf. / Bleib mal locker.	

Theme 2

p.32	**save** [seɪv]	retten	
	brave [breɪv]	mutig	**!** **brave** = *mutig* Molly was **brave**. *brav* = **good** **Good** dog!
	calm [kɑːm]	ruhig, still; besonnen	
	deep [diːp]	tief	He saved his dog from the **deep** water.
	heavy [ˈhevi]	schwer (*Gewicht; Regen*)	**!** **schwer** (*von Gewicht*): a **heavy** box **schwer, schwierig**: a **difficult** question
	work **hard** [hɑːd]	hart arbeiten	
	father [ˈfɑːðə]	Vater	
	speak: he **spoke** [spəʊk]	sprechen: er sprach, er hat gesprochen	
	daughter [ˈdɔːtə]	Tochter	
	have: we've **had** [hæd], [həd]	haben: wir haben gehabt	
	accident [ˈæksɪdənt]	Unfall	
	police officer [pəˈliːs ɒfɪsə]	Polizeibeamter/-beamtin	an English **police officer**
	behave dangerously [bɪˈheɪv]	sich gefährlich verhalten	**!** *English:* **behave** nicely *German:* **sich** nett **verhalten**
	farmer [ˈfɑːmə]	Bauer, Bäuerin; Landwirt/in	
	describe [dɪˈskraɪb]	beschreiben	**!** *English:* **Describe** the picture **to** him/her. *German:* **Beschreibe** ihm/ihr das Bild.
p.33	**message** [ˈmesɪdʒ]	Nachricht, Mitteilung	John isn't at home. Can I take a message?
	take a message	etwas ausrichten	
	Is that the Taylors?	Sind da die Taylors? (*am Telefon*)	
	Who's speaking?	Wer spricht (da)? (*am Telefon*)	I'm afraid I'm not at home right now. You can leave a message after the beep.
	This is Rob Blake.	Hier spricht Rob Blake. (*am Telefon*)	
	right now	gerade jetzt, genau jetzt	

Story

p.34	**across** the fields [əˈkrɒs]	(quer) über die Felder	Birds can fly **across** the sea.

smile [smaɪl]	lächeln; *(das)* Lächeln	❗ **smile** = **1.** lächeln; **2.** *(das/ein)* Lächeln
bush [bʊʃ]	Busch, Strauch	
suddenly [ˈsʌdənli]	plötzlich	
nose [nəʊz]	Nase	
full (of ...) [fʊl]	voll; voller ...	There's too much traffic here. All the streets are **full of** cars.
catch [kætʃ], **caught** [kɔːt], **caught**	(ein)fangen	The cat is trying to **catch** the mouse.
light [laɪt]	Licht; Lampe	
office [ˈɒfɪs]	Büro	
fox [fɒks]	Fuchs	
mouth [maʊθ]	Mund; *(Tier)* Schnauze	
o.35 **quiet** [ˈkwaɪət]	ruhig, still, leise	**quiet** ◄► **loud, noisy**
park (a car) [pɑːk]	parken	You can't **park** your car here!
write down [raɪt ˈdaʊn], **wrote** [rəʊt], **written** [ˈrɪtn]	aufschreiben	
mother [ˈmʌðə]	Mutter	❗ **mother** – **father** **mum** – **dad**
people **who** leave rubbish	Menschen, die Müll zurücklassen	
article [ˈɑːtɪkl]	Artikel	❗ Betonung auf der 1. Silbe: **article** [ˈɑːtɪkl]
put: he has **put**	*(etwas wohin)* tun, legen, stellen, stecken: er hat getan, gelegt, gestellt, gesteckt	

Skills

o.36 **foreground** [ˈfɔːgraʊnd]	Vordergrund	There are two boys in the **foreground**. In the **background**, you can see a river.
background [ˈbækgraʊnd]	Hintergrund	
horse [hɔːs]	Pferd	
o.37 **everywhere** [ˈevriweə]	überall(hin)	There are London taxis **everywhere** in London.
usually [ˈjuːʒəli]	meistens, normalerweise	
ideal [aɪˈdɪəl]	ideal	❗ Betonung auf der 2. Silbe: i**deal** [aɪˈdɪəl]
move (to) [muːv]	(um)ziehen (nach)	They **moved to** York, **to** a nice flat in town.
uncle [ˈʌŋkl]	Onkel	**aunt** ◄► **uncle**
o.38 **little** [ˈlɪtl]	klein	Ellie sometimes has to look after her **little** brother.
o.39 **grandad** [ˈgrædæd]	Opa	

Focus on language

p.40	**questionnaire** [kwestʃə'neə]	Fragebogen	
	ride: I **rode** [rəʊd], I've **ridden** ['rɪdn]	reiten: ich ritt, ich bin geritten; (Rad) fahren: ich fuhr (Rad), ich bin (Rad) gefahren	
	move house	umziehen (an einen neuen Wohnort)	We **moved house** last year. We moved from London to Plymouth.
	once [wʌns]	einmal	
	twice [twaɪs]	zweimal	**once** (1x) – **twice** (2x) – **three times** (3x)
	person ['pɜːsn]	Person	**!** Nur selten wird der Plural **persons** benutzt. Normalerweise: one **person** – five **people**.

> **Irregular verbs**
>
> | | | | | | | | | |
> |---|---|---|---|---|---|---|---|---|
> | buy | bought | **bought** | *kaufen* | put | put | **put** | *legen, stellen* |
> | do | did | **done** | *tun, machen* | ride | rode | **ridden** | *reiten, (Rad) fahren* |
> | catch | caught | **caught** | *fangen* | see | saw | **seen** | *sehen* |
> | find | found | **found** | *finden* | speak | spoke | **spoken** | *sprechen* |
> | have | had | **had** | *haben* | write | wrote | **written** | *schreiben* |
> | meet | met | **met** | *(sich) treffen* | | | | |
>
> ▶ *Unregelmäßige Verben, p. 200*

Unit 3: The world in one city

p.48	**China** ['tʃaɪnə]	China	
	ship [ʃɪp]	Schiff	
	slave [sleɪv]	Sklave, Sklavin	
	Europe ['jʊərəp]	Europa	
	America [ə'merɪkə]	Amerika	
	Australia [ɒ'streɪliə]	Australien	

Theme 1

p.50	**sell** [sel], **sold** [səʊld], **sold**	verkaufen	**buy** ◄► **sell**
	packet (of) ['pækɪt]	Packung, Päckchen, Schachtel	**!** *English:* **a packet of crisps** *German:* **eine Packung Chips**
	cost [kɒst], **cost**, **cost**	kosten	How much did your new computer **cost**?
	bicycle ['baɪsɪkl]	Fahrrad	**bicycle** = **bike**
	back [bæk]	Rücken; Rückseite	

back

	chocolate bar ['tʃɒklət bɑː]	Schokoriegel	
p.51	**more and more**	immer mehr	**more and more** ◄► **less and less** immer mehr immer weniger
	as much **as** [æz], [əz]	so viel wie	Please write **as** many words **as** you can. My photos aren't **as** good **as** Anne's.

possible [ˈpɒsəbl]	möglich	I'd like to finish this today, if **possible**.
son [sʌn]	Sohn	**daughter** ◄► son
bring: he **brought** [brɔːt]	(mit)bringen: er brachte (mit), er hat (mit)gebracht	
against [əˈgenst]	gegen	We're not allowed to use our mobiles at school. It's **against** the school rules.
Yours sincerely [jɔːz sɪnˈsɪəli]	Mit freundlichen Grüßen *(Briefschluss)*	
less [les]	weniger	**less** ◄► more
etc. *(aus dem Lateinischen)* [etˈsetərə]	usw. (und so weiter)	
What sort of …? [sɔːt]	Welche Art/Sorte (von) …?	**What sort of** music do you like?
make money, made, made	Geld verdienen	
biscuit [ˈbɪskɪt]	Keks, Plätzchen	**!** *German:* Keks – *English:* **biscuit** *German:* Kuchen – *English:* **cake**
cereal bar [ˈsɪəriəl bɑː]	Müsliriegel	
energy [ˈenədʒi]	Energie	**!** Betonung auf der 1. Silbe: **energy** [ˈenədʒi]

Theme 2

p.52 **be good at** sth.	etwas gut können, gut sein in etwas	**!** *English:* I'm **good at** maths. *German:* Ich bin **gut in** Mathematik.
Miss [mɪs]	Anrede für Lehrerin in GB	
active [ˈæktɪv]	aktiv	**!** Betonung auf der 1. Silbe: **active** [ˈæktɪv]
term [tɜːm]	Trimester	The school year in Britain has three **terms**.
salesperson [ˈseɪlzpɜːsn], *pl* **salespeople** [ˈseɪlzpiːpl]	Verkäufer/in	
serious [ˈsɪəriəs]	ernst(haft)	This is a **serious** problem. *(ernst)* **Seriously**, Ben, you're a good salesperson. *(ernsthaft, im Ernst)*
hear: I've **heard** [hɜːd]	hören: ich habe gehört	
competition [kɒmpəˈtɪʃn]	Wettbewerb	
take part in sth. [teɪk ˈpɑːt], **took, taken** [ˈteɪkən]	an etwas teilnehmen, bei etwas mitmachen	More than 200 singers **took part in** the concert.
information (about) *(no pl)* [ɪnfəˈmeɪʃn]	Information(en) (über)	**!** Das englische Wort **information** hat keinen Plural: *English:* Here's the **information** about … *German:* Hier sind die Information**en** über …
p.53 the **most** money [məʊst]	das meiste Geld, am meisten Geld	**!** *Steigerung:* **much/many – more – (the) most**
on TV	im Fernsehen	I saw an interesting programme **on TV** last night.
the USA [juː es ˈeɪ]	die USA (= die Vereinigten Staaten von Amerika)	

badge [bædʒ]	Anstecknadel, Button	
balloon [bəˈluːn]	Ballon	
plant [plɑːnt]	Pflanze	a **plant**
cost [kɒst]	Kosten, Preis	**!** *English:* **cost** (Singular!) *German:* **Kost**en

euro (€) [ˈjʊərəʊ]	Euro

Pounds and euros

In **Britain** you pay with **pounds** and **pence**:

You say:	*You write:*
fifty p [piː]/**fifty pence** [pens]	50 p
one pound/a pound	£ 1
two pounds fifty	£ 2.50

In **Germany** you pay with **euros** and **cents**:

You say:	*You write:*
fifty cents [sents]	€0.50
one euro/a euro	€1
two euros fifty	€2.50

---

total [ˈtəʊtl]	Gesamtbetrag, Summe	
per balloon [pɜː], [pə]	pro Ballon	
profit [ˈprɒfɪt]	Gewinn, Profit	I made a **profit** of £ 15 when I sold my bike. **!** Betonung auf der 1 Silbe: **profit** [ˈprɒfɪt]

Story

p.54	**look around** [lʊk əˈraʊnd]	sich umschauen (in)	Let's go to town and **look around** the shops.
	flour [ˈflaʊə]	Mehl	
	break [breɪk], **broke** [brəʊk], **broken** [ˈbrəʊkən]	(zer)brechen	**!** something is **broken** = etwas ist gebrochen, zerbrochen, kaputt
	egg [eg]	Ei	You need **eggs** and flour to make cupcakes.
	impressed [ɪmˈprest]	beeindruckt	Dad was really **impressed** when I hoovered all the house.
	at 16	mit 16, im Alter von 16	In the USA you can learn to drive **at 16**.
	sit down [sɪt ˈdaʊn], **sat** [sæt], **sat**	sich (hin)setzen	
	grandfather [ˈgrænfɑːðə]	Großvater	**grandfather** = **grandad** = **grandpa**
	negative [ˈnegətɪv]	negativ	
	enough [ɪˈnʌf]	genug	It's not perfect, but it's good **enough**.
	mean [miːn], **meant** [ment], **meant**	meinen, sagen wollen	I don't understand. What do you **mean**?
p.55	send: they **sent** [sent]	schicken: sie schickten, sie haben geschickt	

| represent [reprɪ'zent] | repräsentieren, vertreten | Teams from six countries took part in the competition. A team from Kiel **represented** Germany. |
| fantastic [fæn'tæstɪk] | fantastisch | |

Skills

.56	**useful** ['juːsfl]	nützlich	
	underline [ʌndə'laɪn]	unterstreichen	Please **underline** the <u>new words</u>.
	fact [fækt]	Tatsache; Information	
	task [tɑːsk]	Aufgabe	
.57	**opinion** [ə'pɪnjən]	Meinung	
	comment ['kɒment]	Kommentar	
	for lots of reasons ['riːznz]	aus vielen Gründen	I want a good job. **For** this **reason** I work hard at school.
	in my opinion [ə'pɪnjən]	meiner Meinung nach	
	role model ['rəʊl mɒdl]	Vorbild	
	boxing ['bɒksɪŋ]	(das) Boxen	
	Olympic [ə'lɪmpɪk]	olympisch	the **Olympic** Games = die Olympischen Spiele
	even ['iːvn]	sogar, selbst	Everybody tried to help, **even** the children.
	violent ['vaɪələnt]	gewalttätig; gewaltsam	Do you think judo is a **violent** sport?
	fight [faɪt], **fought** [fɔːt], **fought**	kämpfen	
	prefer sth. **to** sth. [prɪ'fɜː]	etwas lieber mögen als etwas, etwas einer Sache vorziehen	I like team sports, so I **prefer** football **to** jogging.
	strong [strɒŋ]	stark	She's very **strong**.

.59	**Get ready. Steady. Go!** [get redi stedi 'gəʊ]	Auf die Plätze, fertig, los!	
	ready ['redi]	bereit, fertig	Are you **ready**? Can we go?
	I guess [ges]	ich glaube, ich nehme an	
	message ['mesɪdʒ]	Botschaft, Aussage	! **message** = **1.** Nachricht, Mitteilung; **2.** Botschaft, Aussage
.61	**be bored** [bɔːd]	Langeweile haben, gelangweilt sein	! The play was **boring**. **langweilig** I was **bored**. **gelangweilt**
	jump [dʒʌmp]	springen; (vor Schreck) zusammenzucken	Can you **jump** on your chair? Suddenly there was a loud noise. We all **jumped**.

Irregular verbs

bring	brought	brought	(mit)bringen	mean	meant	meant	meinen, sagen wollen
break	broke	broken	(zer)brechen	sell	sold	sold	verkaufen
cost	cost	cost	kosten	send	sent	sent	schicken
fight	fought	fought	kämpfen	sit	sat	sat	sitzen
hear	heard	heard	hören	take	took	taken	nehmen
make	made	made	machen				

▶ *Unregelmäßige Verben, p. 200*

Unit 4: Scotland is different

p.68	**Scotland** [ˈskɒtlənd]	Schottland	
	castle [ˈkɑːsl]	Burg	a **castle**

	lake [leɪk]	(Binnen-)See	a **lake**

p.69	**throw** [θrəʊ], **threw** [θruː], **thrown** [θrəʊn]	werfen	
	grey [greɪ]	grau	They're **grey**.

	sky [skaɪ]	Himmel	❗ *English:* clouds **in** the sky *German:* Wolken **am** Himmel
	modern [ˈmɒdn]	modern	❗ Betonung auf der 1. Silbe: **mo**dern [ˈmɒdn]
	building [ˈbɪldɪŋ]	Gebäude	
	capital [ˈkæpɪtl]	Hauptstadt	Berlin is the **capital** of Germany.
	which lake? [wɪtʃ]	welcher See?	
	its **own** flag [əʊn]	seine eigene Fahne	❗ *English:* Do you have **your** own room? *German:* Hast du **ein eigenes** Zimmer?
	parliament [ˈpɑːləmənt]	Parlament	❗ Beachte die Schreibweise: **parli**ament
	language [ˈlæŋgwɪdʒ]	Sprache	
	musical [ˈmjuːzɪkl]	Musik-, musikalisch	The piano is a **musical** instrument.

Theme 1

p.70	**change** [tʃeɪndʒ]	Veränderung, Wechsel	❗ **change** = 1. (ver)ändern, sich (ver)ändern; 2. Veränderung, Wechsel
	for the last time	zum letzten Mal	
	equipment (no pl) [ɪˈkwɪpmənt]	Ausrüstung, Ausstattung	walking **equipment**
	shop [ʃɒp]	(ein)kaufen	❗ **shop** = 1. Geschäft, Laden; 2. (ein)kaufen
	unemployed [ˌʌnɪmˈplɔɪd]	arbeitslos	
	month [mʌnθ]	Monat	
p.71	**meal** [miːl]	Mahlzeit, Essen	Do you eat a hot **meal** at lunchtime? *(warme Mahlzeit)*
	blame sb. **(for)** [bleɪm]	jm. die Schuld geben (an), jm. Vorwürfe machen (wegen)	Don't **blame** me. It wasn't my mistake.
	Don't blame yourself. [jɔːˈself], [jəˈself]	Mach dir keine Vorwürfe.	

myself, yourself, himself … (Reflexivpronomen)

I listen to **myself**.	Ich höre **mir** zu	/ **mich** an.		
You listen to **yourself**.	Du … **dir** …	/ **dich** …		
He listens to **himself**.	Er … **sich** …	/ **sich** …		
She listens to **herself**.	Sie … **sich** …	/ **sich** …	**!** Aussprache und Betonung:
It listens to **itself**.	Es … **sich** …	/ **sich** …		**-self** [-'self]
We listen to **ourselves**.	Wir … **uns** …	/ **uns** …		**-selves** [-'selvz]
You listen to **yourselves**.	Ihr … **euch** …	/ **euch** …		
They listen to **themselves**.	Sie … **sich** …	/ **sich** …		

beautiful ['bjuːtɪfl]	(wunder)schön	Your baby sister is a **beautiful** little girl.
Enjoy yourself/yourselves.	Viel Vergnügen! / Viel Spaß!	
bed and breakfast (B&B)	Frühstückspension; Zimmer mit Frühstück	We stayed at a nice **B&B** in York last year. **Bed and breakfast** can be quite expensive.
teach [tiːtʃ], **taught** [tɔːt], **taught**	unterrichten, lehren	Mr Schwarz is a teacher. He **teaches** English.
get cold, **got, got**	kalt werden	It **gets** very hot here in the summer. **!** **get** = **1.** bekommen, kriegen; **2.** werden
Help yourselves.	Bedient euch! / Greift zu!	I've made cupcakes. **Help yourselves.** Take as many as you like!

Theme 2

p.72 **exhibition** [eksɪ'bɪʃn]	Ausstellung	
guest [gest]	Gast	
twin room [twɪn 'ruːm]	Zweibettzimmer	
single room [sɪŋgl 'ruːm]	Einzelzimmer	

a **single room**   a **twin room**

kettle ['ketl]	Wasserkocher (elektrisch)	
dry [draɪ]	trocknen	
coat [kəʊt]	Mantel; Jacke	
Canadian [kə'neɪdiən]	kanadisch, aus Kanada; Kanadier/in	
book [bʊk]	buchen, reservieren	That restaurant is quite famous. You should **book** a table. **!** **book** = **1.** Buch; **2.** buchen, reservieren
p.73 **confirm** [kən'fɜːm]	bestätigen	
reservation [rezə'veɪʃn]	Reservierung	"I'd like to make a **reservation** for two people for this evening, please."
directions (pl) [də'rekʃnz]	Wegbeschreibung(en)	
just [dʒʌst]	einfach; nur, bloß	**Just** listen to me for five minutes, please. Don't **just** sit there! Get up and help me.
knife [naɪf], pl **knives** [naɪvz]	Messer	**!** Aussprache – das „k" wird nicht gesprochen: **knife** [naɪf]

| sock [sɒk] | Socke | |
| bagpipes (pl) [ˈbægpaɪps] | Dudelsack | |

Story

p.74 ghost [gəʊst]	Gespenst	
exist [ɪgˈzɪst]	existieren	
down [daʊn]	hinunter, runter, nach unten	**up ◄► down**
wave [weɪv]	winken	
land [lænd]	landen	
hire [ˈhaɪə]	mieten, leihen	
driving licence [ˈdraɪvɪŋ laɪsns]	Führerschein	You need a **driving licence** if you want to drive a car.
mine [maɪn]	meine, meiner, meins	Is that Ryan's pencil? – No, it's **mine**.
hoot [huːt]	hupen	
luckily [ˈlʌkɪli]	glücklicherweise	I forgot my homework, but **luckily** our teacher didn't check.
p.75 finger [ˈfɪŋgə]	Finger	! Aussprache: **finger** [ˈfɪŋgə]
ruin (oft auch pl: ruins) [ˈruːɪn]	Ruine	Urquhart Castle is now a **ruin**. ! Betonung auf der 1. Silbe: **ruin** [ˈruːɪn]
car park [ˈkɑː pɑːk]	Parkplatz	
narrow [ˈnærəʊ]	eng, schmal	The road was too **narrow** for the big bus.
yours [jɔːz]	deiner, deine, deins; eurer, eure, eures	Are these yours? No, they're dad's.
not … either [ˈaɪðə]	auch nicht	I hate coffee and I do**n't** like tea **either**.
over there [əʊvə ˈðeə]	da drüben; da hinüber	
accent [ˈæksent]	Akzent	I find it hard to understend people with a strong Scottish **accent**.

Skills

p.76 fly [flaɪ], flew [fluː], flown [fləʊn]	fliegen	
p.77 pride [praɪd]	Stolz	you're very **proud** – you're full of **pride**
born [bɔːn]	geboren	When's your birthday? When were you **born**?
bass guitar [beɪs gɪˈtɑː]	E-Bass	
p.78 skim a text [skɪm]	einen Text überfliegen (um den Inhalt grob zu erfassen)	
region [ˈriːdʒən]	Region	! Betonung auf der 1. Silbe: **region** [ˈriːdʒən]
p.79 salt [sɔːlt]	Salz	
sugar [ˈʃʊgə]	Zucker	

Focus on language

p.80	a thing **that** we use …	ein Ding, das wir … benutzen
	shower [ˈʃaʊə]	Dusche; Schauer
	What do you call …?	Wie nennt man …?
	waiter [ˈweɪtə], **waitress** [ˈweɪtrəs]	Kellner, Kellnerin
	mechanic [mɪˈkænɪk]	Mechaniker/in
	mirror [ˈmɪrə]	Spiegel
	towel [ˈtaʊəl]	Handtuch
p.81	**machine** [məˈʃiːn]	Maschine, Gerät

customers

waiter

She looked at herself in the **mirror**.

Irregular verbs

fly	flew	**flown**	*fliegen*	teach	taught	**taught**	*unterrichten, lehren*
get	got	**got**	*bekommen; werden*	throw	threw	**thrown**	*werfen*

▸ *Unregelmäßige Verben, p. 200*

Grammatical terms (Grammatische Fachbegriffe)

adjective	[ˈædʒɪktɪv]	Adjektiv	*good, red, new, boring, …*
adverb	[ˈædvɜːb]	Adverb	*slowly, happily, well, …*
comparison	[kəmˈpærɪsn]	Steigerung	*old – older – oldest*
conditional sentence	[kənˈdɪʃənl ˈsentəns]	Bedingungssatz	*If we win, we'll go to London.*
future	[ˈfjuːtʃə]	Zukunft, Futur	*Wait, I'll help you!*
infinitive	[ɪnˈfɪnətɪv]	Grundform des Verbs, Infinitiv	*go, open, see, read*
irregular verb	[ɪˈreɡjələ ˈvɜːb]	unregelmäßiges Verb	*go – went – gone*
linker, linking word	[ˈlɪŋkɪŋ wɜːd]	Bindewort (Konjunktion)	*and, because, but, so*
noun	[naʊn]	Nomen, Hauptwort, Substantiv	*Alfie, boy, mother, time, …*
opposite	[ˈɒpəzɪt]	Gegenteil	*hot – cold; start – stop*
past participle	[pɑːst ˈpɑːtɪsɪpl]	Partizip Perfekt, 3. Form des Verbs	*happened, eaten, gone, …*
present perfect	[preznt ˈpɜːfɪkt]	*present perfect*	He **has drunk** your water.
present progressive	[preznt prəˈɡresɪv]	Verlaufsform der Gegenwart	They**'re having** lunch.
question word	[ˈkwestʃən wɜːd]	Fragewort	*what?, when?, where?, how?, …*
reflexive pronoun	[rɪˌfleksɪv ˈprəʊnaʊn]	Reflexivpronomen	*myself, yourself, himself, …*
relative pronoun	[ˌrelətɪv ˈprəʊnaʊn]	Relativpronomen	*who, that*
regular verb	[ˈreɡjələ ˈvɜːb]	regelmäßiges Verb	*help – helped – helped*
simple past	[sɪmpl ˈpɑːst]	einfache Form der Vergangenheit	I **loved** the holidays.
simple present	[sɪmpl ˈpreznt]	einfache Form der Gegenwart	I always **go** to school by bike.
time phrase	[ˈtaɪm freɪz]	Zeitangabe	*yesterday, after school*
***will*-future**	[ˈwɪl fjuːtʃə]	Futur mit *will*	I think our trip **will be** fun.
word building	[ˈwɜːd bɪldɪŋ]	Wortbildung	*sleep – sleepy; run – runner*

Das **DICTIONARY** besteht aus **zwei alphabetischen Wörterlisten**:
English – German (S. 166–182) und **German – English** (S. 183–196)

Das **English – German dictionary** enthält den Wortschatz der Bände 1–3 von *Highlight*.
Wenn du wissen möchtest, was ein englisches Wort bedeutet, wie man es ausspricht oder
wie es genau geschrieben wird, dann kannst du hier nachschlagen.

Im **Dictionary** werden folgende **Abkürzungen und Symbole** verwendet:

sb. = somebody   sth. = something   *pl* = *plural* (Mehrzahl)
infml = *informal* (umgangssprachlich)   *AE* = American English

° Mit diesem Kringel sind Wörter markiert, die nicht zum Lernwortschatz gehören.

Die **Fundstellenangaben** zeigen, wo ein Wort zum ersten Mal vorkommt.
Die Ziffern in Klammern bezeichnen Seitenzahlen:

I   = *Highlight* Band 1
III 1 (17) = *Highlight* Band 3, Unit 1, Seite 17

Tipps zur Arbeit mit einem Wörterbuch findest du im Skills file auf Seite 126.

A

a [ə] ein/e I **£10 a week**
10 Pfund pro Woche II
°**ability** [əˈbɪləti] Fähigkeit,
Können
about [əˈbaʊt]:
1. ungefähr I
2. über I
What about you? Und du? /
Was ist mit dir? I **What's special
about him?** Was ist das Besondere an ihm? II **write about**
schreiben über I
°**abseil** [ˈæbseɪl] sich abseilen
accent [ˈæksent] Akzent III 4 (75)
accident [ˈæksɪdənt] Unfall III 2 (32)
°**accommodation** [əkɒməˈdeɪʃn]
Unterkunft; Wohnung, Zimmer
across the fields [əˈkrɒs] (quer)
über die Felder III 2 (34)
act [ækt] Theater spielen; schauspielern II
°**action** [ˈækʃn] Aktion, Handlung
active [ˈæktɪv] aktiv III 3 (52)
activity [ækˈtɪvəti] Aktivität, Beschäftigung I
°**actor** [ˈæktə] Schauspieler/in
°**add** [æd] hinzufügen, addieren
address [əˈdres] Adresse I
°**adrenaline-filled** [əˈdrenəlɪn fɪld]
voller Adrenalin *(sehr aufregend)*
adult [ˈædʌlt] Erwachsene/r II
adventure [ədˈventʃə] Abenteuer II
advert [ˈædvɜːt] Anzeige, Werbung III 1 (12)
°**advertise sth** [ˈædvətaɪz] Werbung
machen für etwas
Africa [ˈæfrɪkə] Afrika I

after school [ɑːftə ˈskuːl] nach der
Schule I
afternoon [ɑːftəˈnuːn] Nachmittag I
again [əˈgen] wieder, noch einmal I
against [əˈgenst] gegen III 3 (51)
ago [əˈgəʊ]: **two years ago** vor
zwei Jahren III 1 (11)
agree [əˈgriː]: **agree with sb.**
jm. zustimmen II °**agree on**
sich einigen auf
airport [ˈeəpɔːt] Flughafen II
°**alarm clock** [əˈlɑːm klɒk] Wecker
°**alcohol** [ˈælkəhɒl] Alkohol
all [ɔːl] alle(s) I **all day** den ganzen Tag (lang) II
allowed [əˈlaʊd]: **be allowed to
do sth.** etwas tun dürfen III 1 (10)
alone [əˈləʊn] allein(e) II
along the street [əˈlɒŋ] die Straße
entlang II
alphabet [ˈælfəbet] Alphabet I
°**already** [ɔːlˈredi] schon
also [ˈɔːlsəʊ] auch III 1 (10)
always [ˈɔːlweɪz] immer I
am [æm]: **I'm (= I am)** ich bin I
am [eɪˈem]: **5 am** 5 Uhr morgens/
vormittags I
amazed [əˈmeɪzd] erstaunt, verwundert II
amazing [əˈmeɪzɪŋ] erstaunlich
III 1 (10)
America [əˈmerɪkə] Amerika III 3 (48)
°**American** [əˈmerɪkən] amerikanisch
an [ən] ein/e *(vor Vokalen)* I
and [ænd], [ənd] und I
angry [ˈæŋgri] wütend, ärgerlich I
animal [ˈænɪml] Tier I

another [əˈnʌðə] ein/e andere(r, s);
noch ein/e II
answer [ˈɑːnsə]:
1. Antwort I
2. antworten; beantworten III 1 (14)
°**answer the phone** ans Telefon
gehen
any [ˈeni]: **there aren't any trees**
es gibt keine Bäume II
anything [ˈeniθɪŋ]: **Anything else?**
Sonst noch etwas? I **not (…)
anything** nichts II
°**appetite** [ˈæpɪtaɪt] Appetit
apple [ˈæpl] Apfel II
°**appointment** [əˈpɔɪntmənt]
Verabredung
April [ˈeɪprəl] April I
are [ɑː] bist; seid; sind I
The mobiles are £ 10. Die Handys
kosten 10 Pfund. I
°**arena** [əˈriːnə] Arena
°**argument** [ˈɑːgjumənt] Argument
arm [ɑːm] Arm II
around [əˈraʊnd]: **look around**
sich umschauen (in) III 3 (54)
°**around 7** um ca. 7 Uhr
°**around London** durch London,
in London umher
arrive [əˈraɪv] ankommen II
art [ɑːt] Kunst I
article [ˈɑːtɪkl] Artikel III 2 (35)
as [æz], [əz]: **as much as** so viel
wie III 3 (51) °**as a footballer**
als Fußballer/in °**as many as
you can** so viele (wie) du kannst
ask [ɑːsk] fragen I **ask for sth.**
um etwas bitten II

at [æt], [ət]: **at a restaurant** in einem Restaurant ⏐ **at Egg-buckland** auf der Eggbuckland-Schule ⏐ **at Ellie's house** bei Ellie daheim, bei Ellie zu Hause ⏐ **at home** zu Hause ⏐ **at MAR-TINS** bei MARTINS ⏐ **at school** in der Schule ⏐ **at the cinema** im Kino ⏐ **at the top (of)** oben, am oberen Ende (von); an der Spitze (von) II ⏐ °**at least** mindestens, wenigstens

ate [eɪt], [et] *siehe* **eat**

°**athletics** [æθˈletɪks] Sport, Leichtathletik

August [ˈɔːɡəst] August ⏐

aunt [ɑːnt] Tante II

Australia [ɒˈstreɪliə] Australien III 3 (48)

°**available** [əˈveɪləbl] verfügbar; erhältlich; möglich

away [əˈweɪ] weg, fort ⏐

B

baby [ˈbeɪbi] Baby ⏐

babysitter [ˈbeɪbɪsɪtə] Babysitter ⏐

back [bæk]:
1. Rücken; Rückseite III 3 (50)
2. zurück ⏐
°3. hinteres Ende

background [ˈbækɡraʊnd] Hintergrund III 2 (36)

bad [bæd] schlecht; schlimm ⏐

badge [bædʒ] Anstecknadel, Button III 3 (53)

badminton [ˈbædmɪntən] Badminton, Federball II

bag [bæɡ] Tasche ⏐

bagpipes *(pl)* [ˈbæɡpaɪps] Dudelsack III 4 (73)

ball [bɔːl] Ball ⏐

balloon [bəˈluːn] Ballon III 3 (53)

banana [bəˈnɑːnə] Banane ⏐ **banana skin** Bananenschale ⏐

band [bænd] Band, Musikgruppe II

bank [bæŋk] Bank *(Geldinstitut)* II

baseball [ˈbeɪsbɔːl] Baseball II

basketball [ˈbɑːskɪtbɔːl] Basketball ⏐

bass guitar [beɪs ɡɪˈtɑː] E-Bass III 4 (77)

bathroom [ˈbɑːθruːm] Bad(ezimmer) ⏐

battle [ˈbætl] Wettstreit, Battle *(im Rap)* ⏐

be [biː], **was/were, been** sein ⏐

beach [biːtʃ] Strand ⏐

°**bean** [biːn] Bohne

bear [beə] Bär ⏐

°**Beatlemania** [biːtlˈmeɪniə] *extreme Begeisterung für die Beatles*

beautiful [ˈbjuːtɪfl] (wunder-)schön III 4 (71)

because [bɪˈkɒz] weil ⏐

bed [bed] Bett ⏐

bed and breakfast (B&B) [bed ən ˈbrekfəst] Frühstückspension; Zimmer mit Frühstück III 4 (71)

bedroom [ˈbedruːm] Schlafzimmer ⏐

been [biːn], [bɪn] *siehe* **be**

before [bɪˈfɔː] vor *(zeitlich)* ⏐ **before you read** bevor du liest ⏐

began [bɪˈɡæn] *siehe* **begin**

begin [bɪˈɡɪn], **began, begun** beginnen, anfangen III 1 (14)

behave [bɪˈheɪv] sich verhalten III 2 (32) **behave dangerously** sich gefährlich verhalten III 2 (32)

behind [bɪˈhaɪnd] hinter ⏐

believe [bɪˈliːv] glauben III 2 (30)

bell [bel] Glocke; Klingel III 1 (8)

°**below** [bɪˈləʊ] unten; unter(halb von)

best [best] beste(r, s); am besten ⏐ **Best wishes** Viele Grüße, … *(Briefschluss)* ⏐ **like sth. best** etwas am liebsten mögen II

better [ˈbetə] besser II **do better** besser abschneiden II **like sth. better** etwas lieber mögen II

between [bɪˈtwiːn] zwischen II

°**beware of** [bɪˈweər əv] sich in Acht nehmen vor

bicycle [ˈbaɪsɪkl] Fahrrad III 3 (50)

big [bɪɡ] groß ⏐

bike [baɪk] Fahrrad ⏐ **ride a bike** Rad fahren ⏐

bird [bɜːd] Vogel ⏐

birdhouse [ˈbɜːdhaʊs] Nistkasten *(für Vögel)* II

birthday [ˈbɜːθdeɪ] Geburtstag ⏐ **Happy birthday!** Herzlichen Glückwunsch zum Geburtstag! ⏐ **It's her birthday.** Sie hat Geburtstag. ⏐

biscuit [ˈbɪskɪt] Keks, Plätzchen III 3 (51)

bit [bɪt]: **a bit** ein bisschen II

black [blæk] schwarz ⏐

blame sb. (for) [bleɪm] jm. die Schuld geben (an), jm. Vorwürfe machen (wegen) III 4 (71)

blazer [ˈbleɪzə] Blazer *(Jackett, oft Teil der Schuluniform)* III 1 (20)

block of flats [blɒk əv ˈflæts] Mehrfamilienhaus, Wohnblock III 2 (29)

°**blog** [blɒɡ] Blog *(Internet-Tagebuch)*

°**blow** [bləʊ] wehen

blue [bluː] blau ⏐

°**board** [bɔːd] Tafel *(im Klassenraum)*

boat [bəʊt] Boot; Schiff ⏐

°**bold** [bəʊld] fett (gedruckt)

bonfire [ˈbɒnfaɪə] *(Freuden-)*Feuer II

book [bʊk]:
1. Buch ⏐
2. buchen, reservieren III 4 (72)

bookshop [ˈbʊkʃɒp] Buchladen II

boot [buːt] Stiefel II

bored [bɔːd]: **be bored** Langeweile haben, gelangweilt sein III 3 (61)

boring [ˈbɔːrɪŋ] langweilig ⏐

born [bɔːn] geboren III 4 (77) °**she was born** sie wurde geboren

borrow [ˈbɒrəʊ] (aus)leihen, sich borgen ⏐

boss [bɒs] Boss, Chef/in III 4 (70)

bossy [ˈbɒsi] herrisch ⏐

°**both** [bəʊθ] beide

bottle [ˈbɒtl] Flasche ⏐

bought [bɔːt] *siehe* **buy**

bowling [ˈbəʊlɪŋ]: **go bowling** Bowling spielen gehen ⏐

box [bɒks]
1. Box, Kasten ⏐
°2. boxen

°**boxer** [ˈbɒksə] Boxer/in

boxing *(das)* Boxen III 3 (57)

boy [bɔɪ] Junge ⏐

°**boyband** [ˈbɔɪbænd] Boyband

boyfriend [ˈbɔɪfrend] (fester) Freund II

brave [breɪv] mutig III 2 (32)

bread [bred] Brot II

break [breɪk] Pause ⏐

break [breɪk], **broke, broken** (zer)brechen III 3 (54)

breakfast [ˈbrekfəst] Frühstück ⏐

bridge [brɪdʒ] Brücke II

°**bright** [braɪt] hell

bring [brɪŋ], **brought, brought** bringen, mitbringen ⏐

Britain [ˈbrɪtn] Großbritannien II

British [ˈbrɪtɪʃ] britisch ⏐

brochure [ˈbrəʊʃə] Broschüre, Prospekt ⏐

broke [brəʊk] *siehe* **break**

broken [ˈbrəʊkən]:
1. *siehe* **break**
2. zerbrochen, kaputt III 3 (54)

brother [ˈbrʌðə] Bruder ⏐

brought [brɔːt] *siehe* **bring**

brown [braʊn] braun ⏐

°**browse** [braʊz] stöbern in, sich umschauen in, durchstöbern

building [ˈbɪldɪŋ] Gebäude III 4 (69)

bull [bʊl] Bulle I

burger [ˈbɜːgə] Hamburger (Frikadelle) II

bus [bʌs] Bus I

bus stop [ˈbʌs stɒp] Bushaltestelle II

bush [bʊʃ] Busch, Strauch III 2 (34)

business [ˈbɪznəs] Geschäft, Betrieb III 2 (30) **start a business** ein Geschäft aufmachen, einen Betrieb gründen/eröffnen III 2 (30)

°**business studies** (pl) [ˈbɪznəs stʌdiːz] Wirtschaftskunde

busy [ˈbɪzi]:
1. belebt; verkehrsreich III 1 (16)
2. **be busy** beschäftigt sein, (viel) zu tun haben II

but [bʌt] aber I

buy [baɪ], **bought, bought** kaufen I

by [baɪ] **by Sam Holmes** (geschrieben) von Sam Holmes III 1 (10) **go by bus** mit dem Bus fahren I

Bye. [baɪ] Tschüs. I

C

cafe [ˈkæfeɪ] Café I

cake [keɪk] Kuchen II

calculator [ˈkælkjʊleɪtə] Taschenrechner I

calendar [ˈkælɪndə] Kalender I

call [kɔːl]:
1. rufen; nennen; anrufen III 1 (14)
2. (kurz für: **phone call**) (Telefon-)Anruf II

calm [kɑːm] ruhig, still; besonnen III 2 (32)

came [keɪm] siehe **come**

camera [ˈkæmərə] Fotoapparat; Kamera I

°**camping** [ˈkæmpɪŋ]: **go camping** zelten gehen, campen gehen

can [kæn], [kən] können I **can't (= cannot)** nicht können I

Canadian [kəˈneɪdiən] kanadisch, aus Kanada; Kanadier/in III 4 (72)

°**canoe** [kəˈnuː] Kanu, Paddelboot

°**canoeing** [kəˈnuːɪŋ] Paddeln, Kanusport

canteen [kænˈtiːn] (Schul-)Mensa, Kantine I

°**canyoning** [ˈkænjənɪŋ] Canyoning (in Schluchten springen oder sich abseilen)

capital [ˈkæpɪtl] Hauptstadt III 4 (69)

°**captain** [ˈkæptɪn] Kapitän/in

°**caption** [ˈkæpʃn] Bildunterschrift

car [kɑː] Auto I

car park [ˈkɑː pɑːk] Parkplatz III 4 (75)

card [kɑːd] Karte I

careful [ˈkeəfl] vorsichtig; sorgfältig II

carefully [ˈkeəfəli]: **drive carefully** vorsichtig fahren II

°**carriage** [ˈkærɪdʒ] (Eisenbahn-)Wagen

carrot [ˈkærət] Möhre, Karotte II

°**carry out** [kæri ˈaʊt] durchführen

cartoon [kɑːˈtuːn] Zeichentrickfilm; Comic II

castle [ˈkɑːsl] Burg III 4 (68)

cat [kæt] Katze I

catch [kætʃ], **caught, caught** (ein)fangen III 2 (34)

caught [kɔːt] siehe **catch**

°**'cause** [kɔːz] weil (= because)

CCTV [siː siː tiː ˈviː] Überwachungssystem; Überwachungskamera(s) III 2 (30)

CD [siːˈdiː] CD I

CD player [siːˈdiː pleɪə] CD-Spieler II

celebrate [ˈselɪbreɪt] feiern II

cent [sent] Cent III 3 (53)

centre [ˈsentə] Zentrum, (Stadt-)Mitte II

cereal bar [ˈsɪəriəl bɑː] Müsliriegel III 3 (51)

°**ceremony** [ˈserəməni] Zeremonie II

chair [tʃeə] Stuhl I

champion [ˈtʃæmpiən] Meister/in (Sport) III 3 (59)

change [tʃeɪndʒ]:
1. (ver)ändern, sich (ver)ändern II
2. Veränderung, Wechsel III 4 (70)
°3. wechseln

charity [ˈtʃærəti] wohltätige Organisation II **charity shop** Geschäft, das gespendete Waren für wohltätige Zwecke verkauft II

chat [tʃæt]:
1. Gespräch, Unterhaltung; Chat II
2. **chat (with)** plaudern (mit); „chatten" (mit) II

cheap [tʃiːp] billig, preiswert II **It's cheaper than that.** So viel kostet das nicht. II

check [tʃek] (über)prüfen, kontrollieren II

cheese [tʃiːz] Käse I

chicken [ˈtʃɪkɪn] Huhn; (Brat-)Hähnchen I

child, (pl) **children** [tʃaɪld], [ˈtʃɪldrən] Kind I

chill [tʃɪl] (infml) relaxen, sich ausruhen II

China [ˈtʃaɪnə] China III 3 (48)

chipmunk [ˈtʃɪpmʌŋk] Streifenhörnchen I

chips (pl) [tʃɪps] Pommes frites I °**fish and chips** Backfisch mit Pommes frites

chocolate [ˈtʃɒklət] Schokolade; Praline II

chocolate bar [ˈtʃɒklət bɑː] Schokoriegel III 3 (50)

°**choose** [tʃuːz] (aus)wählen

chores [tʃɔːz]: **do chores** (Haus-)Arbeiten erledigen II

°**chorus** [ˈkɔːrəs] Refrain (in einem Lied)

°**Christmas** [ˈkrɪsməs] Weihnachten **Christmas Day** 1. Weihnachtstag (25. 12.) **Christmas pantomime** (GB) Theaterstück zur Weihnachtszeit

church [tʃɜːtʃ] Kirche III 2 (29)

cinema [ˈsɪnəmə] Kino I

°**circle** [ˈsɜːkl] Kreis

circus [ˈsɜːkəs] Zirkus II

city [ˈsɪti] (Groß-)Stadt I

class [klɑːs] (Schul-)Klasse I

class teacher [ˈklɑːs tiːtʃə] Klassenlehrer/in I

classroom [ˈklɑːsruːm] Klassenraum I

clear [klɪə] deutlich, klar II

clearly [ˈklɪəli]: **talk clearly** deutlich sprechen II

clever [ˈklevə] schlau, klug III 1 (14)

°**click** [klɪk] klicken

°**cliff** [klɪf] Klippe, Felsen

climb [klaɪm] klettern (auf) II **climbing** (das) Klettern (Sport) II

clock [klɒk] Uhr I

close [kləʊz] schließen, zumachen III 2 (31) °**close sth. down** etwas schließen, stillegen (Fabrik, Geschäft)

closed [kləʊzd]: **be closed** geschlossen sein, zu sein II

clothes (pl) [kləʊðz] Kleidung, Kleidungsstücke II

cloud [klaʊd] Wolke II

cloudy [ˈklaʊdi] wolkig, bewölkt II

club [klʌb] Klub, Verein I

coat [kəʊt] Mantel; Jacke III 4 (72)

coffee [ˈkɒfi] Kaffee I

cold [kəʊld] kalt II

collect [kəˈlekt] sammeln II

°**collection** [kəˈlekʃn] Abholung, Abhol-

colour [ˈkʌlə] Farbe I

coloured [ˈkʌləd] bunt, farbig II

°**colourful** [ˈkʌləfl] farbenfroh, bunt

°**column** [ˈkɒləm] Spalte *(in einem gedruckten Text)*

come [kʌm], **came, come** (mit) kommen I **Come on!** Komm(t) (schon)! / Ach komm! III 2 (30)

comedy [ˈkɒmədi] Comedyshow; Komödie I

comfortable [ˈkʌmftəbl] bequem, gemütlich II **make yourself comfortable** es sich gemütlich machen III 4 (74)

comic [ˈkɒmɪk] Comic(heft) II

comment [ˈkɒment] Kommentar III 3 (57)

°**community** [kəˈmjuːnəti] Gemeinde(-), Lokal-

°**compare** [kəmˈpeə] vergleichen

°**comparison** [kəmˈpærɪsn] Vergleich

competition [kɒmpəˈtɪʃn] Wettbewerb III 3 (52)

°**complete** [kəmˈpliːt]:
  1. vervollständigen
  2. vollständig

computer [kəmˈpjuːtə] Computer I

concert [ˈkɒnsət] Konzert I

confirm [kənˈfɜːm] bestätigen III 4 (73)

Congratulations (on ...)! [kəngrætʃuˈleɪʃnz] Herzlichen Glückwunsch (zu ...)! I

cook [kʊk] kochen I

°**cooker** [ˈkʊkə] Herd

°**cool** [kuːl] cool I

°**copy** [ˈkɒpi] kopieren, abschreiben

corner [ˈkɔːnə] Ecke I

correct [kəˈrekt]:
  1. korrigieren, berichtigen II
  °**2.** korrekt

cost [kɒst] Kosten, Preis III 3 (53)

cost [kɒst], **cost, cost** kosten III 3 (50)

cottage [ˈkɒtɪdʒ] Häuschen, Hütte II

could [kʊd]:
  1. she could sie konnte II
  2. you could du könntest II

country [ˈkʌntri] Land I **in the country** auf dem Land III 2 (28)

°**course** [kɔːs] Kurs(us)

°**cousin** [ˈkʌzn] Cousin, Cousine I

°**cover** [ˈkʌvə] abdecken, zudecken

cow [kaʊ] Kuh I

crab [kræb] Krebs I

cream [kriːm] Sahne I

°**cream tea** [kriːm ˈtiː] *Tee mit scones, Marmelade und Sahne*

cricket [ˈkrɪkɪt] Cricket *(Mannschaftssportart)* II

crime series, (pl) crime series [ˈkraɪm sɪəriːz] Krimiserie II

crisps *(pl)* [krɪsps] (Kartoffel-)Chips II

crocodile [ˈkrɒkədaɪl] Krokodil I

cross [krɒs] überqueren I

crossroads, (pl) crossroads [ˈkrɒsrəʊdz] (Straßen-)Kreuzung III 2 (29)

°**cruise** [kruːz] Kreuzfahrt, Schiffsreise

cry [kraɪ] weinen II

°**cubic metre** [kjuːbɪk ˈmiːtə] Kubikmeter

culture [ˈkʌltʃə] Kultur III 1 (10)

cup [kʌp] Tasse III 1 (19) **a cup of tea** eine Tasse Tee III 1 (19)

cupcake [ˈkʌpkeɪk] Cupcake *(kleiner runder Kuchen)* III 3 (54)

cushion [ˈkʊʃn] Kissen I

customer [ˈkʌstəmə] Kunde, Kundin I

cut [kʌt], **cut, cut** schneiden; *(Rasen)* mähen II

cute [kjuːt] niedlich, süß I

cycle [ˈsaɪkl] Rad fahren II

D

dad [dæd] Papa, Vati I

dance [dɑːns] tanzen II

dancer [ˈdɑːnsə] Tänzer/in III 1 (17)

dancing [ˈdɑːnsɪŋ] *(das)* Tanzen I

dangerous [ˈdeɪndʒərəs] gefährlich I

dark [dɑːk] dunkel III 1 (21)

date [deɪt] Datum I

daughter [ˈdɔːtə] Tochter III 2 (32)

day [deɪ] Tag I **day out** (Tages-)Ausflug II

deal [diːl] Geschäft; Vereinbarung II **It's a deal!** Abgemacht! II **make a deal** ein Geschäft abschließen, vereinbaren II

dear [dɪə] **Oh dear!** oje! II

Dear ... [dɪə] Liebe ... / Lieber ... I

December [dɪˈsembə] Dezember I

°**decide** [dɪˈsaɪd] sich entscheiden, beschließen

deep [diːp] tief III 2 (32)

°**delivery** [dɪˈlɪvəri] Lieferung; Liefer-

Denmark [ˈdenmɑːk] Dänemark II

°**departure** [dɪˈpɑːtʃə] Abfahrt

describe [dɪˈskraɪb] beschreiben III 2 (32)

desk [desk] Schreibtisch II

°**detail** [ˈdiːteɪl] Detail, Einzelheit

detective [dɪˈtektɪv] Detektiv/in III 1 (8)

°**diagram** [ˈdaɪəgræm] Diagramm

°**dialogue** [ˈdaɪəlɒg] Dialog

°**diary** [ˈdaɪəri] Tagebuch; Kalender

dictionary [ˈdɪkʃənri] Wörterbuch, (alphabetisches) Wörterverzeichnis I

did [dɪd] *siehe* **do** **Did they go?** Gingen sie?/Sind sie gegangen? II **we didn't have a ...** wir hatten kein/keine ... I

die [daɪ] sterben II

difference [ˈdɪfrəns] Unterschied I **make a difference** etwas bewirken, etwas ausmachen I

different [ˈdɪfrənt] unterschiedlich, verschieden, anders I

difficult [ˈdɪfɪkəlt] schwierig, schwer I

diner [ˈdaɪnə] *(AE)* Imbissstube, Lokal II

dinner [ˈdɪnə] Abendessen I

dinosaur [ˈdaɪnəsɔː] Dinosaurier III 1 (14)

directions *(pl)* [dəˈrekʃnz] Wegbeschreibung(en) III 4 (73)

°**disagree** [dɪsəˈgriː] nicht zustimmen, widersprechen

disappointed [dɪsəˈpɔɪntɪd] enttäuscht II

disaster [dɪˈzɑːstə] Katastrophe, Unglück III 1 (14)

°**discover** [dɪˈskʌvə] entdecken

dishwasher [ˈdɪʃwɒʃə] Geschirrspülmaschine II

dive [daɪv] einen Kopfsprung machen I

°**diver** [ˈdaɪvə] Kunst-/Turmspringer/in

diving [ˈdaɪvɪŋ] *(das)* Tauchen *(Sport)* II

do [duː], **did, done** machen, tun I **50p will do** 50 Pence reichen (auch) II **do a trip** einen Ausflug/eine Reise machen II **I do my homework** ich mache (meine) Hausaufgaben I

doctor [ˈdɒktə] Arzt/Ärztin, Doktor/in II

dog [dɒg] Hund I **dogs' home** Hundeheim II

dollar ($) [ˈdɒlə] Dollar III 1 (15) **like a million dollars** fantastisch III 1 (15)

done [dʌn] *siehe* **do**

donkey [ˈdɒŋki] Esel I

door [dɔː] Tür II

°**dormitory** [ˈdɔːmətri] Schlafsaal

°**dossier** [ˈdɒsieɪ] Mappe, Dossier

°**double room** [dʌbl ˈruːm] Doppelzimmer

down [daʊn] hinunter, runter, nach unten III 4 (74)

downside ['daʊnsaɪd] Kehrseite, Nachteil III 1 (10)

°**draft** [drɑːft] Entwurf

drama ['drɑːmə] Schauspiel, darstellende Kunst I

drank [dræŋk] siehe **drink**

°**draw** [drɔː], **drew, drawn** zeichnen I

dream [driːm] Traum II

dress [dres] Kleid II

°**dressing room** ['dresɪŋ ruːm] Umkleide(kabine)

°**drew** [druː] siehe **draw**

drink [drɪŋk] Getränk I

drink [drɪŋk], **drank, drunk** trinken III 1 (15)

°**drip** [drɪp] tropfen

drive [draɪv], **drove, driven** (mit dem Auto) fahren II

driver ['draɪvə] Fahrer/in III 1 (17)

driving licence ['draɪvɪŋ laɪsns] Führerschein III 4 (74)

drove [drəʊv] siehe **drive**

drums [drʌmz] Schlagzeug; Trommeln I

dry [draɪ] trocknen III 4 (72)

duck [dʌk] Ente I

DVD [diːviːˈdiː] DVD I

DVD player [diːviːˈdiː pleɪə] DVD-Player III 4 (72)

E

°**each** [iːtʃ] jede(r, s) (einzelne)

ear [ɪə] Ohr II

early ['ɜːli] früh I

earthquake ['ɜːθkweɪk] Erdbeben III 1 (15)

east [iːst] Osten; östlich; Ost- II

easy ['iːzi] einfach, leicht II **Take it easy!** (infml) Reg dich nicht auf. / Bleib mal locker. III 2 (31)

eat [iːt], **ate, eaten** essen; fressen I

egg [eg] Ei III 3 (54)

eight [eɪt] acht I

either ['aɪðə]: **not … either** auch nicht III 4 (75)

elephant ['elɪfənt] Elefant I

eleven [ɪˈlevən] elf I

else [els]: **Anything else?** Sonst noch etwas? I

email ['iːmeɪl] E-Mail I

empty ['empti]:
1. leer II
2. leeren II

end [end] Ende, Schluss I **in the end** schließlich, zum Schluss II

ending ['endɪŋ] Ende (Text, Geschichte) II **happy ending** Happy End II

energy ['enədʒi] Energie III 3 (51)

energy drink ['enədʒi drɪŋk] Energiegetränk III 3 (51)

England ['ɪŋglənd] England I

English ['ɪŋglɪʃ] Englisch; englisch I

enjoy [ɪnˈdʒɔɪ] genießen II **Enjoy yourself/yourselves.** Viel Vergnügen! / Viel Spaß! III 4 (71) °**Enjoy your meal.** Guten Appetit!

enough [ɪˈnʌf] genug III 3 (54)

°**entertainment** [entəˈteɪnmənt] Unterhaltung

°**entry** ['entri] Eintritt, Zutritt

equipment [ɪˈkwɪpmənt] Ausrüstung, Ausstattung III 4 (70)

e-reader ['iː riːdə] E-Book-Reader II

escalator ['eskəleɪtə] Rolltreppe III 1 (20)

especially [ɪˈspeʃəli] insbesondere III 1 (15)

etc. [etˈsetərə] (aus dem Lateinischen) usw. (und so weiter) III 3 (51)

euro (€) ['jʊərəʊ] Euro III 3 (53)

Europe ['jʊərəp] Europa III 3 (48)

even ['iːvn] sogar, selbst III 3 (57)

evening ['iːvnɪŋ] Abend I

°**event** [ɪˈvent] Ereignis

ever ['evə] je(mals) II **Have you ever been …?** Warst du schon mal …? / Bist du schon mal … gewesen? II

every ['evri] jede(r, s) II °**every 3 minutes** alle 3 Minuten

everybody ['evribɒdi] jeder; alle I

everyone ['evriwʌn] jeder; alle II

°**everything** ['evriθɪŋ] alles

everywhere ['evriweə] überall(hin) III 2 (37)

example [ɪgˈzɑːmpl] Beispiel I **for example** zum Beispiel I

excited [ɪkˈsaɪtɪd] aufgeregt, gespannt I

exciting [ɪkˈsaɪtɪŋ] aufregend II

Excuse me, … [ɪksˈkjuːz mi] Entschuldigung, … II

exercise ['eksəsaɪz] Übung, Aufgabe I **exercise book** Schulheft, Übungsheft I **do exercises** Übungen machen II

exhibition [eksɪˈbɪʃn] Ausstellung III 4 (72)

exist [ɪgˈzɪst] existieren III 4 (74)

expensive [ɪkˈspensɪv] teuer I

°**experience** [ɪkˈspɪəriəns]:
1. erfahren, erleben
2. Erfahrung, Erlebnis

°**expert** ['ekspɜːt] fachmännisch, ausgezeichnet

°**explain** [ɪkˈspleɪn] erklären

°**explore** [ɪkˈsplɔː] erforschen, erkunden

°**explorer** [ɪkˈsplɔːrə] Forschungsreisende/r, Entdecker/in

°**express** [ɪkˈspres] ausdrücken, zum Ausdruck bringen

°**expression** [ɪkˈspreʃn] Ausdruck

eye [aɪ] Auge III 1 (9)

F

face [feɪs] Gesicht I

fact [fækt] Tatsache; Information III 3 (56)

fall [fɔːl], **fell, fallen** fallen; hinfallen I

false [fɔːls] falsch, unrichtig II

family ['fæməli] Familie I **family tree** (Familien-)Stammbaum I **family-friendly** familienfreundlich III 4 (72)

famous (for) ['feɪməs] berühmt (für, wegen) III 1 (8)

fan [fæn] Fan III 1 (11)

°**fancy** ['fænsi] Lust haben auf

fantastic [fænˈtæstɪk] fantastisch III 3 (55)

far [fɑː] weit III 1 (16)

farm [fɑːm] Bauernhof I

farmer ['fɑːmə] Bauer, Bäuerin; Landwirt/in III 2 (32)

fashion ['fæʃn] Mode(trend) III 1 (10)

°**fast** [fɑːst] schnell

father ['fɑːðə] Vater III 2 (32)

favourite ['feɪvərɪt] Lieblings- I **favourite thing** Lieblingssache I

February ['februəri] Februar I

fed up [fed ʌp] **feel fed up** genervt sein, sauer sein; die Nase voll haben I

feed [fiːd] füttern I

feel [fiːl], **felt, felt** sich fühlen; fühlen I

°**feeling** ['fiːlɪŋ] Gefühl

fell [fel] siehe **fall**

felt [felt] siehe **feel**

°**female** ['fiːmeɪl] weiblich; Frau

ferry ['feri] Fähre I

festival ['festɪvl] Fest II

°**few** [fjuː]: **a few** ein paar, einige

field [fiːld] Feld; Weide I

fifty ['fɪfti] fünfzig I

fight [faɪt], **fought, fought** kämpfen III 3 (57)

°**file** [faɪl] Datei

fill [fɪl] füllen II

film [fɪlm] Film I

film star ['fɪlm stɑː] Filmstar III 1 (8)

find [faɪnd], **found, found** finden II **find out** herausfinden II

fine [faɪn] gut, schön I **I'm fine.** Es geht mir gut. I

finger ['fɪŋgə] Finger III 4 (75)

finish ['fɪnɪʃ]:
1. beenden, enden II
°**2.** Ende, Ziel II

fire ['faɪə] Feuer II

firefighter ['faɪəfaɪtə] Feuerwehrmann, Feuerwehrfrau I

firework ['faɪəwɜːk] Feuerwerkskörper II **fireworks** *(pl)* Feuerwerk II

first [fɜːst]:
1. zuerst I
2. first (= 1st) erste, erster, erstes I

first aid [fɜːst 'eɪd] Erste Hilfe II

first-aid kit [fɜːst 'eɪd kɪt] Erste-Hilfe-Set, Verbandkasten II

fish, *(pl)* **fish** [fɪʃ] Fisch I °**fish and chips** Backfisch mit Pommes frites

fit [fɪt] fit III 3 (57)

five [faɪv] fünf I **Give me five!** Gib mir fünf! *(Aufforderung, gegen die erhobene Hand des Gegenübers zu klatschen, Geste der Freude/Begrüßung)* II

flag [flæg] Fahne, Flagge II

flat [flæt] Wohnung I **block of flats** Mehrfamilienhaus, Wohnblock III 2 (29)

flat-screen TV ['flæt skriːn tiː viː] Flachbildfernseher I

flew [fluː] *siehe* **fly**

flour ['flaʊə] Mehl III 3 (54)

flown [fləʊn] *siehe* **fly**

fly [flaɪ], **flew, flown** fliegen III 4 (76)

°**focus** ['fəʊkəs] Schwerpunkt **focus on language** *(etwa)* Schwerpunkt: Sprache

fog [fɒg] Nebel II

foggy ['fɒgi] nebelig II

°**follow** ['fɒləʊ] folgen **follow in sb.'s footsteps** in js. Fußstapfen treten

food [fuːd] Essen, Lebensmittel; Futter I

°**foot,** *(pl)* **feet** [fʊt], [fiːt] Fuß **on foot** zu Fuß

football ['fʊtbɔːl] Fußball I **football club (FC)** Fußballverein

III 1 (11) **playing football** Fußballspielen I

footballer ['fʊtbɔːlə] Fußballspieler/in III 1 (17)

°**footstep** ['fʊtstep]: **follow in sb.'s footsteps** in js. Fußstapfen treten

for [fɔː], [fə] für I **for 100 metres** 100 Meter weit II **for lots of reasons** aus vielen Gründen III 3 (57) **for the last time** zum letzten Mal III 4 (70) °**for miles and miles** meilenweit

°**forecast** ['fɔːkɑːst]: **(weather) forecast** (Wetter-)Vorhersage

foreground ['fɔːgraʊnd] Vordergrund III 2 (36)

forget [fə'get], **forgot, forgotten** vergessen II

forgot [fə'gɒt] *siehe* **forget** **I forgot my homework.** Ich habe meine Hausaufgaben vergessen. I

°**form** [fɔːm] Form I

°**forum** ['fɔːrəm] Forum I

fought [fɔːt] *siehe* **fight**

found [faʊnd] *siehe* **find**

four [fɔː] vier I

fox [fɒks] Fuchs III 2 (34)

France [frɑːns] Frankreich I

free [friː]:
1. frei III 4 (72)
Are you free at one o'clock? Hast du um ein Uhr Zeit? I
2. kostenlos I

French [frentʃ] Französisch; französisch I

°**fresh** [freʃ] frisch I

°**freshwater** ['freʃwɔːtə] Süßwasser-

Friday ['fraɪdeɪ], ['fraɪdi] Freitag I

friend [frend] Freund/in I **make friends** Freunde finden II

friendly ['frendli] freundlich, nett II

from [frɒm] aus I **from Monday to Friday** von Montag bis Freitag I **a text from mum** eine SMS von Mama I

front [frʌnt]: **in front of** vor I

fruit [fruːt] Früchte, Obst; Frucht II

full [fʊl] voll III 2 (34) **full of ...** voller ... III 2 (34) °**(half-)full** (halb)voll

°**fully guided** [fʊli 'gaɪdɪd] geführt

fun [fʌn]: **they're fun** es macht Spaß, mit ihnen zusammen zu sein I

°**fun run** ['fʌn rʌn] Spaß(wett)lauf

funny ['fʌni] lustig I

future ['fjuːtʃə] Zukunft II

G

game [geɪm] Spiel I

garage ['gærɑːʒ] Garage I **garage sale** Garagenflohmarkt *(privater Flohmarkt)* I

garden ['gɑːdn] Garten I

gate [geɪt] Tor III 2 (29)

gave [geɪv] *siehe* **give**

geek [giːk] *jemand, der sich sehr stark für etwas begeistert (und manchmal von anderen deswegen belächelt wird)* III 1 (14)

°**general** ['dʒenrəl] allgemein

geography [dʒi'ɒgrəfi] Geografie, Erdkunde I

German ['dʒɜːmən]:
1. Deutsch; deutsch I
2. Deutsche/r II

Germany ['dʒɜːməni] Deutschland I

get [get], **got, got**:
1. bekommen, kriegen I
get the bus den Bus nehmen I
get up aufstehen I
2. get cold kalt werden III 4 (71)

ghost [gəʊst] Gespenst III 4 (74)

ginger ['dʒɪndʒə] Ingwer; rotblond *(Haare)* II

girl [gɜːl] Mädchen I

girlfriend ['gɜːlfrend] (feste) Freundin II

give [gɪv], **gave, given** geben II **give a talk** einen Vortrag halten II **Give me five!** Gib mir fünf! *(Aufforderung, gegen die erhobene Hand des Gegenübers zu klatschen, Geste der Freude/Begrüßung)* II

glad [glæd]: **I'm glad** ich bin froh II

glasses *(pl)* ['glɑːsɪz] Brille II

glove [glʌv] Handschuh II

go [gəʊ], **went, gone** gehen; fahren I **go away** weggehen I **go out** ausgehen; hinausgehen II **I'm going to ask ...** ich werde ... fragen/bitten II

°**goal** [gəʊl] Tor *(Sport)*

good [gʊd] gut I **Good luck.** Viel Glück! I **Good morning.** Guten Morgen. I **be good at sth.** etwas gut können, gut sein in etwas III 3 (52) **Have a good day.** Ich wünsche dir einen schönen Tag. / Schönen Tag noch. I

Goodbye. [gʊd'baɪ] Auf Wiedersehen. I

got [gɒt] *siehe* **get**

GPS [dʒiː piː 'es] GPS III 4 (73)

grandad ['grændæd] Opa III 2 (39)

grandfather ['grænfɑːðə] Groß-vater III 3 (54)

grandma ['grænmɑː] Oma I

grandpa ['grænpɑː] Opa I

grass [grɑːs] Gras II

great [greɪt] großartig, toll I

Great Britain [greɪt 'brɪtn] Groß-britannien II

Greek [griːk] griechisch; Grie-chisch; Grieche/Griechin III 1 (10)

green [griːn] grün I

grey [greɪ] grau III 4 (69)

ground [graʊnd] Erde *(Erdboden)* II

group [gruːp] Gruppe I **group work** Gruppenarbeit I

guess [ges]:
1. I guess ich glaube, ich nehme an III 3 (59)
°**2.** (er)raten

guest [gest] Gast III 4 (72)

°**guide** [gaɪd] Reiseleiter/in, Fremdenführer/in

guitar [gɪ'tɑː] Gitarre I

°**guitarist** [gɪ'tɑːrɪst] Gitarrist/in

guy [gaɪ] Guy-Fawkes-Puppe II
guys Leute *(als Anrede ver-wendet)* II

gymnastics [dʒɪm'næstɪks] Turnen, Gymnastik II

H

had [hæd], [həd] *siehe* **have**

hair [heə] Haar, Haare II

hairdresser ['heədresə] Frisör/in II

hairdryer ['heədraɪə] Föhn, Haar-trockner II

°**half,** *(pl)* **halves** [hɑːf], [hɑːvz] Hälfte **half the class** die halbe Klasse

Halloween [hæləʊ'iːn] Halloween *(Abend des 31. 10.)* II

hamster ['hæmstə] Hamster I

hand [hænd] Hand II

hang-gliding ['hæŋ glaɪdɪŋ] Drachenfliegen II

happen ['hæpən] geschehen, passieren II

happy ['hæpi] glücklich, froh I
Happy birthday! Herzlichen Glückwunsch zum Geburtstag! I
happy ending Happy End II

harbour ['hɑːbə] Hafen I

hard [hɑːd] schwer; schwierig; hart I **work hard** hart arbeiten III 2 (32)

has [hæz], [həz]: **he/she/it has** er/sie/es hat I

hat [hæt] Hut, Mütze II

have [hæv], **had, had** haben I
Have a good day. Ich wünsche dir einen schönen Tag. / Schönen Tag noch. I **have a salad** einen Salat nehmen, essen II **have to do sth.** etwas tun müssen III 1 (20) **I've lived here all my life.** Ich wohne hier schon mein ganzes Leben (lang). III 1 (10) **not have to do sth.** etwas nicht tun müssen / brauchen III 1 (20)

he [hiː] er I

headache ['hedeɪk]: **have a head-ache** Kopfschmerzen haben II

°**heading** ['hedɪŋ] Überschrift

°**headline** ['hedlaɪn] Überschrift

healthy ['helθi] gesund II

hear [hɪə], **heard, heard** hören I

heard [hɜːd] *siehe* **hear**

°**heart** [hɑːt] Herz

heavy ['hevi] schwer *(Gewicht; Regen)* III 2 (32)

Hello. [hə'ləʊ] Hallo. I

help [help]:
1. helfen I
Help yourselves. Bedient euch! / Greift zu! III 4 (71)
2. Hilfe I

helper ['helpə] Helfer/in II

her [hɜː]:
1. her dad ihr Vater I
2. with her mit ihr II
3. for her für sie *(weibliche Per-son)* II

here [hɪə] hier; hierher I **Here you are.** Bitte schön. / Hier, bitte. I

herself [hɜː'self] sie/sich selbst *(weibliche Person)* III 4 (71)

Hi! [haɪ] Hallo. I

high [haɪ] hoch III 1 (9)

high school ['haɪ skuːl] *(GB etwa:)* Gesamtschule I

high street ['haɪ striːt] Hauptstra-ße; Einkaufsstraße III 2 (29)

°**highlight** ['haɪlaɪt] Höhepunkt, Schlaglicht

hiking ['haɪkɪŋ] *(das)* Wandern II

hill [hɪl] Hügel II

hilly ['hɪli] hügelig III 1 (17)

him [hɪm] ihn; ihm I

himself [hɪm'self] er/sich selbst III 4 (71)

hip hop ['hɪp hɒp] Hip-Hop I

hire ['haɪə] mieten, leihen III 4 (74)
°**for hire** zum Mieten, Miet-

his [hɪz] sein/e I

history ['hɪstri] Geschichte I

hit [hɪt] Hit III 4 (77)

hobby ['hɒbi] Hobby I **do a hobby** einem Hobby nachgehen II

hockey ['hɒki] (Feld-)Hockey II

°**hold: hold it together** durchhalten **hold sth. back** etwas zurückhalten

holiday ['hɒlədeɪ] Urlaub II
a week's / six weeks' holiday eine Woche / sechs Wochen Urlaub II

holidays ['hɒlədeɪz] Ferien I

home [həʊm]:
1. nach Hause I
at home zu Hause I
2. Heim, Zuhause II
dogs' home Hundeheim II

homework ['həʊmwɜːk] Hausaufgabe/n I **I do my homework** ich mache (meine) Hausaufgaben I

°**honest** ['ɒnɪst] ehrlich

hoodie ['hʊdi] Kapuzenpullover I

°**Hooray!** [hu'reɪ] Hurra!

hoot [huːt] hupen III 4 (74)

hoover ['huːvə] staubsaugen II

hope [həʊp] hoffen I

horse [hɔːs] Pferd III 2 (36)

hospital ['hɒspɪtl] Krankenhaus I

°**host** [həʊst] Gastgeber/in **host family** Gastfamilie **host mother** Gastmutter

hot [hɒt]:
1. heiß, warm II
°**2.** cool, (brand)heiß

°**hot chocolate** [hɒt 'tʃɒklət] Kakao, heiße (Trink-)Schokolade

hot dog ['hɒt dɒg] Hot Dog *(hei-ßes Würstchen in einem Brötchen)* III 3 (51)

hotel [həʊ'tel] Hotel III 4 (71)

hour [aʊə] Stunde III 1 (9)

house [haʊs] Haus I

how [haʊ] wie I **How are you?** Wie geht's? / Wie geht es dir/euch? I

hundred ['hʌndrəd]: **a hundred, one hundred** (ein)hundert I

hungry ['hʌŋgri]: **be hungry** Hun-ger haben, hungrig sein II

°**hurt** [hɜːt]: **be hurt** verletzt sein **get hurt** sich verletzen

I

I [aɪ] ich I **I'm (= I am)** ich bin I

°**ice** [aɪs] Eis *(gefrorenes Wasser)*

ice cream [aɪs 'kriːm] (Speise-)Eis II

°**ice hockey** ['aɪs hɒki] Eishockey

ice skating ['aɪs skeɪtɪŋ] Schlitt-schuhlaufen II

°**iceberg** ['aɪsbɜːg] Eisberg

ICT (information and communi-cation technology) [aɪ siː 'tiː], [ɪnfəmeɪʃn ənd kəmjuːnɪkeɪʃn tekˈnɒlədʒɪ] Informations- und Kommunikationstechnologie I

idea [aɪˈdɪə] Idee I

ideal [aɪˈdɪəl] ideal III 2 (37)

idiot [ˈɪdɪət] Idiot/in III 1 (15)

if [ɪf] wenn, falls II

ill [ɪl] krank II

°**imagine sth.** [ɪˈmædʒɪn] sich etwas vorstellen

important [ɪmˈpɔːtənt] wichtig I

impressed [ɪmˈprest] beeindruckt III 3 (54)

in [ɪn] in I   **in English** auf Englisch I   **in my opinion** meiner Meinung nach III 3 (57)   **in the country** auf dem Land III 2 (28)   **in the morning/afternoon/evening** am Morgen/Nachmittag/Abend I   °**in a word** mit einem Wort   °**in other words** mit anderen Worten

°**include** [ɪnˈkluːd] einschließen

°**including** [ɪnˈkluːdɪŋ] einschließlich, inklusive

information (about) [ɪnfəˈmeɪʃn] Information(en) (über) III 3 (52)

inside [ɪnˈsaɪd] (nach) drinnen II

instrument [ˈɪnstrəmənt] Instrument I

interested [ˈɪntrəstɪd]: **be interested in** sich interessieren für, interessiert sein an II   °**if interested** falls man interessiert ist, bei Interesse

interesting [ˈɪntrəstɪŋ] interessant II

°**international** [ɪntəˈnæʃnəl] international

internet [ˈɪntənet] Internet II

interview [ˈɪntəvjuː]:
1. Interview I
°2. befragen, interviewen

into [ˈɪntu], [ˈɪntə] in (... hinein) II   **into the classroom** in den Klassenraum (hinein) II

invitation (to) [ɪnvɪˈteɪʃn] Einladung (zu, nach) I

Irish [ˈaɪrɪʃ] irisch, aus Irland III 1 (10)

is [ɪz] (er/sie/es) ist I   **The calculator is £ 1.** Der Taschenrechner kostet 1 Pfund. I

it [ɪt] es, (bei Dingen und Tieren) er, sie I   **it's (= it is)** es ist (bei Dingen und Tieren auch: er ist, sie ist) I

°**Italian** [ɪˈtælɪən] Italiener/in; italienisch

its [ɪts] sein/e; ihr/e (bei Dingen und Tieren) III 1 (11)

itself [ɪtˈself] es/sich selbst III 4 (71)

J

jacket [ˈdʒækɪt] Jacke, Jackett II

jam [dʒæm] Marmelade I

January [ˈdʒænjuərɪ] Januar I

jeans [dʒiːnz] Jeans I

°**jewel** [ˈdʒuːəl] Juwel

jigsaw [ˈdʒɪgsɔː] Puzzle II

job [dʒɒb] Job II

jogging [ˈdʒɒgɪŋ] Jogging II

join [dʒɔɪn] mitmachen (bei); (einem Klub) beitreten II

joke [dʒəʊk]:
1. Witz, Scherz II
2. Witze machen, scherzen III 2 (30)
You're joking! Du machst wohl Witze! / Spitzenwitz! III 2 (30)

judo [ˈdʒuːdəʊ] Judo II

juice [dʒuːs] Saft I

July [dʒuˈlaɪ] Juli I

jump [dʒʌmp] springen, (vor Schreck) zusammenzucken III 3 (61)

June [dʒuːn] Juni I

junk food [ˈdʒʌŋk fuːd] Junkfood (ungesundes Essen) II

just [dʒʌst]:
1. einfach; nur, bloß III 4 (73)
°2. gerade (eben)
3. **just like Berry** genau wie Berry II

K

°**kangaroo** [kæŋgəˈruː] Känguru

karate [kəˈrɑːti] Karate II

keep [kiːp], **kept, kept** behalten III 1 (15)

kept [kept] siehe **keep**

kettle [ˈketl] Wasserkocher (elektrisch) III 4 (72)

kick [kɪk] treten, schießen III 1 (15)

kid [kɪd] Kind, Jugendliche/r I

kilometre (km) [ˈkɪləmiːtə] Kilometer II

kilt [kɪlt] Kilt (Schottenrock) III 4 (73)

kind [kaɪnd] freundlich, nett II

°**kind (of)** [kaɪnd]: **all kinds of ...** alle Arten/Sorten (von) ...

king [kɪŋ] König III 1 (8)

kiss [kɪs] Kuss I

kitchen [ˈkɪtʃɪn] Küche I

kitten [ˈkɪtn] Kätzchen, junge Katze II

°**knee** [niː] Knie

°**knew** [njuː] siehe **know**

knife, (pl) **knives** [naɪf], [naɪvz] Messer III 4 (73)

know [nəʊ], **knew, known** wissen; kennen I

L

lake [leɪk] (Binnen-)See III 4 (68)

lamp [læmp] Lampe I

land [lænd] landen III 4 (74)

°**landmark** [ˈlændmɑːk] Wahrzeichen

language [ˈlæŋgwɪdʒ] Sprache III 4 (69)   °**language file** Anhang zum Thema Sprache

lantern [ˈlæntən] Laterne II

laptop [ˈlæptɒp] Laptop I

lasagne [ləˈzænjə] Lasagne II

last [lɑːst] letzte(r, s) I   **last week** vorige Woche II   **at last** schließlich, endlich III 1 (15)

late [leɪt] (zu) spät I   **my bus is late** mein Bus hat Verspätung I   °**sleep late** lange schlafen

later [ˈleɪtə] später I

laugh [lɑːf] lachen I

leader [ˈliːdə] Leiter/in, (An-)Führer/in I

learn [lɜːn] lernen II

°**learner log** [ˈlɜːnə lɒg] Lern-Tagebuch

leave [liːv], **left, left** (jn.) verlassen; weggehen; abfahren; zurücklassen II

left [left]:
1. siehe **leave**
2. links; nach links I
on the left links, auf der linken Seite I

leg [leg] Bein I

°**legend** [ˈledʒənd] Legende, Sage

lemonade [leməˈneɪd] Limonade II

less [les] weniger III 3 (51)   **less and less** immer weniger III 3 (51)

lesson [ˈlesn] (Unterrichts-)Stunde I

let's (= let us) [lets], [ˈlet əs] lass(t) uns I   **Let's see.** Lass(t) uns (mal) sehen. II

letter [ˈletə] Brief I

life, (pl) **lives** [laɪf], [laɪvz] Leben I

lifestyle [ˈlaɪfstaɪl] Lebensstil II

light [laɪt] Licht; Lampe III 2 (34)

like [laɪk] mögen I   **I'd like (= I would like)** ich hätte gern, ich möchte (...) haben I   **I'd like to (= I would like to) join** ich würde / möchte gern mitmachen II   °**she likes living in ...** sie lebt/wohnt gern in ...

like [laɪk] wie ‖ **I don't feel like it.** Mir ist nicht danach. ‖ **just like Berry** genau wie Berry ‖ **What's the weather like?** Wie ist das Wetter? ‖

line [laɪn]:
1. Zeile ı
°2. Reihe

°**lion** [ˈlaɪən] Löwe

°**list** [lɪst] Liste

listen [ˈlɪsn] zuhören ı ‖ **listen for sth.** auf etwas horchen, *(beim Zuhören)* auf etwas achten ‖

listener [ˈlɪsənə] Zuhörer/in III 1 (17)

little [ˈlɪtl] klein III 2 (38)

°**little-known** [lɪtl ˈnəʊn] wenig bekannt

live [lɪv] leben, wohnen ı

living room [ˈlɪvɪŋ ruːm] Wohnzimmer ı

°**local** [ˈləʊkəl] einheimisch, am/vom Ort

°**located** [ləʊˈkeɪtɪd]: **be located in …** in … liegen

°**lodge** [lɒdʒ] (Berg., Ski-)Hütte

Londoner [ˈlʌndənə] Londoner/in III 1 (10)

lonely [ˈləʊnli] einsam ‖

long [lɒŋ] lang ‖

look [lʊk]:
1. aussehen ‖
2. sehen, schauen ı
look after sich kümmern um; aufpassen auf ı **look at** anschauen ı **look for** suchen ‖

lose [luːz], **lost, lost** verlieren ‖

°**loser** [ˈluːzə] Verlierer/in

lost [lɒst] *siehe* **lose**

lot [lɒt]:
1. **lots (of); a lot of** viel(e) ı; III 1 (18)
2. **I worry a lot** ich mache mir große Sorgen, ich bin sehr besorgt III 1 (21)

loud [laʊd] laut III 1 (15)

love [lʌv] lieben, sehr mögen ı **I'd love to come. (= I would love to come.)** Ich komme sehr gern. / Ich würde sehr gern kommen. ı

°**lovely** [ˈlʌvli] wunderschön, herrlich

luck [lʌk]: **Good luck.** Viel Glück! ı

luckily [ˈlʌkɪli] glücklicherweise III 4 (74)

lucky [ˈlʌki]: **Lucky you!** Du Glückliche/r! ‖ **you're lucky** du hast Glück ı

lunch [lʌntʃ] Mittagessen ı **have lunch** (zu) Mittag essen ı

lunchtime [ˈlʌntʃtaɪm]: **at lunchtime** mittags, zur Mittagszeit ‖

M

machine [məˈʃiːn] Maschine, Gerät III 4 (81)

made [meɪd] *siehe* **make**

madhouse [ˈmædhaʊs] Irrenhaus ı

magazine [mægəˈziːn] Zeitschrift ‖

°**main** [meɪn] Haupt-

make [meɪk], **made, made** machen, herstellen ı **make a deal** ein Geschäft abschließen, vereinbaren ‖ **make friends** Freunde finden ‖ **make money** Geld verdienen III 3 (51) **What makes a perfect weekend?** Was macht ein perfektes Wochenende aus? ‖ °**make sth. up** etwas erfinden, sich etwas ausdenken

make-up [ˈmeɪkʌp] Make-up ‖

man, *(pl)* **men** [mæn], [men] Mann ı

°**manage (to do sth.)** [ˈmænɪdʒ] (es) schaffen (etwas zu tun) ı

manager [ˈmænɪdʒə] Geschäftsführer/in, Manager/in III 4 (70)

many [ˈmeni] viele ‖ **How many …?** Wie viele …? ı

map [mæp] Landkarte, Stadtplan ‖

March [mɑːtʃ] März ı

°**maritime** [ˈmærɪtaɪm] See-, Schiff-fahrts-

market [ˈmɑːkɪt] Markt ı

mask [mɑːsk] Maske ı

°**match with** [ˈmætʃ wɪð] zuordnen

°**match** [mætʃ] Spiel *(z.B. Fußball)*

maths [mæθs] Mathematik ı

May [meɪ] Mai ı

maybe [ˈmeɪbiː] vielleicht ‖

°**mayonnaise** [meɪəˈneɪz] Mayonnaise

me [mi] mir; mich ı **It's me.** Ich bin's. ı

meal [miːl] Mahlzeit, Essen III 4 (71)

mean [miːn]:
1. geizig ‖
2. gemein, fies ı

mean [miːn], **meant, meant** meinen, sagen wollen III 3 (54)

°**meaning** [ˈmiːnɪŋ] Bedeutung ı

meant [ment] *siehe* **mean**

meat [miːt] Fleisch ‖

mechanic [mɪˈkænɪk] Mechaniker/in III 4 (80)

°**mediation** [miːdiˈeɪʃn] Vermittlung, Sprachmittlung

meet [miːt], **met, met** kennenlernen; (sich) treffen ı

men [men] *Plural von* **man** ı

menu [ˈmenjuː] Speisekarte ı

message [ˈmesɪdʒ]:
1. Botschaft, Aussage III 3 (59)
2. Nachricht, Mitteilung III 2 (33) **take a message** etwas ausrichten III 2 (33)

messy [ˈmesi] unordentlich ı

met [met] *siehe* **meet**

metre [ˈmiːtə] Meter ‖

°**mice** [maɪs] *Plural von* **mouse**

middle [ˈmɪdl] Mitte ı **in the middle** in der Mitte ı

mile [maɪl] Meile *(ca. 1,6 km)* ‖

milk [mɪlk] Milch ı

milkshake [ˈmɪlkʃeɪk] Milchshake ‖

million [ˈmɪljən] Million III 1 (15) **like a million dollars** fantastisch III 1 (15)

mine [maɪn] meine, meiner, meins III 4 (74)

minute [ˈmɪnɪt] Minute ı

mirror [ˈmɪrə] Spiegel III 4 (80)

miss [mɪs] vermissen ı

Miss Borowski [mɪs] Frau Borowski ı

Miss [mɪs] *Anrede für Lehrerin in GB* III 3 (52)

missing [ˈmɪsɪŋ] vermisst ‖

°**mistake** [mɪˈsteɪk] Fehler ı

°**mobile** [ˈməʊbaɪl] mobil ı

mobile (phone) [məʊbaɪl ˈfəʊn] Handy ı

model [ˈmɒdl] Modell **model car** [mɒdl ˈkɑː] Modellauto ‖

modern [ˈmɒdn] modern III 4 (69)

Monday [ˈmʌndeɪ], [ˈmʌndi] Montag ı

money [ˈmʌni] Geld ı **make money** Geld verdienen III 3 (51)

monitor [ˈmɒnɪtə] Monitor III 2 (34)

monkey [ˈmʌŋki] Affe ı

monster [ˈmɒnstə] Monster III 4 (69)

month [mʌnθ] Monat III 4 (70)

more [mɔː]:
1. mehr, weitere ‖ **more and more** immer mehr III 3 (51)
2. **more popular** beliebter, populärer ‖

morning [ˈmɔːnɪŋ] Morgen ı **Good morning.** Guten Morgen. ı

most [məʊst]:
1. **the most money** das meiste Geld, am meisten Geld III 3 (53) °**most students** die meisten Schüler/innen

2. most popular der/die/das beliebteste/populärste, am beliebtesten/populärsten II

mother ['mʌðə] Mutter III 2 (35/157)

°**motto** ['mɒtəʊ] Motto

mountain ['maʊntən] Berg II

°**mountain biker** ['maʊntən baɪkə] Mountainbiker/in

°**mountain biking** ['maʊntən baɪkɪŋ] (das) Mountainbikefahren

°**mouse, (pl) mice** [maʊs], [maɪs] Maus

mouth [maʊθ] Mund; (Tier) Schnauze III 2 (34)

move (to) [muːv] (um)ziehen (nach) III 2 (37) **move house** umziehen (an einen neuen Wohnort) III 2 (40)

Mr Smith ['mɪstə] Herr Smith I

Mrs Smith ['mɪsɪz] Frau Smith I

Ms Lee [mɪz] Frau Lee I

much [mʌtʃ] viel II **miss/like/ love sb. so much** jn. so sehr vermissen/mögen/lieben II **Thanks very much.** Vielen Dank. II

mud [mʌd] Matsch, Schlamm II

°**muddy** ['mʌdi] matschig

muffin ['mʌfɪn] Muffin (kleiner runder Kuchen) II

mum [mʌm] Mama, Mutti I

museum [mjuˈziːəm] Museum III 1 (14)

music ['mjuːzɪk] Musik I

musical ['mjuːzɪkl]:
  1. Musik-, musikalisch III 4 (69)
  °**2.** Musical

°**musician** [mjuˈzɪʃn] Musiker/in

must [mʌst] müssen I

mustn't do ['mʌsnt] nicht tun dürfen II

my [maɪ] mein/e I

myself [maɪˈself] ich/mich/mir selbst III 4 (71)

°**mystery** ['mɪstri] Geheimnis

N

name [neɪm] Name I **What's your name?** Wie heißt du? I

narrow ['nærəʊ] eng, schmal III 4 (75)

national ['næʃnəl] national II

national park [næʃnəl 'paːk] Nationalpark (staatliches Naturschutzgebiet) II

natural ['nætʃrəl] natürlich, Natur- III 1 (14)

natural history [nætʃrəl 'hɪstri] Naturkunde III 1 (14)

near [nɪə] in der Nähe von, nahe (bei) II

need [niːd] brauchen I

negative ['negətɪv] negativ III 3 (54)

neighbour ['neɪbə] Nachbar/in II

neighbourhood ['neɪbəhʊd] Nachbarschaft, Viertel, Gegend II

nervous ['nɜːvəs] nervös, aufgeregt I

°**net** [net] Netz (Sport)

network ['netwɜːk] Netz; Wortnetz I

never ['nevə] nie, niemals I

new [njuː] neu I

news [njuːz] Nachrichten I

newsletter ['njuːzletə] Mitteilungsblatt, Informationsblatt II

newspaper ['njuːzpeɪpə] (Tages-)Zeitung II

next [nekst]:
  1. als Nächstes III 1 (15)
  2. nächste(r, s) I

next to ['nekst tə] neben I

nice [naɪs] nett, schön I **Nice to be together again.** Schön, wieder zusammenzusein. II

night [naɪt] Nacht I **at night** nachts, in der Nacht I

nine [naɪn] neun I

nineties ['naɪntiz]: **the 90s** die Neunzigerjahre II

no [nəʊ] kein/e I

no [nəʊ] nein I

nobody ['nəʊbədi] niemand II

noise [nɔɪz] Geräusch; Lärm I

noisy ['nɔɪzi] laut, voller Lärm I

normal ['nɔːml] normal I

north [nɔːθ] Norden; nördlich; Nord- II **north-east** Nordosten, nordöstlich II **north-west** Nordwesten, nordwestlich II

nose [nəʊz] Nase III 2 (34)

not [nɒt] nicht; kein/e I

°**note** [nəʊt] notieren

°**notepad** ['nəʊtpæd] Notizblock

°**notes** [nəʊts] Notizen **take notes** (sich) Notizen machen

°**note-taking** ['nəʊt teɪkɪŋ] sich Notizen machen

nothing ['nʌθɪŋ] nichts I

°**notice** ['nəʊtɪs] Anschlag, Bekanntmachung (an einem Schwarzen Brett)

November [nəʊˈvembə] November I

now [naʊ] nun, jetzt I **right now** gerade jetzt, genau jetzt III 2 (33)

°**nowhere** ['nəʊweə] nirgendwo(hin)

number ['nʌmbə]:
  1. Anzahl III 4 (72)
  2. Nummer I

O

o'clock [əˈklɒk]: **at one o'clock** um 1 Uhr / um 13 Uhr I

October [ɒkˈtəʊbə] Oktober I

of [ɒv], [əv] von I **the last day of the holidays** der letzte Tag der Ferien I

of course [əv ˈkɔːs] natürlich, selbstverständlich I

°**offer** ['ɒfə] anbieten

office ['ɒfɪs] Büro III 2 (34)

°**off-road** ['ɒf rəʊd] abseits der Straße

often ['ɒfn], ['ɒftən] oft I

oh [əʊ] Null (im gesprochenen Englisch) I

OK [əʊˈkeɪ]: **I'm OK.** Es geht mir gut. I

old [əʊld] alt I

Olympic [əˈlɪmpɪk] olympisch III 3 (57) **Olympic Games** Olympische Spiele III 3 (57) °**the Olympics** die olympischen Spiele

on [ɒn] auf I **on Monday** am Montag I **on my birthday** an meinem Geburtstag I **on the bus** im Bus I **on TV** im Fernsehen III 3 (53) °**work on sth.** an etwas arbeiten

once [wʌns] einmal III 2 (40)

one [wʌn] eins I

online [ɒnˈlaɪn] online, Online- II

only ['əʊnli]:
  1. nur, bloß I
  2. the only student der einzige Schüler / die einzige Schülerin I

°**onto** ['ɒntu] auf (… hinauf)

open ['əʊpən]:
  1. öffnen, aufmachen II
  2. sich öffnen, aufgehen III 1 (9)
  3. offen, geöffnet II

opinion [əˈpɪnjən] Meinung III 3 (57) **in my opinion** meiner Meinung nach III 3 (57)

°**option** ['ɒpʃn] Wahl(möglichkeit), Option

or [ɔː] oder I

orange ['ɒrɪndʒ]:
  1. Orange I
  2. orange(farben) I

°**order** ['ɔːdə] Reihenfolge

°**organic eggs** [ɔːˈgænɪk] **Bio-Eier**

°**organised** ['ɔːgənaɪzd] organisiert

other ['ʌðə] andere(r, s) I

our ['aʊə], [ɑː] unser/e I

ourselves [aʊəˈselvz] wir/uns selbst III 4 (71)

out [aʊt] hinaus, heraus, raus II
go out ausgehen; hinausgehen II
°**outdoor sport** ['aʊtdɔː] Sport für draußen / der draußen stattfindet
outside [aʊt'saɪd] draußen; nach draußen I
°**over 16** ['əʊvə] über 16
over there [əʊvə 'ðeə] da drüben; da hinüber III 4 (75)
own [əʊn]: **its own flag** seine eigene Fahne III 4 (69)
°**owner** ['əʊnə] Besitzer/in

P

p [piː]: **50p** 50 Pence I
pack [pæk] packen, einpacken II
°**packed lunch** [pækt 'lʌntʃ] Lunchpaket
packet (of) ['pækɪt] Packung, Päckchen, Schachtel III 3 (50)
page (= p.) [peɪdʒ] (Buch-, Heft-) Seite I
paid [peɪd] siehe **pay**
pain [peɪn]: **What a pain!** (infml) So ein Mist! / Es nervt! III 2 (30)
°**painting** ['peɪntɪŋ] Gemälde, (gemaltes) Bild
°**pair** [peə] Paar
palace ['pæləs] Palast III 1 (8)
paper ['peɪpə] Zeitung II **do a paper round** Zeitungen austragen II
°**paragraph** ['pærəgrɑːf] (Text-) Abschnitt
parents ['peərənts] Eltern I
park [pɑːk] Park I
park (a car) [pɑːk] parken III 2 (35)
parliament ['pɑːləmənt] Parlament III 4 (69)
part [pɑːt] Teil II **take part in sth.** an etwas teilnehmen, bei etwas mitmachen III 3 (52)
partner ['pɑːtnə] Partner/in I **partner work** Partnerarbeit I
party ['pɑːti] Party I **have a party** eine Party feiern I
past the shop [pɑːst] am Geschäft vorbei II
pasty ['pæsti] Pastete (mit Fleisch- oder Gemüsefüllung) II
pay [peɪ], **paid, paid** (be)zahlen II
PE (physical education) [piː 'iː], [fɪzɪkl edʒuˈkeɪʃn] (Schul-)Sport I
pen [pen] Kugelschreiber, Stift; Füller I
pence [pens] Pence III 3 (53)
pencil ['pensl] Bleistift I
pencil case ['pensl keɪs] Federmäppchen I

pencil sharpener ['pensl ʃɑːpnə] Bleistiftanspitzer I
penny ['peni] Penny (kleinste britische Münze) II
people ['piːpl] Leute, Menschen I
per balloon [pɜː], [pə] pro Ballon III 3 (53)
perfect ['pɜːfɪkt] perfekt II
perhaps [pə'hæps] vielleicht II
person ['pɜːsn] Person III 2 (40)
pet [pet] Haustier I **pets corner** Streichelzoo I
phone [fəʊn]:
  1. anrufen I
  2. Telefon I
°**answer the phone** ans Telefon gehen
phone call ['fəʊn kɔːl] (Telefon-) Anruf II
phone number ['fəʊn nʌmbə] Telefonnummer I
photo ['fəʊtəʊ] Foto I **take a photo** ein Foto machen I
phrase [freɪz] Ausdruck, (Rede-) Wendung I
piano [pi'ænəʊ] Klavier I
pick [pɪk] (aus)wählen, aussuchen II **pick sb. up** jn. abholen III 1 (21)
pickpocket ['pɪkpɒkɪt] Taschendieb/in III 1 (20)
picnic ['pɪknɪk] Picknick II **have a picnic** ein Picknick machen II
picture ['pɪktʃə] Bild I
°**piece** [piːs] Stück I
pig [pɪg] Schwein I
°**pilates** [pɪ'lɑːtiːz] Pilates (Fitnessprogramm)
pink [pɪŋk] rosa I
°**place** [pleɪs] Ort, Platz, Stelle I
°**placemat** ['pleɪsmæt] Platzdeckchen
plan [plæn]:
  1. Plan II
  2. planen II
plane [pleɪn] Flugzeug III 1 (16)
°**plankton** ['plæŋktən] Plankton (Kleinstlebewesen im Wasser)
plant [plɑːnt] Pflanze III 3 (53)
plastic ['plæstɪk] Plastik, Kunststoff II **plastic bag** Plastiktüte II
platform ['plætfɔːm] Bahnsteig II
play [pleɪ]:
  1. spielen I
  playing football Fußballspielen I
  playing games Spiele spielen I
  2. Theaterstück II
°**player** ['pleɪə] Spieler/in I
please [pliːz] bitte I

pm [piː'em]: **5 pm** 5 Uhr nachmittags/abends / 17 Uhr I
pocket ['pɒkɪt] Tasche (an Kleidungsstücken) II
pocket money ['pɒkɪt mʌni] Taschengeld II
poem ['pəʊɪm] Gedicht I
°**poet** ['pəʊɪt] Dichter/in
°**point** [pɔɪnt] Punkt I
police (pl) [pə'liːs] Polizei III 1 (15)
police officer [pə'liːs ɒfɪsə] Polizeibeamter/-beamtin III 2 (32)
pony ['pəʊni] Pony I
°**pony-trekking** ['pəʊni trekɪŋ] Wanderreiten
poor [pʊə] arm II **poor Mrs Trent** (die) arme Mrs Trent II **Poor you!** Du Arme/r! II
°**pop (music)** ['pɒp mjuːzɪk] Pop(musik)
popular ['pɒpjələ] beliebt, populär II
°**possible** ['pɒsəbl] möglich III 3 (51)
post [pəʊst] Post (Briefe etc.) III 1 (17)
post office ['pəʊst ɒfɪs] Post(amt) II
postcard ['pəʊstkɑːd] Postkarte III 1 (17)
poster ['pəʊstə] Poster I
postman, (pl) **postmen** ['pəʊstmən] Briefträger III 1 (17)
postwoman, (pl) **postwomen** ['pəʊstwʊmən], ['pəʊstwɪmɪn] Briefträgerin III 1 (17)
°**pot** [pɒt] Topf I
potato, (pl) **potatoes** [pə'teɪtəʊ] Kartoffel I
pound (£) [paʊnd] Pfund (britische Währung) I
°**practice** ['præktɪs] Übung; Training
practise ['præktɪs] üben I
prefer sth. to sth. [prɪ'fɜː] etwas lieber mögen als etwas, etwas einer Sache vorziehen III 3 (57)
°**prepare (for)** [prɪ'peə] vorbereiten; sich vorbereiten (auf)
present ['preznt]:
  1. Geschenk I
  °**2.** präsentieren, vorstellen
°**presentation** [prezn'teɪʃn] Referat, Präsentation
president ['prezɪdənt] Präsident/in III 1 (8)
price [praɪs] (Kauf-)Preis I
pride [praɪd] Stolz III 4 (77)
prince [prɪns] Prinz I
principal ['prɪnsəpl] Schulleiter/in I
prize [praɪz] Preis (Gewinn) I

problem ['prɒbləm] Problem I

°**profile** ['prəʊfaɪl] Profil; Beschreibung, Portrait

profit ['prɒfɪt] Gewinn, Profit III 3 (53)

programme ['prəʊgræm] (Fernseh-)Sendung I

proud (of) [praʊd] stolz (auf) I

°**provide** [prə'vaɪd] (an)bieten, zur Verfügung stellen

pub [pʌb] Kneipe III 2 (29)

pullover ['pʊləʊvə] Pullover I

put [pʊt], **put, put** (etwas wohin) tun, legen, stellen II **He puts it with the other things.** Er legt sie zu den anderen Dingen. II **put on trousers** eine Hose anziehen II

Q

°**quad bike** ['kwɒd baɪk] Quad (vierrädriges Motorrad)

°**quad biking** ['kwɒd baɪkɪŋ] Quad fahren

queen [kwiːn] Königin III 1 (8)

question ['kwestʃən] Frage I

questionnaire [kwestʃə'neə] Fragebogen III 2 (40)

quick [kwɪk] schnell II

quiet ['kwaɪət] ruhig, still, leise III 2 (35)

quiz [kwɪz] Quiz I

R

rabbit ['ræbɪt] Kaninchen I

°**radio** ['reɪdiəʊ] Radio

°**rafting** ['rɑːftɪŋ]: **(whitewater) rafting** Rafting, Wildwasserfahren

rain [reɪn]:
1. Regen II
2. regnen II

rain jacket ['reɪn dʒækɪt] Regenjacke II

rain trousers (pl) ['reɪn traʊzəz] Regenhose II

rainy ['reɪni] regnerisch II

ran [ræn] siehe **run**

rang [ræŋ] siehe **ring**

ranger ['reɪndʒə] Aufseher/in in einem Nationalpark II

rap [ræp]:
1. Rap I
2. rappen I

rat [ræt] Ratte I

°**rather** ['rɑːðə]: **I'd rather be ...** ich wäre lieber ...

read [riːd], **read, read** lesen I **reading** (das) Lesen I

read [red] siehe **read**

reader ['riːdə] Leser/in III 1 (17)

ready ['redi] bereit, fertig III 3 (59) **Get ready. Steady. Go!** Auf die Plätze, fertig, los! III 3 (59)

real [rɪəl] echt, wirklich I

reality [ri'æliti] Realität, Wirklichkeit I

really nice ['rɪəli] wirklich nett I

reason ['riːzn] Grund, Begründung III 3 (57) **for lots of reasons** aus vielen Gründen III 3 (57)

recipe ['resəpi] (Koch-)Rezept II

red [red] rot I

region ['riːdʒən] Region III 4 (78)

remember [rɪ'membə] daran denken, nicht vergessen; sich erinnern an I

°**repair** [rɪ'peə] Reparatur

°**repeat** [rɪ'piːt] wiederholen

°**report** [rɪ'pɔːt] Bericht

reporter [rɪ'pɔːtə] Reporter/in III 1 (10)

represent [reprɪ'zent] repräsentieren, vertreten III 3 (55)

reservation [rezə'veɪʃn] Reservierung III 4 (73)

°**respect** [rɪ'spekt] respektieren

°**rest** [rest] Rest

restaurant ['restrɒnt] Restaurant I

°**revision** [rɪ'vɪʒn] Wiederholung (von Lernstoff)

reward [rɪ'wɔːd] Belohnung II

°**rewrite** [riː'raɪt] noch einmal schreiben, neu schreiben

°**rhyme** [raɪm] Reim

°**rice** [raɪs] Reis

ridden ['rɪdn] siehe **ride**

°**ride** [raɪd] Fahrt

ride [raɪd], **rode, ridden**:
1. reiten I **ride a pony** auf einem Pony/ ein Pony reiten I **riding** (das) Reiten I
2. fahren I **ride a bike** Rad fahren I

right [raɪt]:
1. richtig I **be right** Recht haben III 1 (18) **that's right** das stimmt, das ist richtig I
2. rechts I **on the right** rechts, auf der rechten Seite I
3. **right now** gerade jetzt, genau jetzt III 2 (33)

ring [rɪŋ], **rang, rung** läuten, klingeln II

ringtone ['rɪŋtəʊn] Klingelton (Handy) III 1 (19)

river ['rɪvə] Fluss II

road [rəʊd] Straße (Landstraße zwischen Orten / Straße in Orten) I

rock (music) ['rɒk mjuːzɪk] Rock(musik) I

rode [rəʊd] siehe **ride**

°**role** [rəʊl] Rolle (Theater, Rollenspiel)

role model ['rəʊl mɒdl] Vorbild III 3 (57)

room [ruːm] Raum, Zimmer I

°**route** [ruːt] Route, Weg

°**royal** ['rɔɪəl] königlich

rubber ['rʌbə] Radiergummi I

rubbish ['rʌbɪʃ]:
1. Müll, Abfall I
2. Unsinn, dummes Zeug III 1 (18)

rubbish bin ['rʌbɪʃ bɪn] Mülleimer II

rucksack ['rʌksæk] Rucksack I

rugby ['rʌgbi] Rugby (Ballsportart) II

ruins (oft auch pl: ruins) ['ruːɪn] Ruine III 4 (75)

rule [ruːl] Regel, Vorschrift II

ruler ['ruːlə] Lineal I

run [rʌn], **ran, run** rennen II

runner ['rʌnə] Läufer/in III 1 (17)

S

sad [sæd] traurig II

safe [seɪf] sicher (gefahrlos); in Sicherheit III 1 (20)

said [sed] siehe **say**

salad ['sæləd] Salat (als Gericht oder Beilage) I

sale [seɪl] Verkauf; Schlussverkauf I

salesperson, (pl) **salespeople** ['seɪlzpɜːsn], ['seɪlzpiːpl] Verkäufer/in III 3 (52)

salt [sɔːlt] Salz III 4 (79)

same [seɪm]: **the same** dasselbe / das gleiche; gleich II

sandwich ['sænwɪtʃ] Sandwich I

sang [sæŋ] siehe **sing**

sat [sæt] siehe **sit**

Saturday ['sætədeɪ], ['sætədi] Samstag I

sausage ['sɒsɪdʒ] Wurst, Würstchen II

save [seɪv] retten III 2 (32)

saw [sɔː] siehe **see**

say [seɪ], **said, said** sagen I

scared [skeəd]: **be scared (of)** Angst haben (vor) II

scary ['skeəri] unheimlich, gruselig II

scene [siːn]:
 1. Szene I
 °**2.** Schauplatz
school [skuːl] Schule I
science ['saɪəns] Naturwissenschaft I
°**scientist** ['saɪəntɪst] (Natur-)Wis-
 senschaftler/in
scone [skɒn] *Milchbrötchen, leicht
 süß, oft mit Rosinen* I
°**Scot** [skɒt] Schotte/Schottin
Scotland ['skɒtlənd] Schottland
 III 4 (68)
Scottish ['skɒtɪʃ] schottisch,
 aus Schottland III 1 (10)
scream [skriːm] schreien II
sea [siː] Meer II
°**seafaring** ['siːfeərɪŋ] Seefahrer-
seaside ['siːsaɪd]: **at the seaside**
 am Meer II
second ['sekənd] zweite(r, s) I
second-hand shop [sekənd 'hænd]
 Second-Hand-Laden II
security [sɪ'kjʊərəti] Sicherheit
 III 1 (14)
see [siː], **saw, seen** sehen I
 See you. Bis dann. / Tschüs. I
seen [siːn] *siehe* **see**
°**self-catering** [self 'keɪtərɪŋ] Selbst-
 versorgung, für Selbstversorger
sell [sel], **sold, sold** verkaufen
 III 3 (50)
send [send] **sent, sent** schicken,
 senden I
sent [sent] *siehe* **send**
sentence ['sentəns] Satz I
September [sep'tembə] September I
serious ['sɪəriəs] ernst(haft) II 3 (52)
 seriously im Ernst III 3 (52)
°**serve** [sɜːv] servieren
°**service** ['sɜːvɪs] Service; *(bei Fahr-
 zeugen etc.)* Wartung, Inspektion
°**setting** ['setɪŋ] Umgebung;
 Schauplatz
seven ['sevn] sieben I
°**several** ['sevrəl] mehrere, einige
°**share** [ʃeə] teilen; austauschen
sharpener ['ʃɑːpnə] Anspitzer I
she [ʃiː] sie *(weibliche Person)* I
 she's (= she is) sie ist I
sheep, *(pl)* **sheep** [ʃiːp] Schaf I
°**shine** [ʃaɪn] leuchten, glänzen,
 strahlen
ship [ʃɪp] Schiff III 3 (48)
°**shipping** ['ʃɪpɪŋ] Schifffahrt(s-)
shirt [ʃɜːt] Hemd I
°**shock** [ʃɒk] Schock, Schreck
°**shocked** [ʃɒkt] schockiert

shoe [ʃuː] Schuh I
shop [ʃɒp]:
 1. (ein)kaufen III 4 (70)
 2. Geschäft, Laden I
°**shopper** ['ʃɒpə] Käufer/in
shopping ['ʃɒpɪŋ]: **go shopping**
 einkaufen gehen I
shopping centre ['ʃɒpɪŋ sentə]
 Einkaufszentrum III 1 (10)
short [ʃɔːt] kurz; klein *(Person)* II
should [ʃʊd]: **you should** du solltest II
shoulder ['ʃəʊldə] Schulter I
shout [ʃaʊt] rufen II
show [ʃəʊ]:
 1. Show, Vorführung, Aufführung I
 2. zeigen II
shower ['ʃaʊə] Dusche; Schauer
 III 4 (80)
Shut up! [ʃʌt 'ʌp] Halt den Mund! I
°**sightseeing** ['saɪtsiːɪŋ] Besichti-
 gungen *(von Sehenswürdigkeiten)*
sign [saɪn] Schild; Zeichen I
silly ['sɪli] albern, dumm, blöd I
sincerely [sɪn'sɪəli]: **Yours sincerely**
 Mit freundlichen Grüßen *(Briefschluss)* III 3 (51)
sing [sɪŋ], **sang, sung** singen I
singer ['sɪŋə] Sänger/in I
single room [sɪŋgl 'ruːm] Einzelzimmer III 4 (72)
sister ['sɪstə] Schwester I
sit [sɪt], **sat, sat** sitzen; sich (hin)
 setzen II **sit down** sich (hin)
 setzen III 3 (54)
°**site** [saɪt]: **on site** vor Ort, an Ort
 und Stelle
six [sɪks] sechs I
skateboard ['skeɪtbɔːd] Skateboard I
skateboarding ['skeɪtbɔːdɪŋ] *(das)*
 Skateboardfahren I
skiing ['skiːɪŋ] *(das)* Skilaufen II
°**skill** [skɪl] Fähigkeit, Fertigkeit;
 Lern- und Arbeitstechnik **skills
 file** Anhang mit Lern- und Ar-
 beitstechniken
skim a text [skɪm] einen Text
 überfliegen *(um den Inhalt grob
 zu erfassen)* III 4 (78)
°**skipping** ['skɪpɪŋ] *(das)* Seilspringen
skirt [skɜːt] Rock II
°**skive** [skaɪv] *(infml)* schwänzen
 (Schule) II
°**skiver** ['skaɪvə] (Schul-)Schwän-
 zer/in III 1 (17)
sky [skaɪ] Himmel III 4 (69)
slave [sleɪv] Sklave, Sklavin III 3 (48)
°**slavery** ['sleɪvəri] Sklaverei

sleep [sliːp] Schlaf II
sleep [sliːp], **slept, slept** schlafen
 II °**sleep late** lange schlafen
sleeping bag ['sliːpɪŋ bæg] Schlafsack II
sleepover ['sliːpəʊvə] Schlafparty I
°**sleepwalker** ['sliːpwɔːkə] Schlaf-
 wandler/in
sleepy ['sliːpi] verschlafen, müde
 III 1 (17)
slept [slept] *siehe* **sleep**
°**slice** [slaɪs] Scheibe *(z.B. Brot)*;
 Stück *(z.B. Kuchen)*
slow [sləʊ] langsam II
small [smɔːl] klein I
°**smell** [smel] riechen, duften II
smile [smaɪl] lächeln; *(das)* Lächeln
 III 2 (34)
°**smoothie** ['smuːði] cremiges
 Fruchtgetränk
snack [snæk] Snack, kleine Mahlzeit I
snake [sneɪk] Schlange I
so [səʊ]:
 1. also II
 2. so II
 so much so sehr II
soap [səʊp] Seife; *(infml auch:)*
 Seifenoper II
sock [sɒk] Socke III 4 (73)
sofa ['səʊfə] Sofa II
°**soft drink** ['sɒft drɪŋk] alkohol-
 freies Getränk
sold [səʊld] *siehe* **sell**
some [sʌm], [səm] einige, ein
 paar; etwas II
somebody ['sʌmbədi] jemand II
someone ['sʌmwʌn] jemand II
something ['sʌmθɪŋ] etwas I
sometimes ['sʌmtaɪmz] manchmal I
son [sʌn] Sohn III 3 (51)
song [sɒŋ] Lied I
soon [suːn] bald I
sore [sɔː] schmerzhaft II **a sore
 throat** Halsschmerzen II **Her leg
 was sore.** Ihr Bein tat weh. II
sorry ['sɒri]: **Sorry. / I'm sorry.**
 Tut mir leid. / Entschuldigung. I
 be/feel sorry for sb. Mitleid
 mit jm. haben II
sort [sɔːt]: **What sort of …?**
 Welche Art/Sorte (von) …? III 3 (51)
sound [saʊnd] klingen, sich anhören I **Sounds fun.** Hört sich gut
 an. / Klingt, als ob es Spaß macht. I
°**sound file** ['saʊnd faɪl] Tondatei
soup [suːp] Suppe I
south [saʊθ] Süden; südlich; Süd- II
 south-east Südosten, südöstlich II

south-west Südwesten, südwestlich II

space [speɪs] Platz II

Spain [speɪn] Spanien II

speak [spiːk], **spoke, spoken** sprechen I **speak to** sprechen mit I **Who's speaking?** Wer spricht (da)? *(am Telefon)* III 2 (33)

special [ˈspeʃl] besondere(r, s) II

°**spectacular** [spekˈtækjələ] spektakulär

°**speech bubble** [ˈspiːtʃ bʌbl] Sprechblase

spell [spel] buchstabieren I

spend money/time (on) [spend], **spent, spent** Geld ausgeben (für); Zeit verbringen (mit) III 1 (18)

spent [spent] *siehe* **spend**

°**spine** [spaɪn] Wirbelsäule, Rückgrat

spoke [spəʊk] *siehe* **speak**

spoken [ˈspəʊkən] *siehe* **speak**

sport [spɔːt] Sport; Sportart I **sports shop** Sportgeschäft I

°**sportswoman, (pl) sportswomen** [ˈspɔːtswʊmən], [ˈspɔːtswɪmɪn] Sportlerin

sporty [ˈspɔːti] sportlich II

spot [spɒt]:
   1. Tupfen *(Leopard)*; Pickel II
   °**2.** Stelle, Fleck

stadium [ˈsteɪdɪəm] Stadion II

°**stall** [stɔːl] (Markt-)Stand, Bude II

stand [stænd], **stood, stood** stehen II **stand up** aufstehen II

star [stɑː] Star III 1 (8)

start [stɑːt] anfangen I

°**statement** [ˈsteɪtmənt] Aussage I

station [ˈsteɪʃn] Bahnhof II

°**statue** [ˈstætʃuː] Statue I

stay [steɪ] bleiben I

steady [ˈstedi]: **Get ready. Steady. Go!** Auf die Plätze, fertig, los! III 3 (59)

°**steam** [stiːm] Dampf I

°**step** [step] Schritt; Stufe I

stepbrother [ˈstepbrʌðə] Stiefbruder I

stepdad [ˈstepdæd] Stiefvater I

stepmum [ˈstepmʌm] Stiefmutter I

stepsister [ˈstepsɪstə] Stiefschwester I

still [stɪl] (immer) noch; trotzdem II

stood [stʊd] *siehe* **stand**

stop [stɒp] anhalten; stehen bleiben; aufhören (mit) II

°**store** [stɔː] Geschäft I

story [ˈstɔːri] Geschichte I

straight [streɪt]: **Go straight on.** Geh geradeaus (weiter). II

street [striːt] Straße *(in Ortschaften)* I

street surfing [ˈstriːt sɜːfɪŋ] Waveboarden II

strict [strɪkt] streng, strikt II

strong [strɒŋ] stark III 3 (57)

student [ˈstjuːdnt] Schüler/in; Student/in I

stuff [stʌf] *(infml)* Zeug, Kram II

°**stumble** [ˈstʌmbl] stolpern II

stupid [ˈstjuːpɪd] dumm, blöd; albern II

subway [ˈsʌbweɪ] Unterführung III 1 (20)

suck [sʌk]: **It sucks!** *(infml)* Es nervt / Es ist Mist! III 2 (30)

suddenly [ˈsʌdənli] plötzlich III 2 (34)

sugar [ˈʃʊgə] Zucker III 4 (79)

°**summary** [ˈsʌməri] Zusammenfassung

summer [ˈsʌmə] Sommer I

sun [sʌn] Sonne III 1 (17)

Sunday [ˈsʌndeɪ], [ˈsʌndi] Sonntag I

sunglasses *(pl)* [ˈsʌnglɑːsɪz] Sonnenbrille II

sunny [ˈsʌni] sonnig II

supermarket [ˈsuːpəmɑːkɪt] Supermarkt II

sure [ʃʊə] sicher I

surprise [səˈpraɪz] Überraschung I

surprised [səˈpraɪzd] überrascht II

°**swap** [swɒp] tauschen II

°**sweat** [swet] Schweiß II

sweets [swiːts] Bonbons, Süßigkeiten I

°**swim** [swɪm] schwimmen (durch) I

swimming [ˈswɪmɪŋ]: **go swimming** schwimmen gehen I

swimming pool [ˈswɪmɪŋ puːl] Schwimmbad II

T

table [ˈteɪbl] Tisch I

table tennis [ˈteɪbl tenɪs] Tischtennis II

tae kwon do [taɪ kwɒn ˈdəʊ] Taekwondo II

tag rugby [ˈtæg rʌgbi] Tag Rugby *(kontaktlose Rugby-Variante)* II

tail [teɪl] Schwanz II

take [teɪk], **took, taken** nehmen II **take a photo** ein Foto machen II **take part in sth.** an etwas teilnehmen, bei etwas mitmachen III 3 (52)

taken [ˈteɪkən] *siehe* **take**

°**talent** [ˈtælənt] Talent

talk about [tɔːk] sprechen über I

talk [tɔːk] Vortrag, Rede; Gespräch II **give a talk** einen Vortrag halten II **talk show** Talkshow II

talker [ˈtɔːkə] Redner/in III 1 (17)

tall [tɔːl] groß *(Person)*; hoch *(Gebäude)* II

task [tɑːsk] Aufgabe III 3 (56)

taught [tɔːt] *siehe* **teach**

taxi [ˈtæksi] Taxi III 1 (9)

tea [tiː] Tee I

teach [tiːtʃ], **taught, taught** unterrichten, lehren III 4 (71)

teacher [ˈtiːtʃə] Lehrer/in I

team [tiːm] Team, Mannschaft II

technology [tekˈnɒlədʒi] Technik, Technologie I

teen [tiːn] Teenager II

teenage kids [ˈtiːneɪdʒ] Kinder im Teenageralter III 4 (72)

teenager [ˈtiːneɪdʒə] Teenager I

telephone [ˈtelɪfəʊn] Telefon III 4 (72)

tell [tel], **told, told** erzählen, berichten II **tell about** erzählen von, berichten über II **tell sb. the way** jm. den Weg beschreiben II

temperature [ˈtemprətʃə] Temperatur; Fieber II **I have a temperature.** Ich habe Fieber. II

ten [ten] zehn I

tennis [ˈtenɪs] Tennis II

tent [tent] Zelt II

term [tɜːm] Trimester III 3 (52)

terrible [ˈterəbl] schrecklich I

test [test] Test; Klassenarbeit II

text (message) [ˈtekst mesɪdʒ] SMS I

text [tekst] eine SMS schicken I

than [ðæn]: **It's cheaper than that.** So viel kostet das nicht. II **older than me** älter als ich II

thank you [ˈθæŋk juː] danke (schön) I

thanks [θæŋks] danke I

that [ðæt]:
   1. das (da) I
   Is that the Taylors? Sind da die Taylors? *(am Telefon)* III 2 (33)
   2. der, die, das *(Relativpronomen)* III 4 (80)
   a thing that we use … ein Ding, das wir … benutzen III 4 (80)
   3. dass II
   they think that … sie denken, dass … II

the [ðə] der, die, das I

theatre ['θɪətə] Theater I
their [ðeə] ihr/e *(Plural)* II
them [ðem], [ðəm] sie, ihnen *(Plural)* II
°**theme** [θiːm] Thema
themselves [ðəm'selvz] sie/sich selbst *(Plural)* III 4 (71)
then [ðen] dann I
there [ðeə] da, dort; dahin, dort-hin I **there are …** es sind … / es gibt … I **there's** es ist … / es gibt … I
these people [ðiːz] diese Men-schen (hier) II
they [ðeɪ] sie *(Plural)* I **they're (= they are)** sie sind I
thing [θɪŋ] Ding, Sache I
think [θɪŋk], **thought, thought** denken, meinen, glauben I **think of/about** halten von, denken über III 1 (10)
third [θɜːd] dritte(r, s) I
this [ðɪs] diese(r, s) I **This is Rob Blake.** Hier spricht Rob Blake. *(am Telefon)* III 2 (33) **This is …** Dies ist … I **this morning/af-ternoon/evening** heute Mor-gen/Nachmittag/Abend I
those CDs [ðəʊz] die CDs dort, jene CDs II
thought [θɔːt] *siehe* **think**
°**thousand** ['θaʊznd] tausend I
three [θriː] drei I
threw [θruː] *siehe* **throw**
throat [θrəʊt] Hals II **a sore throat** Halsschmerzen II
through [θruː] durch I °**all through the match** das ganze Spiel hindurch
throw [θrəʊ], **threw, thrown** werfen III 4 (69)
thrown [θrəʊn] *siehe* **throw**
Thursday ['θɜːzdeɪ], ['θɜːzdi] Donnerstag I
ticket ['tɪkɪt] Eintrittskarte, Fahrkarte I
tidy ['taɪdi]:
1. aufräumen II
2. ordentlich II
tie [taɪ] Krawatte I
tiger ['taɪgə] Tiger I
time [taɪm]:
1. Zeit; Uhrzeit I **on time** pünktlich II **What's the time?** Wie spät ist es? I
2. Mal II **next time** nächstes Mal II
timetable ['taɪmteɪbl] Stunden-plan I

°**tip** [tɪp] Tipp I
tired ['taɪəd] müde I
to [tu], [tə] zu, nach, in I **to the country** aufs Land I **from Monday to Friday** von Montag bis Freitag I **go to dad's flat** in Papas Wohnung gehen I **Have you ever been to London?** Warst du schon mal in London? II **time to eat** Zeit zu essen I **write to** schreiben an I °**ideas what to do** Ideen, was man tun könnte
toast [təʊst] Toast(brot) II
today [tə'deɪ] heute I
together [tə'geðə] zusammen II
toilet ['tɔɪlət] Toilette I
toilet roll ['tɔɪlət rəʊl] Rolle Toilet-tenpapier I
told [təʊld] *siehe* **tell**
°**tomato, *(pl)* tomatoes** [tə'mɑːtəʊ] Tomate
tomorrow [tə'mɒrəʊ] morgen I
too [tuː] auch I
too small [tuː] zu klein I
took [tʊk] *siehe* **take**
top [tɒp]: **at the top (of)** oben, am oberen Ende (von); an der Spitze (von) I
°**torch** [tɔːtʃ] Fackel I
total ['təʊtl] Gesamtbetrag, Summe III 3 (53)
tour [tʊə] Tour; Rundfahrt III 1 (9)
°**tour guide** Reiseleiter/in, Fremdenführer/in
tourist ['tʊərɪst] Tourist/in III 1 (9)
towel ['taʊəl] Handtuch III 4 (80)
tower ['taʊə] Turm III 1 (9)
town [taʊn] Stadt I **in town** in der Stadt I
toy [tɔɪ] Spielzeug II
toy animal [tɔɪ 'ænɪml] Kuschel-tier II
track [træk] Pfad, (Feld-)Weg II
°**tractor** ['træktə] Traktor I
°**tradition** [trə'dɪʃn] Tradition I
°**traditional** [trə'dɪʃənl] traditionell
traffic lights *(pl)* ['træfɪk laɪts] Verkehrsampel II
°**trail** [treɪl] Weg, Pfad, Route I
train [treɪn] Zug, Eisenbahn II
train station ['treɪn steɪʃn] Bahn-hof II
trainer ['treɪnə] Sportschuh I
°**training** ['treɪnɪŋ] Training I
trampoline ['træmpəliːn] Trampo-lin I
transport ['trænspɔːt] Verkehrs-mittel; Transport(wesen) III 1 (16)

travel ['trævl] reisen; fahren, sich fortbewegen III 1 (8)
°**travelcard** ['trævlkɑːd] Ein- oder Mehrtagesfahrkarte *(London)*
travel-sick ['trævlsɪk] reisekrank III 1 (17)
tree [triː] Baum I
trick [trɪk] Trick, Kunststück II
trip [trɪp] Ausflug, Reise II
trouble ['trʌbl] Ärger, Schwierigkeit(en) I
trousers *(pl)* ['traʊzəz] Hose II
true [truː] wahr II
°**truth** [truːθ] Wahrheit I
try [traɪ] versuchen, (aus)probieren II
T-shirt ['tiːʃɜːt] T-Shirt I
Tube [tjuːb]: **the Tube** die U-Bahn *(in London)* III 1 (8)
Tuesday ['tjuːzdeɪ], ['tjuːzdi] Dienstag I
°**tunnel** ['tʌnl] Tunnel I
Turkey ['tɜːki] die Türkei II
°**Turkish** ['tɜːkɪʃ] türkisch; Türkisch I
turn right/left [tɜːn] (nach) rechts/links abbiegen II
TV [tiː'viː] Fernseher I
twelve [twelv] zwölf I
twice [twaɪs] zweimal III 2 (40)
twin room [twɪn 'ruːm] Zweibett-zimmer III 4 (72)
two [tuː] zwei I

U

uncle ['ʌŋkl] Onkel III 2 (37)
uncool [ʌn'kuːl] uncool II
under ['ʌndə] unter I
underground ['ʌndəgraʊnd] U-Bahn III 1 (8)
underline [ʌndə'laɪn] unter-streichen III 3 (56) °**underlined** unterstrichen
understand [ʌndə'stænd], **under-stood, understood** verstehen II
understood [ʌndə'stʊd] *siehe* **un-derstand**
unemployed [ʌnɪm'plɔɪd] arbeits-los III 4 (70)
°**unfair** [ʌn'feə] unfair I
unfriendly [ʌn'frendli] unfreund-lich II
unhappy [ʌn'hæpi] unglücklich I
unhealthy [ʌn'helθi] ungesund II
uniform ['juːnɪfɔːm] (Schul-)Uni-form I
uninteresting [ʌn'ɪntrəstɪŋ] unin-teressant II
°**unique** [juːniːk] einmalig I
unit ['juːnɪt] Unit I
unsure [ʌn'ʃʊə] unsicher II

until [ən'tɪl] bis (zeitlich) II
not (...) until they're 13 erst, wenn sie 13 sind II
°**untold** [ʌn'təʊld] (noch) nicht erzählt, unbekannt
up [ʌp] hinauf, hoch II
upstairs [ʌp'steəz] oben; nach oben II
°**up-to-the-minute** [ʌp tə ðə 'mɪnɪt] brandaktuell, allerneueste(r, s)
us [ʌs], [əs] uns I
USA [ju: es 'eɪ]: **the USA** die USA (= die Vereinigten Staaten von Amerika) III 3 (53)
use [ju:z] benutzen I ° **they were used** sie wurden benutzt
useful ['ju:sfl] nützlich III 3 (56)
usual ['ju:ʒəl] normal, üblich III 3 (54)
usually ['ju:ʒəli] meistens, normalerweise III 2 (37)

V

van [væn] Transporter, Lieferwagen III 2 (30)
°**variety (of)** [və'raɪəti] Auswahl (an)
°**various** ['veəriəs] (mehrere) verschiedene
vegetables, *infml auch* **veg** ['vedʒtəblz], [vedʒ] Gemüse I
°**verse** [vɜːs] Vers, Strophe (Lied)
°**version** ['vɜːʃn] Version
very ['veri] sehr I **Thanks very much.** Vielen Dank. II
°**viaduct** ['vaɪədʌkt] Viadukt (Talbrücke)
video ['vɪdiəʊ] Video II
video chat ['vɪdiəʊ tʃæt] Videochat, „Cammen" (Internet-Telefonegespräch mit Bildübertragung) II
°**viewing** ['vju:ɪŋ] (das) Anschauen (von DVDs, Filmen usw.)
village ['vɪlɪdʒ] Dorf I
°**village hall** ['vɪlɪdʒ hɔːl] Gemeindesaal
violent ['vaɪələnt] gewalttätig; gewaltsam III 3 (57)
visit ['vɪzɪt]:
1. besuchen II
°2. zu Besuch kommen
visitor ['vɪzɪtə] Besucher/in, Gast I
°**voice** [vɔɪs] Stimme
volleyball ['vɒlibɔːl] Volleyball II
vote for sb. [vəʊt] für jn. stimmen II

W

wait (for) [weɪt] warten (auf) II
Wait for this. (infml) Stell

dir nur vor! / Du wirst es kaum glauben! II
waiter ['weɪtə] Kellner/in III 4 (80)
waitress ['weɪtrəs] Kellnerin III 4 (80)
wake [weɪk] wecken I
°**wake-up call** ['weɪk ʌp kɔːl] Weckruf
walk [wɔːk] (zu Fuß) gehen, wandern I
walker ['wɔːkə] Wanderer/Wanderin, Fußgänger/in III 1 (17)
wall [wɔːl] Wand; Mauer II
want [wɒnt] wollen I **want to buy** kaufen wollen I
wardrobe ['wɔːdrəʊb] Kleiderschrank I
warm [wɔːm] warm II
°**warning** ['wɔːnɪŋ] Warnung
was [wɒz], [wəz]: **he/she/it was** Vergangenheitsform von **be** I
°**wash** [wɒʃ] (sich) waschen I
wash up [wɒʃ 'ʌp] abwaschen I
waste [weɪst]:
1. verschwenden III 1 (18/153)
2. Verschwendung III 1 (18)
watch [wɒtʃ] sich etwas anschauen; beobachten I **watching TV** Fernsehen I
water ['wɔːtə] Wasser I
°**waterfall** ['wɔːtəfɔːl] Wasserfall
wave [weɪv] winken III 4 (74)
way [weɪ] Weg II **ask sb. the way** jn. nach dem Weg fragen II **tell sb. the way** jm. den Weg beschreiben II °**a long way (from)** weit entfernt (von)
we [wiː] wir I **we're (= we are)** wir sind I
°**weak** [wiːk] schwach
wear [weə]**, wore, worn** tragen, anhaben (Kleidung) II
weather ['weðə] Wetter II
website ['websaɪt] Website III 4 (72)
Wednesday ['wenzdeɪ], ['wenzdi] Mittwoch I
°**wee** [wiː] klein (schottisches Englisch)
week [wiːk] Woche I
weekday ['wiːkdeɪ] Werktag, Wochentag I
weekend [wiːk'end] Wochenende I
welcome ['welkəm]:
1. **Welcome to Plymouth.** Willkommen in Plymouth! I
2. **You're welcome.** Bitte, gern geschehen. / Nichts zu danken. I
well [wel] gut (Adv.) II **Well done.** Gut gemacht! I **do well** es gut machen; gut abschneiden,

erfolgreich sein III 3 (52) **she can't walk well** sie kann nicht gut gehen/laufen II
°**well-known** [wel 'nəʊn] bekannt
went [went] siehe **go**
were [wɜː], [wə]: **we/you/they were** Vergangenheitsform von **be** I
west [west] Westen; westlich; West- II
wet [wet] nass I
what [wɒt]:
1. was I
2. welche(r, s) I
What about you? Und du? / Was ist mit dir? I **What do you call ...?** Wie nennt man ...? III 4 (80) **What's the time?** Wie spät ist es? I **What's your name?** Wie heißt du? I
wheelchair ['wiːltʃeə] Rollstuhl I
when [wen]:
1. wann I
When's (= when is) your birthday? Wann hast du Geburtstag? I
2. wenn I
3. als I
where [weə] wo(hin) I
which [wɪtʃ]:
1. **which lake?** welcher See? III 4 (69)
°2. **a magazine which ...** eine Zeitschrift, die ...
whistle ['wɪsl] (Triller-)Pfeife II
white [waɪt] weiß I
who [huː]:
1. wer I
Who are you? Wer bist du? / Wer seid ihr? I
2. wem?; wen? I
Who did Adam meet? Wen hat Adam getroffen? / Wen traf Adam? II
3. der, die (Relativpronomen, Person) III 2 (35)
people who leave rubbish Menschen, die Müll zurücklassen III 2 (35)
°**whole** [həʊl] ganze(r, s)
why [waɪ] warum I
Wi-fi ['waɪ faɪ] WLAN, kabellose Datenübertragung III 4 (72)
wild [waɪld] wild; wild lebend I
will [wɪl]: **50p will do** 50 Pence reichen (auch) II **the weather will be good** das Wetter wird gut sein II
°**win** [wɪn] Gewinn
win [wɪn]**, won, won** gewinnen II
wind [wɪnd] Wind II
window ['wɪndəʊ] Fenster III 1 (9)

windy ['wɪndi] windig II

winner ['wɪnə] Gewinner/in III 1 (17)

winter ['wɪntə] Winter II

wish [wɪʃ]: **Best wishes** Viele Grüße, … *(Briefschluss)* I

with [wɪð] mit I **with Ellie** bei Ellie I **He puts it with the other things.** Er legt sie zu den anderen Dingen. II

without [wɪ'ðaʊt] ohne II

woman, *(pl)* **women** ['wʊmən], ['wɪmɪn] Frau I

won [wʌn] *siehe* **win**

won't [wəʊnt]: **it won't rain** es wird nicht regnen II

wood [wʊd] Wald; Holz III 2 (29)

word [wɜːd] Wort I °**in a word** mit einem Wort °**in other words** mit anderen Worten

°**wordbank** ['wɜːdbæŋk] Wortbank *(Sammlung von Wörtern zu einem Thema)*

wore [wɔː] *siehe* **wear**

work [wɜːk]:
1. Arbeit I **at work** bei der Arbeit, am Arbeitsplatz I
2. arbeiten I °**work on sth.** an etwas arbeiten
3. funktionieren I

worker ['wɜːkə] Arbeiter/in; Arbeitskraft III 1 (17)

world [wɜːld] Welt III 1 (17)

worried ['wʌrid]: **be worried (about)** beunruhigt sein, besorgt sein (wegen) II

worry (about) ['wʌri] sich Sorgen machen (wegen, um) III 1 (21)

would [wʊd]: **I'd love to come. (= I would love to come.)** Ich komme sehr gern. / Ich würde sehr gern kommen. I **I'd like (= I would like)** ich hätte gern, ich möchte (…) haben I **I'd like to (= I would like to) join** ich würde / möchte gern mitmachen II

write [raɪt], **wrote, written** schreiben I **write down** aufschreiben III 2 (35)

writer ['raɪtə] Autor/in, Verfasser/in III 1 (17)

written ['rɪtn] *siehe* **write**

wrong [rɒŋ] falsch I **be wrong** Unrecht haben III 1 (18) **that's wrong** das stimmt nicht, das ist falsch I **What's wrong with …?** Was stimmt nicht mit …? II

wrote [rəʊt] *siehe* **write**

Y

yeah [jeə] ja *(infml für „yes")* I

year [jɪə] Jahr(gang) II

yellow ['jeləʊ] gelb I

yes [jes] ja I

yesterday ['jestədeɪ] gestern II

yet [jet]: **not … yet** noch nicht III 2 (30)

yippee [jɪ'piː] hurra I

°**yoga** ['jəʊgə] Yoga

yogurt ['jɒgət] Joghurt II

you [juː]:
1. du; ihr; Sie I **you're (= you are)** du bist, ihr seid, Sie sind I **Lucky you! / Poor you!** Du Glückliche/r! / Du Arme/r! II
2. dich; dir; euch; Sie; Ihnen I
3. man III 4 (80)

young [jʌŋ] jung II

your [jɔː] dein/e, euer/eure I

yours [jɔːz] deine, deiner, deins; eurer, eure, eures III 4 (75)

yourself [jɔː'self] du/dir/dich selbst III 4 (71) **Don't blame yourself.** Mach dir keine Vorwürfe. III 4 (71)

yourselves [jɔː'selvz] ihr/euch selbst; Sie/sich selbst III 4 (71)

°**youth** [juːθ] Jugend

°**youth club** ['juːθ klʌb] Jugendklub

yum! [jʌm] lecker! II

Z

zip wire ['zɪp waɪə] Seilrutsche I

zoo [zuː] Zoo I

°**zumba** ['zʊmbə] Zumba

English sounds

[iː]	green, he, sea	[eə]	where, pair, share, their	[s]	six, poster, yes
[ɑː]	ask, class, car, park	[ʊə]	tour	[z]	zoo, quiz, his, music, please
[ɔː]	or, ball, door, four, morning	[ɪə]	here, dear	[ʃ]	she, station, English
[uː]	ruler, blue, too, two, you			[ʒ]	ususally, revision, garage
[ɜː]	early, her, girl, work, T-shirt	[b]	bike, table, verb	[tʃ]	child, teacher, watch
[ɪ]	in, big, expensive	[p]	pen, paper, shop	[dʒ]	job, German, project, orange
[e]	yes, bed, again, breakfast	[d]	day, window, good	[θ]	thing, three, bathroom, both
[æ]	animal, apple, black, cat	[t]	ten, letter, at	[ð]	the, father, with
[ʌ]	mum, bus, colour	[g]	go, again, bag	[h]	house, who, behind
[ɒ]	song, on, dog, what	[k]	kitchen, car, back		
[ʊ]	book, good, pullover	[m]	man, remember, mum		
[ə]	again, today, a sister	[n]	no, one, ten		
[i]	happy, monkey	[ŋ]	wrong, young, uncle, thanks		
		[l]	like, old, small		
[eɪ]	name, eight, play, great	[r]	ruler, friend, sorry		
[aɪ]	I, time, right, my	[w]	we, where, one		
[ɔɪ]	boy, toilet, noise	[j]	yes, you, uniform		
[əʊ]	old, no, road, yellow	[f]	family, after, laugh		
[aʊ]	now, house	[v]	very, seven, have		

Am besten kannst du dir die Aussprache der einzelnen Lautzeichen einprägen, wenn du dir zu jedem Zeichen ein einfaches Wort merkst – das [iː] ist der **green**-Laut, das [eɪ] ist der **name**-Laut usw.

Das **German – English dictionary** enthält den **Lernwortschatz** der Bände 1 und 2 von *Highlight*.
Es kann dir eine erste Hilfe sein, wenn du vergessen hast, wie etwas auf Englisch heißt.

Wenn du wissen möchtest, wo das englische Wort zum ersten Mal in *Highlight* vorkommt,
dann kannst du im **English – German dictionary** (S. 166 – 182) nachschlagen.

Es werden folgende **Abkürzungen** verwendet:

sb. = somebody   sth. = something   jn. = jemanden   jm. = jemandem
pl = plural (Mehrzahl)   *infml = informal* (umgangssprachlich)

A

abbiegen: (nach) rechts/links abbiegen turn right/left [tɜːn]

Abend evening [ˈiːvnɪŋ]

Abendessen dinner [ˈdɪnə]

Abenteuer adventure [ədˈventʃə]

aber but [bʌt]

abfahren leave [liːv]

Abfall rubbish [ˈrʌbɪʃ]

abholen: jn. abholen pick sb. up [pɪk ˈʌp]

abschneiden: gut abschneiden do well [wel] **besser abschneiden** do better [ˈbetə]

abwaschen wash up [wɒʃ ˈʌp]

acht eight [eɪt]

achten: auf etwas achten *(beim Zuhören)* listen for sth. [ˈlɪsn fə]

Adresse address [əˈdres]

Affe monkey [ˈmʌŋki]

Afrika Africa [ˈæfrɪkə]

aktiv active [ˈæktɪv]

Aktivität activity [ækˈtɪvəti]

Akzent accent [ˈæksent]

albern silly [ˈsɪli]; stupid [ˈstjuːpɪd]

alle *(jeder)* everybody [ˈevribɒdi]; everyone [ˈevriwʌn] **alle(s)** all [ɔːl]

allein(e) alone [əˈləʊn]

Alphabet alphabet [ˈælfəbet]

alphabetisches Wörterverzeichnis dictionary [ˈdɪkʃənri]

als
1. *(zeitlich)* when [wen]
2. **älter als ich** older than me [ðən]

also so [səʊ]

alt old [əʊld]

Alter: im Alter von 16 at 16

am: am Arbeitsplatz at work **am besten** best [best] **am Montag** on Monday **am Morgen/Nachmittag/Abend** in the morning/afternoon/evening

Amerika America [əˈmerɪkə]

an: an meinem Geburtstag on my birthday **schreiben an** write to

andere(r, s) other [ˈʌðə] **ein/e andere(r, s)** another [əˈnʌðə]

ändern; sich ändern change [tʃeɪndʒ]

anders different [ˈdɪfrənt]

anfangen start [stɑːt]; begin [bɪˈgɪn]

Anführer/in leader [ˈliːdə]

Angst haben (vor) be scared (of) [skeəd]

anhaben *(Kleidung)* wear [weə]

anhalten stop [stɒp]

anhören: (sich etwas) anhören listen to [ˈlɪsn] **sich anhören** sound [saʊnd] **Hört sich gut an.** Sounds fun.

ankommen arrive [əˈraɪv]

annehmen: ich nehme an I guess [ges]

Anruf *(Telefon)* (phone) call [ˈfəʊn kɔːl]

anrufen phone [fəʊn]; call [kɔːl]

anschauen look at [ˈlʊk ət] **sich etwas anschauen** *(beobachten)* watch [wɒtʃ]

Anspitzer sharpener [ˈʃɑːpnə]

Anstecknadel badge [bædʒ]

Antwort answer [ˈɑːnsə]

antworten answer [ˈɑːnsə]

Anzahl number [ˈnʌmbə]

Anzeige advert [ˈædvɜːt]

anziehen: eine Hose anziehen put on trousers [pʊt ˈɒn]

Apfel apple [ˈæpl]

April April [ˈeɪprəl]

Arbeit work [wɜːk]

arbeiten work [wɜːk]

Arbeiten erledigen *(im Haus)* do chores [tʃɔːz]

Arbeiter/in worker [ˈwɜːkə]

Arbeitskraft worker [ˈwɜːkə]

arbeitslos unemployed [ˌʌnɪmˈplɔɪd]

Arbeitsplatz: am Arbeitsplatz at work [wɜːk]

Ärger trouble [ˈtrʌbl]

ärgerlich angry [ˈæŋgri]

Arm arm [ɑːm]

arm poor [pʊə] **(die) arme Mrs Trent** poor Mrs Trent **Du Arme/r!** Poor you!

Art: Welche Art (von) …? What sort of …? [sɔːt]

Artikel article [ˈɑːtɪkl]

Arzt/Ärztin doctor [ˈdɒktə]

auch also [ˈɔːlsəʊ]; too [tuː] **auch nicht** not … either [ˈeɪðə]

auf on [ɒn] **auf dem Foto** in the photo **auf dem Land** in the country **auf der Eggbuckland-Schule** at Eggbuckland **auf Englisch** in English **aufs Land** to the country **Auf Wiedersehen.** Goodbye. [gʊdˈbaɪ]

Aufführung show [ʃəʊ]

Aufgabe task [tɑːsk]; exercise [ˈeksəsaɪz]

aufgehen *(sich öffnen)* open [ˈəʊpən]

aufgeregt *(gespannt)* excited [ɪkˈsaɪtɪd]; *(nervös)* nervous [ˈnɜːvəs]

aufhören (mit) stop [stɒp]

aufmachen open [ˈəʊpən]

aufpassen auf look after [lʊk ˈɑːftə]

aufräumen tidy [ˈtaɪdi]

aufregen: Reg dich nicht auf. Take it easy!

aufregend exciting [ɪkˈsaɪtɪŋ]

aufschreiben write down [raɪt ˈdaʊn]

Aufseher/in *(in einem Nationalpark)* ranger [ˈreɪndʒə]

aufstehen *(aus dem Bett)* get up [get ˈʌp]; *(sich hinstellen)* stand up [stænd ˈʌp]

Auge eye [aɪ]

August August [ˈɔːgəst]

aus from [frɒm]

Ausdruck phrase [freɪz]

Ausflug trip [trɪp]; *(Tagesausflug)* day out [deɪ ˈaʊt] **einen Ausflug machen** do a trip

ausgeben: Geld ausgeben (für) spend money (on) [spend]

ausgehen go out [gəʊ ˈaʊt]

ausleihen: sich etwas (aus)leihen borrow sth. [ˈbɒrəʊ]

ausmachen: etwas ausmachen
make a difference ['dɪfrəns]
**Was macht ein perfektes
Wochenende aus?** What makes
a perfect weekend?
ausprobieren try [traɪ]
ausrichten: etwas ausrichten
take a message ['mesɪdʒ]
ausruhen: sich ausruhen chill [tʃɪl]
Ausrüstung equipment
['ɪ'kwɪpmənt]
Aussage (Botschaft) message
['mesɪdʒ]
aussehen look [lʊk]
Ausstattung equipment
['ɪ'kwɪpmənt]
Ausstellung exhibition [eksɪ'bɪʃn]
aussuchen pick [pɪk]
austragen: Zeitungen austragen
do a paper round ['peɪpə raʊnd]
Australien Australia [ɒ'streɪliə]
auswählen pick [pɪk]
Auto car [kɑː]
Autor/in writer ['raɪtə]

B

Baby baby ['beɪbi]
Babysitter babysitter ['beɪbɪsɪtə]
Bad(ezimmer) bathroom
['bɑːθruːm]
Badminton badminton ['bædmɪntən]
Bahnhof (train) station
['treɪn steɪʃn]
Bahnsteig platform ['plætfɔːm]
bald soon [suːn]
Ball ball [bɔːl]
Ballon balloon [bə'luːn]
Banane banana [bə'nɑːnə]
Bananenschale banana skin
[bə'nɑːnə skɪn]
Band (Musikgruppe) band [bænd]
Bank (Geldinstitut) bank [bæŋk]
Bär bear [beə]
Baseball baseball ['beɪsbɔːl]
Basketball basketball ['bɑːskɪtbɔːl]
Battle (im Rap) battle ['bætl]
Bauer, Bäuerin farmer ['fɑːmə]
Bauernhof farm [fɑːm]
Baum tree [triː]
beantworten answer ['ɑːnsə]
Bedient euch! (Greift zu!) Help
yourselves. [jɔː'selvz]
beeindruckt impressed [ɪm'prest]
beenden finish ['fɪnɪʃ]
beginnen begin [bɪ'gɪn]
behalten keep [kiːp]
bei with [wɪð] **bei der Arbeit** at
work **bei Ellie daheim/zu Hause**

at Ellie's house **bei MARTINS**
at MARTINS
Bein leg [leg]
Beispiel example [ɪg'zɑːmpl]
zum Beispiel for example
beitreten (einem Klub) join [dʒɔɪn]
bekommen get [get]
belebt busy ['bɪzi]
beliebt popular ['pɒpjələ]
Belohnung reward [rɪ'wɔːd]
benutzen use [juːz]
beobachten watch [wɒtʃ]
bequem comfortable ['kʌmftəbl]
bereit ready ['redi]
Berg mountain ['maʊntən]
berichten tell (about) [tel]
berichtigen correct [kə'rekt]
berühmt (für, wegen) famous
(for) ['feɪməs]
beschäftigt sein be busy ['bɪzi]
Beschäftigung activity [æk'tɪvəti]
beschreiben describe [dɪ'skraɪb]
jm. den Weg beschreiben
tell sb. the way
besondere(r, s) special ['speʃl]
Was ist das Besondere an ihm?
What's special about him?
besonnen calm [kɑːm]
besorgt sein (wegen) be worried
(about) ['wʌrid]
besser better ['betə] **besser abschneiden** do better
bestätigen confirm [kən'fɜːm]
beste(r, s), am besten best [best]
besuchen visit ['vɪzɪt]
Besucher/in visitor ['vɪzɪtə]
Betrieb (Geschäft) business
['bɪznəs] **einen Betrieb gründen/
eröffnen** start a business
Bett bed [bed]
beunruhigt sein (wegen) be worried (about) ['wʌrid]
bevor before [bɪ'fɔː]
bewirken: etwas bewirken make
a difference ['dɪfrəns]
bewölkt cloudy ['klaʊdi]
bezahlen pay [peɪ]
Bild picture ['pɪktʃə]
billig (preiswert) cheap [tʃiːp]
Binnensee lake [leɪk]
bis (zeitlich) until [ən'tɪl] **Bis
dann.** See you. **von Montag bis
Freitag** from Monday to Friday
bisschen: ein bisschen a bit [bɪt]
bitte
1. (in Fragen und Aufforderungen)
please [pliːz]
2. Bitte schön. / Hier, bitte.
Here you are.

3. (Nichts zu danken.) You're
welcome. ['welkʌm]
bitten um ask for [ɑːsk]
blau blue [bluː]
Blazer (Jackett, oft Teil der Schuluniform) blazer ['bleɪzə]
bleiben stay [steɪ]
Bleistift pencil ['pensl]
Bleistiftanspitzer pencil sharpener ['pensl ʃɑːpnə]
blöd silly ['sɪli]; stupid ['stjuːpɪd]
bloß just [dʒʌst]; only ['əʊnli]
Bonbon sweet [swiːt]
Boot boat [bəʊt]
borgen: sich etwas borgen borrow sth. ['bɒrəʊ]
Boss boss [bɒs]
Botschaft (Aussage) message
['mesɪdʒ]
Bowling spielen gehen go bowling ['bəʊlɪŋ]
Box box [bɒks]
Boxen (Boxsport) boxing ['bɒksɪŋ]
Brathähnchen chicken ['tʃɪkɪn]
brauchen need [niːd] **etwas nicht
(zu) tun brauchen** not have to
do sth.
braun brown [braʊn]
brechen break [breɪk]
Brief letter ['letə]
Briefträger postman, (pl) postmen
['pəʊstmən]
Briefträgerin postwoman, (pl)
postwomen ['pəʊstwʊmən],
['pəʊstwɪmɪn]
Brille glasses (pl) ['glɑːsɪz]
bringen bring [brɪŋ]
britisch British ['brɪtɪʃ]
Broschüre brochure ['brəʊʃə]
Brot bread [bred]
Brücke bridge [brɪdʒ]
Bruder brother ['brʌðə]
Buch book [bʊk]
buchen book [bʊk]
Buchladen bookshop ['bʊkʃɒp]
Buchseite page [peɪdʒ]
buchstabieren spell [spel]
Bulle bull [bʊl]
bunt coloured ['kʌləd]
Burg castle ['kɑːsl]
Büro office ['ɒfɪs]
Bus bus [bʌs] **den Bus nehmen**
get the bus **im Bus** on the bus
Busch bush [bʊʃ]
Bushaltestelle bus stop ['bʌs stɒp]
Button (Anstecknadel) badge
[bædʒ]

C

Café cafe ['kæfeɪ]
Cammen *(Internet-Telefongespräch mit Bildübertragung)* video chat ['vɪdiəʊ tʃæt]
CD CD [si:'di:]
CD-Spieler CD player [si:'di: pleɪə]
Cent cent [sent]
Champion champion ['tʃæmpiən]
Chat chat [tʃæt]
chatten (mit) chat (with) [tʃæt]
Chef/in boss [bɒs]
chillen chill [tʃɪl]
China China ['tʃaɪnə]
Chips crisps *(pl)* [krɪsps]
Comedyshow comedy ['kɒmədi]
Comic cartoon [kɑ:'tu:n]
Comic(heft) comic ['kɒmɪk]
Computer computer [kəm'pju:tə]
cool cool [ku:l]
Cricket *(Mannschaftssportart)* cricket ['krɪkɪt]
Cupcake *(kleiner runder Kuchen)* cupcake ['kʌpkeɪk]

D

da *(dort)* there [ðeə] **Sind da die Taylors?** *(am Telefon)* Is that the Taylors?
daheim: bei Ellie daheim at Ellie's house
daheim: bei Ellie daheim at Ellie's house
dahin there [ðeə]
danach: Mir ist nicht danach. I don't feel like it.
Dänemark Denmark ['denmɑ:k]
Dank: Vielen Dank. Thanks very much.
danke thanks [θæŋks] **danke (schön)** thank you ['θæŋk ju:]
danken: Nichts zu danken. *(Gern geschehen.)* You're welcome. ['welkʌm]
dann then [ðen]
darstellende Kunst drama ['drɑ:mə]
das *(Artikel)* the [ðə]
das (da) that [ðæt]
das *(Relativpronomen)* that [ðæt]
dass that [ðæt]
dasselbe the same [seɪm]
Datum date [deɪt]
dein/e your [jɔ:]
deine, deiner, deins yours [jɔ:z]
denken think [θɪŋk] **denken über** think of/about **daran denken** remember [rɪ'membə]
der *(Artikel)* the [ðə]

der *(Relativpronomen)* that [ðæt] *(Person)* who [hu:]
Detektiv/in detective [dɪ'tektɪv]
deutlich clear [klɪə] **deutlich sprechen** talk clearly ['klɪəli]
Deutsch; deutsch German ['dʒɜ:mən]
Deutsche/r German ['dʒɜ:mən]
Deutschland Germany ['dʒɜ:məni]
Dezember December [dɪ'sembə]
dich you [ju:] **dich selbst** yourself [jɔ:'self]
die *(Artikel)* the [ðə]
die *(Relativpronomen)* that [ðæt] *(Person)* who [hu:]
Dienstag Tuesday ['tju:zdeɪ], ['tju:zdi]
diese(r, s) this [ðɪs] **diese Menschen (hier)** these people [ði:z] **Dies ist …** This is …
Ding thing [θɪŋ]
Dinosaurier dinosaur ['daɪnəsɔ:]
dir you [ju:] **dir selbst** yourself [jɔ:'self]
Doktor/in doctor ['dɒktə]
Dollar dollar ($) ['dɒlə]
Donnerstag Thursday ['θɜ:zdeɪ], ['θɜ:zdi]
Dorf village ['vɪlɪdʒ]
dort there [ðeə] **die (CDs) dort** those (CDs) [ðəʊz]
dorthin there [ðeə]
Drachenfliegen hang-gliding ['hæŋ glaɪdɪŋ]
draußen, nach draußen outside [aʊt'saɪd]
drei three [θri:]
drinnen; nach drinnen inside [ɪn'saɪd]
dritte(r, s) third [θɜ:d]
drüben: da drüben over there [əʊvə 'ðeə]
du you [ju:] **du selbst** yourself [jɔ:'self]
Dudelsack bagpipes *(pl)* ['bægpaɪps]
dumm silly ['sɪli]; stupid ['stju:pɪd]
dunkel dark [dɑ:k]
durch through [θru:]
dürfen: etwas tun dürfen be allowed to do sth. [ə'laʊd] **nicht tun dürfen** mustn't do ['mʌsnt]
Dusche shower ['ʃaʊə]
DVD DVD [di:vi:'di:]
DVD-Player DVD player [di:vi:'di: pleɪə]

E

E-Bass bass guitar [beɪs gɪ'tɑ:]
E-Book-Reader e-reader ['i: ri:də]
echt real [rɪəl]
Ecke corner ['kɔ:nə]
Ei egg [eg]
eigene(r, s): seine eigene Fahne its own flag [əʊn]
ein/e a [ə]; *(vor Vokalen)* an [ən]
einfach *(nicht schwierig)* easy ['i:zi] **Tu es einfach!** Just do it! [dʒʌst]
einfangen catch [kætʃ]
einhundert a hundred, one hundred ['hʌndrəd]
einige some [sʌm], [səm]
einkaufen shop [ʃɒp] **einkaufen gehen** go shopping
Einkaufsstraße high street ['haɪ stri:t]
Einkaufszentrum shopping centre ['ʃɒpɪŋ sentə]
Einladung (zu, nach) invitation (to) [ɪnvɪ'teɪʃn]
einmal once [wʌns]
einpacken pack [pæk]
eins one [wʌn]
einsam lonely ['ləʊnli]
Eintrittskarte ticket ['tɪkɪt]
Einzelzimmer single room [sɪŋgl 'ru:m]
einzige(r, s) only ['əʊnli]
Eis ice cream [aɪs 'kri:m]
Eisenbahn train [treɪn]
Elefant elephant ['elɪfənt]
elf eleven [ɪ'levən]
Eltern parents ['peərənts]
E-Mail email ['i:meɪl]
Ende end [end]; *(Text, Geschichte)* ending ['endɪŋ] **am oberen Ende (von)** at the top (of) [tɒp]
enden finish ['fɪnɪʃ]
endlich at last [ət 'lɑ:st]
Energie energy ['enədʒi]
Energiegetränk energy drink ['enədʒi drɪŋk]
eng narrow ['nærəʊ]
England England ['ɪŋglənd]
Englisch; englisch English ['ɪŋglɪʃ]
Ente duck [dʌk]
entlang: die Straße entlang along the street [ə'lɒŋ]
Entschuldigung. *(Darf ich mal stören?)* Excuse me, … [ɪks'kju:z mi]; *(Tut mir leid.)* Sorry. / I'm sorry. ['sɒri]
enttäuscht disappointed [dɪsə'pɔɪntɪd]

er
1. he [hiː] **er/sich selbst** himself [hɪmˈself]
2. *(bei Dingen und Tieren)* it [ɪt] **er/sich selbst** itself [ɪtˈself]
Erdbeben earthquake [ˈɜːθkweɪk]
Erde *(Erdboden)* ground [graʊnd]
Erdkunde geography [dʒiˈɒgrəfi]
erfolgreich sein do well [wel]
erinnern: sich erinnern an re- member [rɪˈmembə]
Ernst: im Ernst seriously [ˈsɪəriəsli]
ernst(haft) serious [ˈsɪəriəs]
erst, wenn sie 13 sind not (…) until they're 13 [ənˈtɪl]
erstaunlich amazing [əˈmeɪzɪŋ]
erstaunt amazed [əˈmeɪzd]
Erste Hilfe first aid [fɜːst ˈeɪd]
Erste-Hilfe-Set first-aid kit [fɜːst ˈeɪd kɪt]
erste(r, s) first (= 1st) [fɜːst]
Erwachsene/r adult [ˈædʌlt]
erzählen (von) tell (about) [tel]
es it [ɪt] **es/sich selbst** itself [ɪtˈself]
Esel donkey [ˈdɒŋki]
Essen food [fuːd]
essen eat [iːt] **einen Salat essen** have a salad
Essen *(Mahlzeit)* meal [miːl]
etwas something [ˈsʌmθɪŋ]; *(ein bisschen)* some [sʌm], [səm]
Sonst noch etwas? Anything else? [ˈeniθɪŋ]
euch you [juː] **euch selbst** yourselves [jɔːˈselvz]
euer/eure your [jɔː]
Euro euro (€) [ˈjʊərəʊ]
Europa Europe [ˈjʊərəp]
existieren exist [ɪgˈzɪst]

F

Fahne flag [flæg]
Fähre ferry [ˈferi]
fahren go [gəʊ]; *(mit dem Auto)* drive [draɪv]; *(reisen)* travel [ˈtrævl] **mit dem Bus fahren** go by bus **Rad fahren** cycle [ˈsaɪkl]; ride a bike
Fahrer/in driver [ˈdraɪvə]
Fahrkarte ticket [ˈtɪkɪt]
Fahrrad bicycle [ˈbaɪsɪkl]; bike [baɪk]
fallen fall [fɔːl]
falls if [ɪf]
falsch wrong [rɒŋ]; false [fɔːls] **das ist falsch** that's wrong
Familie family [ˈfæməli]
familienfreundlich family-friendly

Familienstammbaum family tree
Fan fan [fæn]
fangen catch [kætʃ]
fantastisch fantastic [fænˈtæstɪk]; like a million dollars
Farbe colour [ˈkʌlə]
farbig coloured [ˈkʌləd]
Februar February [ˈfebruəri]
Federball badminton [ˈbædmɪntən]
Federmäppchen pencil case [ˈpensl keɪs]
feiern celebrate [ˈselɪbreɪt] **eine Party feiern** have a party
Feld field [fiːld]
Fenster window [ˈwɪndəʊ]
Ferien holidays [ˈhɒlədeɪz]
Fernsehen, Fernsehgerät TV [tiːˈviː] *(das)* **Fernsehen** watch- ing TV **im Fernsehen** on TV
Fernsehsendung programme [ˈprəʊgræm]
fertig *(bereit)* ready [ˈredi] **Auf die Plätze, fertig, los!** Get ready. Steady. Go! [get redi stedi ˈgəʊ]
Fest festival [ˈfestɪvl]
Feuer fire [ˈfaɪə]; *(Freudenfeuer)* bonfire [ˈbɒnfaɪə]
Feuerwehrmann/-frau firefighter [ˈfaɪəfaɪtə]
Feuerwerk fireworks
Feuerwerkskörper firework [ˈfaɪəwɜːk]
Fieber temperature [ˈtemprətʃə] **Ich habe Fieber.** I have a tem- perature.
fies mean [miːn]
Film film [fɪlm]
Filmstar film star [ˈfɪlm stɑː]
finden find [faɪnd] **Freunde fin- den** make friends [meɪk]
Finger finger [ˈfɪŋgə]
Fisch fish, *(pl)* fish [fɪʃ]
fit fit [fɪt]
Flachbildfernseher flat-screen TV [ˈflæt skriːn tiː viː]
Flagge flag [flæg]
Flasche bottle [ˈbɒtl]
Fleisch meat [miːt]
fliegen fly [flaɪ]
Flughafen airport [ˈeəpɔːt]
Flugzeug plane [pleɪn]
Fluss river [ˈrɪvə]
Föhn hairdryer [ˈheədraɪə]
fort away [əˈweɪ]
fortbewegen: sich fortbewegen travel [ˈtrævl]
Foto photo [ˈfəʊtəʊ] **ein Foto machen** take a photo

Fotoapparat camera [ˈkæmərə]
Frage question [ˈkwestʃən]
Fragebogen questionnaire [kwestʃəˈneə]
fragen ask [ɑːsk] **jn. nach dem Weg fragen** ask sb. the way
Frankreich France [frɑːns]
Französisch; französisch French [frentʃ]
Frau
1. woman, *(pl)* women [ˈwʊmən], [ˈwɪmɪn]
2. *(allgemeine Anrede f. Frauen)* Ms … [mɪz], [məz]
3. *(Anrede f. unverheiratete Frau- en)* Miss … [mɪs]
4. *(Anrede f. verheiratete Frauen)* Mrs … [ˈmɪsɪz]
frei free [friː]
Freitag Friday [ˈfraɪdeɪ], [ˈfraɪdi]
fressen eat [iːt]
Freund/in friend [frend]; *(feste Freundin)* girlfriend [ˈgɜːlfrend]; *(fester Freund)* boyfriend [ˈbɔɪfrend]
freundlich friendly [ˈfrendli]; kind [kaɪnd] **Mit freundlichen Grüßen** *(Briefschluss)* Yours sincerely [jɔːz sɪnˈsɪəli]
Frisör/in hairdresser [ˈheədresə]
froh happy [ˈhæpi] **ich bin froh** I'm glad [glæd]
Frucht, Früchte fruit [fruːt]
früh early [ˈɜːli]
Frühstück breakfast [ˈbrekfəst]
Frühstückspension bed and breakfast (B&B)
Fuchs fox [fɒks]
fühlen; sich fühlen feel [fiːl]
Führerschein driving licence [ˈdraɪvɪŋ laɪsns]
füllen fill [fɪl]
Füller pen [pen]
fünf five [faɪv]
funktionieren work [wɜːk]
für for [fɔː], [fə]
Fußball football [ˈfʊtbɔːl]
Fußballspielen playing football
Fußballspieler/in footballer [ˈfʊtbɔːlə]
Fußballverein football club (FC)
Fußgänger/in walker [ˈwɔːkə]
Futter food [fuːd]
füttern feed [fiːd]

G

ganz: den ganzen Tag (lang) all day [ɔːl ˈdeɪ]
Garage garage [ˈgærɑːʒ]

Garagenflohmarkt *(privater Floh-markt)* garage sale ['gærɑːʒ seɪl]
Garten garden ['gɑːdn]
Gast guest [gest]; visitor ['vɪzɪtə]
Gebäude building ['bɪldɪŋ]
geben give [gɪv] **es gibt** there are … ['ðeər ɑː]; **there's** [ðeəz] **es gibt keine Bäume** there aren't any trees ['eni]
geboren born [bɔːn]
gebrochen *(kaputt)* broken ['brəʊkən]
Geburtstag birthday ['bɜːθdeɪ] **Herzlichen Glückwunsch zum Geburtstag!** Happy birthday! **Sie hat Geburtstag.** It's her birthday. **Wann hast du Ge-burtstag?** When's (= when is) your birthday?
Gedicht poem ['pəʊɪm]
gefährlich dangerous ['deɪndʒərəs]
gegen against [ə'genst]
Gegend neighbourhood ['neɪbəhʊd]
gehen go [gəʊ] **Wie geht's? / Wie geht es dir/euch?** How are you? **(zu Fuß) gehen** walk [wɔːk]
geizig mean [miːn]
gelangweilt sein be bored [bɔːd]
gelb yellow ['jeləʊ]
Geld money ['mʌni] **Geld ver-dienen** make money
gemein mean [miːn]
Gemüse vegetables, *infml auch* veg ['vedʒtəblz], [vedʒ]
gemütlich comfortable ['kʌmftəbl] **es sich gemütlich machen** make yourself comfortable
genau: genau jetzt right now [raɪt 'naʊ] **genau wie Berry** just like Berry [laɪk]
genervt sein feel fed up [fed 'ʌp]
genießen enjoy [ɪn'dʒɔɪ]
genug enough [ɪ'nʌf]
geöffnet open ['əʊpən]
Geografie geography [dʒi'ɒgrəfi]
gerade jetzt right now [raɪt 'naʊ]
geradeaus: Geh geradeaus (wei-ter). Go straight on. [streɪt]
Gerät *(Maschine)* machine [mə'ʃiːn]
Geräusch noise [nɔɪz]
gern: ich hätte gern I'd like (= I would like) [laɪk] **ich würde gern mitmachen** I'd like to (= I would like to) join **Ich würde sehr gern kommen.** I'd love to come. [lʌv]
Gesamtbetrag total ['təʊtl]

Gesamtschule *(GB)* high school ['haɪ skuːl]
Geschäft
1. shop [ʃɒp]; *(verkauft gespende-te Waren für wohltätige Zwecke)* charity shop ['tʃærəti ʃɒp]
2. *(Betrieb)* business ['bɪznəs] **ein Geschäft aufmachen** start a business
3. *(Vereinbarung)* deal [diːl] **ein Geschäft abschließen, vereinbaren** make a deal
Geschäftsführer/in manager ['mænɪdʒə]
geschehen happen ['hæpən] **Bitte, gern geschehen.** You're welcome. ['welkʌm]
Geschenk present ['preznt]
Geschichte *(Erzählung)* story ['stɔːri]; *(vergangene Zeiten)* history ['hɪstri]
Geschirrspülmaschine dishwasher ['dɪʃwɒʃə]
geschlossen sein be closed [kləʊzd]
Gesicht face [feɪs]
gespannt excited [ɪk'saɪtɪd]
Gespenst ghost [gəʊst]
Gespräch talk [tɔːk]; *(Unterhaltung)* chat [tʃæt]
gestern yesterday ['jestədeɪ]
gesund healthy ['helθi]
Getränk drink [drɪŋk]
gewaltsam violent ['vaɪələnt]
gewalttätig violent ['vaɪələnt]
Gewinn *(Profit)* profit ['prɒfɪt]
gewinnen win [wɪn]
Gewinner/in winner ['wɪnə]
Gitarre guitar [gɪ'tɑː]
glauben believe [bɪ'liːv]; think [θɪŋk] **Du wirst es kaum glauben!** Wait for this. *(infml)* ['weɪt] **ich glaube** I guess [ges]
gleich, das gleiche the same [seɪm]
Glocke bell [bel]
Glück: du hast Glück you're lucky ['lʌki] **Viel Glück!** Good luck. [lʌk]
glücklich happy ['hæpi] **Du Glückliche/r!** Lucky you! ['lʌki]
glücklicherweise luckily ['lʌkɪli]
Glückwunsch: Herzlichen Glück-wunsch (zu …)! Congratulations (on …)! [kəngrætʃu'leɪʃnz] **Herz-lichen Glückwunsch zum Geburtstag!** Happy birthday! [hæpi 'bɜːθdeɪ]
GPS GPS [dʒiː piː 'es]

Gras grass [grɑːs]
grau grey [greɪ]
Grieche/Griechin Greek [griːk]
griechisch; Griechisch Greek [griːk]
groß big [bɪg]; *(Person)* tall [tɔːl] **ich mache mir große Sorgen** I worry a lot [ə 'lɒt]
großartig great [greɪt]
Großbritannien (Great) Britain ['brɪtn]
Großstadt city ['sɪti]
Großvater grandfather ['grænfɑːðə]
grün green [griːn]
Grund *(Begründung)* reason ['riːzn] **aus vielen Gründen** for lots of reasons
Gruppe group [gruːp]
Gruppenarbeit group work ['gruːp wɜːk]
gruselig scary ['skeəri]
Grüße: Mit freundlichen Grüßen *(Briefschluss)* Yours sincerely [jɔːz sɪn'sɪəli] **Viele Grüße, …** Best wishes ['wɪʃɪz]
gut good [gʊd]; fine [faɪn]; *(Ad-verb)* well [wel] **gut abschnei-den** do well **Guten Morgen.** Good morning. **Gut gemacht!** Well done. **gut sein in etwas** be good at sth. **Es geht mir gut.** I'm fine.; I'm OK. **es gut machen** do well **Hört sich gut an.** Sounds fun.
Guy-Fawkes-Puppe guy [gaɪ]
Gymnastik gymnastics [dʒɪm'næstɪks]

H

Haar, Haare hair [heə]
Haartrockner hairdryer ['heədraɪə]
haben have [hæv]
Hafen harbour ['hɑːbə]
Hähnchen chicken ['tʃɪkɪn]
Hallo. Hello. [hə'ləʊ]; Hi! [haɪ]
Halloween *(Abend des 31.10.)* Halloween [hæləʊ'iːn]
Hals throat [θrəʊt] **Mir tut der Hals weh.** I have a sore throat. [sɔː 'θrəʊt]
Halsschmerzen a sore throat [sɔː 'θrəʊt]
halten: halten von think of/about [θɪŋk] **Halt den Mund!** Shut up! [ʃʌt 'ʌp]
Hamburger *(Frikadelle)* burger ['bɜːgə]
Hamster hamster ['hæmstə]
Hand hand [hænd]

Handschuh glove [glʌv]
Handtuch towel ['taʊəl]
Handy mobile (phone) [məʊbaɪl 'fəʊn]
Happy End *(glückliches Ende)* happy ending [hæpi 'endɪŋ]
hart hard [hɑːd] **hart arbeiten** work hard
Hauptstadt capital ['kæpɪtl]
Hauptstraße high street ['haɪ striːt]
Haus house [haʊs] **nach Hause** home [həʊm]
Hausarbeiten erledigen *(Haushalt)* do chores [tʃɔːz]
Hausaufgabe/n homework ['həʊmwɜːk] **ich mache (meine) Hausaufgaben** I do my homework
Häuschen cottage ['kɒtɪdʒ]
Haustier pet [pet]
Heftseite page [peɪdʒ]
Heim *(Zuhause)* home [həʊm]
heiß hot [hɒt]
heißen: Wie heißt du? What's your name?
helfen help [help]
Helfer/in helper ['helpə]
Hemd shirt [ʃɜːt]
heraus out [aʊt]
herausfinden find out [faɪnd 'aʊt]
Herr Smith Mr Smith ['mɪstə]
herrisch bossy ['bɒsi]
herstellen make [meɪk]
herzlich: Herzlichen Glückwunsch (zu …)! Congratulations (on …)! [kəngrætʃʊ'leɪʃnz] **Herzlichen Glückwunsch zum Geburtstag!** Happy birthday! [hæpi 'bɜːθdeɪ]
heute today [tə'deɪ] **heute Morgen/Nachmittag/Abend** this morning/afternoon/evening
hier here [hɪə] **Hier, bitte.** Here you are. **Hier spricht Rob Blake.** *(am Telefon)* This is Rob Blake.
hierher here [hɪə]
Hilfe help [help]
Himmel sky [skaɪ]
hinauf up [ʌp]
hinaus out [aʊt]
hinausgehen go out [gəʊ 'aʊt]
hinfallen fall [fɔːl]
hinsetzen: sich hinsetzen sit [sɪt]; sit down
hinter behind [bɪ'haɪnd]
Hintergrund background ['bækgraʊnd]
hinüber: da hinüber over there [əʊvə 'ðeə]

hinunter down [daʊn]
Hip-Hop hip hop ['hɪp hɒp]
Hit hit [hɪt]
Hobby hobby ['hɒbi] **einem Hobby nachgehen** do a hobby
hoch high [haɪ]; *(nach oben)* up [ʌp]; *(z.B. große Gebäude)* tall [tɔːl]
Hockey hockey ['hɒki]
hoffen hope [həʊp]
Holz wood [wʊd]
horchen auf listen for ['lɪsn fə]
hören hear [hɪə]
Hose trousers (pl) ['traʊzəz]
Hot Dog *(heißes Würstchen in einem Brötchen)* hot dog ['hɒt dɒg]
Hotel hotel [həʊ'tel]
Hügel hill [hɪl]
hügelig hilly ['hɪli]
Huhn chicken ['tʃɪkɪn]
Hund dog [dɒg]
Hundeheim dogs' home
hundert a hundred, one hundred ['hʌndrəd]
Hunger haben be hungry ['hʌŋgri]
hungrig hungry ['hʌŋgri]
hupen hoot [huːt]
hurra yippee [jɪ'piː]
Hut hat [hæt]
Hütte cottage ['kɒtɪdʒ]

I

ich I [aɪ] **Ich bin's.** It's me.
ich selbst myself [maɪ'self]
ideal ideal [aɪ'dɪəl]
Idee idea [aɪ'dɪə]
Idiot/in idiot ['ɪdɪət]
ihm him [hɪm]
ihn him [hɪm]
ihnen them [ðem], [ðəm]
Ihnen *(höfliche Anrede)* you [juː]
ihr: mit ihr with her [hɜː]
ihr *(Plural von „du")* you [juː]
ihr selbst yourselves [jɔː'selvz]
Ihr/e *(vor Nomen; besitzanzeigend) (zu höflichen Anrede „you")* your [jɔː]
ihr/e *(vor Nomen; besitzanzeigend)*
1. *(zu „she")* her [hɜː]
2. *(zu „it")* its [ɪts]
3. *(zu „they")* their [ðeə]
im: im Bus on the bus **im Fernsehen** on TV **im Kino** at the cinema
Imbissstube diner *(AE)* ['daɪnə]
immer always ['ɔːlweɪz] **immer noch** still [stɪl]
in in [ɪn] **in den Klassenraum (hinein)** into the classroom ['ɪntu], ['ɪntə] **in der Schule** at

school **in der Stadt** in town **in einem Restaurant** at a restaurant **in England** in England **in Papas Wohnung gehen** go to dad's flat **Warst du schon mal in London?** Have you ever been to London?
Information fact [fækt]
Information(en) (über) information (about) *(no pl)* [ɪnfə'meɪʃn]
Informations- und Kommunikationstechnologie ICT (information and communication technology) [aɪ siː 'tiː], [ɪnfəmeɪʃn ənd kəmjuːnɪkeɪʃn tek'nɒlədʒi]
Informationsblatt newsletter ['njuːzletə]
Ingwer ginger ['dʒɪndʒə]
insbesondere especially [ɪ'speʃəli]
Instrument instrument ['ɪnstrəmənt]
interessant interesting ['ɪntrəstɪŋ]
interessieren: sich interessieren für be interested in ['ɪntrəstɪd]
interessiert sein an be interested in ['ɪntrəstɪd]
Internet internet ['ɪntənet]
Interview interview ['ɪntəvjuː]
irisch, aus Irland Irish ['aɪrɪʃ]
Irrenhaus madhouse ['mædhaʊs]

J

ja yes [jes]; yeah *(infml)* [jeə]
Jacke coat [kəʊt]; jacket ['dʒækɪt]
Jackett jacket ['dʒækɪt]
Jahr(gang) year [jɪə]
Januar January ['dʒænjuəri]
Jeans jeans [dʒiːnz]
jeder everybody ['evribɒdi]; everyone ['evriwʌn]
jede(r, s) every ['evri]
je(mals) ever ['evə]
jemand somebody ['sʌmbədi]; someone ['sʌmwʌn]
jene (CDs) those (CDs) [ðəʊz]
jetzt now [naʊ] **gerade/genau jetzt** right now [raɪt 'naʊ]
Job job [dʒɒb]
Jogging jogging ['dʒɒgɪŋ]
Joghurt yogurt ['jɒgət]
Judo judo ['dʒuːdəʊ]
Jugendliche/r kid [kɪd]
Juli July [dʒuː'laɪ]
jung young [jʌŋ]
Junge boy [bɔɪ]
Juni June [dʒuːn]
Junkfood *(ungesundes Essen)* junk food ['dʒʌŋk fuːd]

K

Kaffee coffee ['kɒfi]
Kalender calendar ['kælɪndə]
kalt cold [kəʊld]
Kamera camera ['kæmərə]
kämpfen fight [faɪt]
Kanada: aus Kanada Canadian [kə'neɪdɪən]
Kanadier/in Canadian [kə'neɪdɪən]
kanadisch Canadian [kə'neɪdɪən]
Kaninchen rabbit ['ræbɪt]
Kantine canteen [kæn'tiːn]
kaputt broken ['brəʊkən]
Kapuzenpullover hoodie ['hʊdi]
Karate karate [kə'rɑːti]
Karotte carrot ['kærət]
Karte card [kɑːd]
Kartoffel potato, (pl) potatoes [pə'teɪtəʊ]
Kartoffelchips crisps (pl) [krɪsps]
Käse cheese [tʃiːz]
Kasten box [bɒks]
Katastrophe disaster [dɪ'zɑːstə]
Kätzchen kitten ['kɪtn]
Katze cat [kæt] **junge Katze** kitten ['kɪtn]
kaufen buy [baɪ]; shop [ʃɒp]
Kaufpreis price [praɪs]
Kehrseite downside ['daʊnsaɪd]
kein/e no [nəʊ] **es gibt keine Bäume** there aren't any trees ['eni] **Ich bin kein Junge.** I'm not a boy.
Keks biscuit ['bɪskɪt]
Kellner waiter ['weɪtə]
Kellnerin waitress ['weɪtrəs]
kennen know [nəʊ]
kennenlernen meet [miːt]
Kilometer kilometre (km) ['kɪləmiːtə]
Kilt (Schottenrock) kilt [kɪlt]
Kind child, (pl) children [tʃaɪld], ['tʃɪldrən]; kid [kɪd]
Kino cinema ['sɪnəmə]
Kirche church [tʃɜːtʃ]
Kissen cushion ['kʊʃn]
klar clear [klɪə]
Klasse class [klɑːs]
Klassenarbeit test [test]
Klassenlehrer/in class teacher ['klɑːs tiːtʃə]
Klassenraum classroom ['klɑːsruːm]
Klavier piano [pi'ænəʊ]
Kleid dress [dres]
Kleiderschrank wardrobe ['wɔːdrəʊb]
Kleidung(sstücke) clothes (pl) [kləʊðz]

klein little ['lɪtl]; small [smɔːl]; (Person) short [ʃɔːt]
klettern (auf) climb [klaɪm] **Klettern** (Sport) climbing
Klingel bell [bel]
klingeln ring [rɪŋ]
Klingelton (Handy) ringtone ['rɪŋtəʊn]
klingen sound [saʊnd] **Klingt, als ob es Spaß macht.** Sounds fun.
Klub club [klʌb]
klug clever ['klevə]
Kneipe pub [pʌb]
kochen cook [kʊk]
Kochrezept recipe ['resəpi]
kommen come [kʌm] **Ich würde sehr gern kommen.** I'd love to come. **Komm(t) (schon)! / Ach komm!** Come on!
Kommentar comment ['kɒment]
Komödie comedy ['kɒmədi]
König king [kɪŋ]
Königin queen [kwiːn]
können can [kæn], [kən] **nicht können** can't (= cannot) **etwas gut können** be good at sth. **du könntest** you could [kʊd] **sie konnte** she could
kontrollieren check [tʃek]
Konzert concert ['kɒnsət]
Kopfschmerzen haben have a headache ['hedeɪk]
Kopfsprung: einen Kopfsprung machen dive [daɪv]
korrigieren correct [kə'rekt]
Kosten cost [kɒst]
kosten cost [kɒst] **Der Taschenrechner kostet 1 Pfund.** The calculator is £ 1. **Die Handys kosten 10 Pfund.** The mobiles are £ 10.
kostenlos free [friː]
Kram (Zeug) stuff [stʌf]
krank ill [ɪl]
Krankenhaus hospital ['hɒspɪtl]
Krawatte tie [taɪ]
Krebs crab [kræb]
Kreuzung (Straßenkreuzung) crossroads, (pl) crossroads ['krɒsrəʊdz]
kriegen get [get]
Krimiserie crime series, (pl) crime series ['kraɪm sɪəriːz]
Krokodil crocodile ['krɒkədaɪl]
Küche kitchen ['kɪtʃɪn]
Kuchen cake [keɪk]
Kugelschreiber pen [pen]
Kuh cow [kaʊ]
Kultur culture ['kʌltʃə]

kümmern: sich kümmern um look after [lʊk 'ɑːftə]
Kunde, Kundin customer ['kʌstəmə]
Kunst art [ɑːt]
Kunststoff plastic ['plæstɪk]
Kunststück trick [trɪk]
kurz short [ʃɔːt]
Kuscheltier toy animal [tɔɪ 'ænɪml]
Kuss kiss [kɪs]

L

lächeln; (das) **Lächeln** smile [smaɪl]
lachen laugh [lɑːf]
Laden shop [ʃɒp]
Lampe lamp [læmp]; light [laɪt]
Land country ['kʌntri] **auf dem Land** in the country **aufs Land** to the country
landen land [lænd]
Landkarte map [mæp]
Landwirt/in farmer ['fɑːmə]
lang long [lɒŋ]
Langeweile haben be bored [bɔːd]
langsam slow [sləʊ]
langweilig boring ['bɔːrɪŋ]
Laptop laptop ['læptɒp]
Lärm noise [nɔɪz]
Lasagne lasagne [lə'zænjə]
lassen let [let] **lass(t) uns** let's (= let us) **Lass(t) uns (mal) sehen.** Let's see.
Laterne lantern ['læntən]
Läufer/in runner ['rʌnə]
laut loud [laʊd]; noisy ['nɔɪzi]
läuten ring [rɪŋ]
Leben life, (pl) lives [laɪf], [laɪvz]
leben live [lɪv]
Lebensmittel food [fuːd]
Lebensstil lifestyle ['laɪfstaɪl]
lecker! yum! [jʌm]
leer empty ['empti]
leeren empty ['empti]
legen put [pʊt] **Er legt sie zu den anderen Dingen.** He puts it with the other things.
lehren teach [tiːtʃ]
Lehrer/in teacher ['tiːtʃə]
leicht (einfach) easy ['iːzi]
leidtun: Tut mir leid. Sorry. / I'm sorry. ['sɒri]
leihen hire ['haɪə] **sich etwas (aus)leihen** borrow sth. ['bɒrəʊ]
leise quiet ['kwaɪət]
Leiter/in leader ['liːdə]
lernen learn [lɜːn]
lesen read [riːd]; (das) **Lesen** reading ['riːdɪŋ]
Leser/in reader ['riːdə]

Letterbox (Behälter, der beim Letterboxing versteckt wird) letterbox ['letəbɒks]
Letterboxing (Spiel, eine Art Schnitzeljagd) letterboxing ['letəbɒksɪŋ]
letzte(r, s) last [lɑːst]
Leute people ['piːpl]; (als Anrede verwendet) guys [gaɪz]
Licht light [laɪt]
Liebe/r ... Dear ... [dɪə]
lieben love [lʌv]
lieber: etwas lieber mögen like sth. better ['betə] **etwas lieber mögen als etwas** prefer sth. to sth. [prɪˈfɜː]
Lieblings- favourite ['feɪvərɪt] **Lieblingssache** favourite thing
Lied song [sɒŋ]
Lieferwagen van [væn]
Limonade lemonade [leməˈneɪd]
Lineal ruler ['ruːlə]
links left [left] **auf der linken Seite** on the left **nach links** left
locker: Bleib mal locker. Take it easy!
Lokal diner (AE) ['daɪnə]
Londoner/in Londoner ['lʌndənə]
los: Auf die Plätze, fertig, los! Get ready. Steady. Go! [get redi stedi 'gəʊ]
lustig funny ['fʌni]

M

machen do [duː]; make, [meɪk] **Gut gemacht!** Well done. [wel 'dʌn] **ich mache (meine) Hausaufgaben** I do my homework ['həʊmwɜːk]
Mädchen girl [gɜːl]
mähen (Rasen) cut [kʌt]
Mahlzeit meal [miːl] **kleine Mahlzeit** snack [snæk]
Mai May [meɪ]
Make-up make-up ['meɪkʌp]
Mal time [taɪm] **nächstes Mal** next time **zum letzten Mal** for the last time
Mama mum [mʌm]
man you
Manager/in manager ['mænɪdʒə]
manchmal sometimes ['sʌmtaɪmz]
Mann man, (pl) men [mæn], [men]
Mannschaft team [tiːm]
Mantel coat [kəʊt]
Markt market ['mɑːkɪt]
Marmelade jam [dʒæm]
März March [mɑːtʃ]
Maschine machine [məˈʃiːn]

Maske mask [mɑːsk]
Mathematik maths [mæθs]
Matsch mud [mʌd]
Mauer wall [wɔːl]
Mechaniker/in mechanic [mɪˈkænɪk]
Meer sea [siː] **am Meer** at the seaside ['siːsaɪd]
Mehl flour ['flaʊə]
mehr more [mɔː] **immer mehr** more and more
Mehrfamilienhaus block of flats [blɒk əv 'flæts]
Meile (ca. 1,6 km) mile [maɪl]
mein/e (vor Nomen) my [maɪ]
meine/r; meins mine [maɪn]
meinen (denken, glauben) think [θɪŋk]; (sagen wollen) mean [miːn]
Meinung opinion [əˈpɪnjən] **meiner Meinung nach** in my opinion
meistens usually ['juːʒʊəli]
meiste(r, s): das meiste Geld, am meisten Geld the most money [məʊst]
Meister/in (Sport) champion ['tʃæmpiən]
Mensa canteen [kænˈtiːn]
Menschen people ['piːpl]
Messer knife, (pl) knives [naɪf]
Meter metre ['miːtə]
mich me [mi] **mich selbst** myself [maɪˈself]
mieten hire ['haɪə]
Milch milk [mɪlk]
Milchshake milkshake ['mɪlkʃeɪk]
Million million ['mɪljən]
Minute minute ['mɪnɪt]
mir me [mi] **Mir ist nicht danach.** I don't feel like it. **mir selbst** myself [maɪˈself]
Mist: Es ist Mist! It sucks! [sʌks] **So ein Mist!** What a pain! [peɪn]
mit with [wɪð] **mit 16** at 16 **mit dem Bus fahren** go by bus
mitbringen bring [brɪŋ]
mitkommen come [kʌm]
Mitleid mit jm. haben be/feel sorry for sb. ['sɒri]
mitmachen: bei etwas mitmachen take part in sth. [teɪk 'pɑːt]
mitmachen (bei) join [dʒɔɪn]
Mittag: (zu) Mittag essen have lunch [lʌntʃ]
Mittagessen lunch [lʌntʃ]
mittags at lunchtime ['lʌntʃtaɪm]
Mittagszeit: zur Mittagszeit at lunchtime ['lʌntʃtaɪm]
Mitte centre ['sentə]; middle ['mɪdl] **in der Mitte** in the middle

Mitteilung message ['mesɪdʒ]
Mitteilungsblatt newsletter ['njuːzletə]
Mittwoch Wednesday ['wenzdeɪ], ['wenzdi]
möchten: ich möchte (...) haben I'd like (= I would like) [laɪk] **ich möchte gern mitmachen** I'd like to (= I would like to) join
Modell model ['mɒdl] **Modellauto** model car [mɒdl 'kɑː]
modern modern ['mɒdn]
Mode(trend) fashion ['fæʃn]
mögen like [laɪk] **etwas am liebsten mögen** like sth. best **etwas lieber mögen** like sth. better **etwas lieber mögen als etwas** prefer sth. to sth. [prɪˈfɜː] **sehr mögen** love [lʌv]
möglich possible ['pɒsəbl]
Möhre carrot ['kærət]
Monat month [mʌnθ]
Monitor monitor ['mɒnɪtə]
Monster monster ['mɒnstə]
Montag Monday ['mʌndeɪ], ['mʌndi]
morgen tomorrow [təˈmɒrəʊ]
Morgen morning ['mɔːnɪŋ]
müde tired ['taɪəd]; sleepy ['sliːpi]
Muffin muffin ['mʌfɪn]
Müll rubbish ['rʌbɪʃ]
Mülleimer rubbish bin ['rʌbɪʃ bɪn]
Mund mouth [maʊθ] **Halt den Mund!** Shut up! [ʃʌt 'ʌp]
Museum museum [mjuˈziːəm]
Musik music ['mjuːzɪk]
Musik- musical ['mjuːzɪkl]
musikalisch musical ['mjuːzɪkl]
Musikgruppe band [bænd]
Müsliriegel cereal bar ['sɪəriəl bɑː]
müssen must [mʌst] **etwas tun müssen** have to do sth. ['hæv tə] **etwas nicht tun müssen** not have to do sth.
mutig brave [breɪv]
Mutter mother ['mʌðə]
Mutti mum [mʌm]
Mütze hat [hæt]

N

nach (örtlich) to [tu], [tə]; (zeitlich) after ['ɑːftə] **nach Hause** home [həʊm]
Nachbar/in neighbour ['neɪbə]
Nachbarschaft neighbourhood ['neɪbəhʊd]
nachgehen: einem Hobby nachgehen do a hobby

Nachmittag afternoon [ɑːftəˈnuːn]
Nachricht *(Botschaft)* message ['mesɪdʒ]
Nachrichten news [njuːz]
nächste(r, s), als Nächstes next
Nacht night [naɪt] **in der Nacht** at night
Nachteil downside ['daʊnsaɪd]
nachts at night [ət 'naɪt]
Nähe: in der Nähe von near [nɪə]
nahe (bei) near [nɪə]
Name name [neɪm]
Nase nose [nəʊz] **die Nase voll haben** feel fed up [fed 'ʌp]
nass wet [wet]
national national ['næʃnəl]
Nationalpark national park [næʃnəl 'pɑːk]
Natur- natural ['nætʃrəl]
Naturkunde natural history [nætʃrəl 'hɪstri]
natürlich natural ['nætʃrəl]; of course [əv 'kɔːs]
Naturwissenschaft science ['saɪəns]
Nebel fog [fɒg]
nebelig foggy ['fɒgi]
neben next to ['nekst tə]
negativ negative ['negətɪv]
nehmen take [teɪk] **den Bus nehmen** get the bus **einen Salat nehmen** have a salad
nein no [nəʊ]
nennen call [kɔːl] **Wie nennt man …?** What do you call …?
nerven: Es nervt! It sucks! [sʌks]; What a pain! [peɪn]
nervös nervous ['nɜːvəs]
nett nice [naɪs]; *(freundlich)* friendly ['frendli]; kind [kaɪnd]
Netz network ['netwɜːk]
neu new [njuː]
neun nine [naɪn]
Neunzigerjahre 90s ['naɪntiz]
nicht not [nɒt] **auch nicht** not … either ['aɪðə] **noch nicht** not … yet [jet]
nichts not (…) anything ['eniθɪŋ]; nothing ['nʌθɪŋ]
niedlich cute [kjuːt]
nie(mals) never ['nevə]
niemand nobody ['nəʊbədi]
Nistkasten birdhouse ['bɜːdhaʊs]
noch still [stɪl] **noch ein/e** another [ə'nʌðə] **noch einmal** again [ə'gen] **noch nicht** not … yet [jet]
Norden, Nord- north [nɔːθ]
nördlich north [nɔːθ]

Nordosten, nordöstlich north-east [nɔːθ'iːst]
Nordwesten, nordwestlich north-west [nɔːθ'west]
normal normal ['nɔːml]; usual ['juːʒəl]
normalerweise usually ['juːʒəli]
November November [nəʊ'vembə]
Null *(im gesprochenen Englisch)* oh [əʊ]
Nummer number ['nʌmbə]
nun now [naʊ]
nur just [dʒʌst]; only ['əʊnli]
nützlich useful ['juːsfl]

O

oben upstairs [ʌp'steəz]; *(am oberen Ende)* at the top [tɒp] **nach oben** upstairs
Obst fruit [fruːt]
oder or [ɔː]
offen open ['əʊpən]
öffnen, sich öffnen open ['əʊpən]
oft often ['ɒfn], ['ɒftən]
ohne without [wɪ'ðaʊt]
Ohr ear [ɪə]
oje! Oh dear! [dɪə]
Oktober October [ɒk'təʊbə]
olympisch Olympic [ə'lɪmpɪk] **Olympische Spiele** Olympic Games
Oma grandma ['grænmɑː]
Onkel uncle ['ʌŋkl]
online, Online- online [ɒn'laɪn]
Opa grandad ['grændæd]; grandpa ['grænpɑː]
Orange orange ['ɒrɪndʒ]
orange(farben) orange ['ɒrɪndʒ]
ordentlich tidy ['taɪdi]
Ort place [pleɪs]
Osten, Ost- east [iːst]
östlich east [iːst]

P

paar: ein paar some [sʌm], [səm]
Päckchen packet (of) ['pækɪt]
packen pack [pæk]
Packung packet (of) ['pækɪt]
Palast palace ['pæləs]
Papa dad [dæd]
Park park [pɑːk]
parken park (a car) [pɑːk]
Parkplatz car park ['kɑː pɑːk]
Parlament parliament ['pɑːləmənt]
Partner/in partner ['pɑːtnə]
Partnerarbeit partner work ['pɑːtnə wɜːk]
Party party ['pɑːti] **eine Party feiern** have a party

passieren *(geschehen)* happen ['hæpən]
Pastete *(mit Fleisch-/Gemüse-füllung)* pasty ['pæsti]
Pause break [breɪk]
Pence pence [pens] **50 Pence** 50p [piː]
Penny *(kleinste britische Münze)* penny ['peni]
perfekt perfect ['pɜːfɪkt]
Person person ['pɜːsn]
Pfad track [træk]
Pfeife *(Trillerpfeife)* whistle ['wɪsl]
Pferd horse [hɔːs]
Pflanze plant [plɑːnt]
Pfund *(britische Währung)* pound (£) [paʊnd]
Pickel spot [spɒt]
Picknick picnic ['pɪknɪk] **ein Picknick machen** have a picnic
Plan plan [plæn]
planen plan [plæn]
Plastik plastic ['plæstɪk]
Plastiktüte plastic bag [plæstɪk 'bæg]
Platz *(Stelle, Ort)* place [pleɪs]; *(freier Raum)* space [speɪs] **Auf die Plätze, fertig, los!** Get ready. Steady. Go! [get redi stedi 'gəʊ]
Plätzchen *(Keks)* biscuit ['bɪskɪt]
plaudern (mit) chat (with) [tʃæt]
plötzlich suddenly ['sʌdənli]
Polizei police *(pl)* [pə'liːs]
Polizeibeamter/-beamtin police officer [pə'liːs ɒfɪsə]
Pommes frites chips *(pl)* [tʃɪps]
Pony pony ['pəʊni]
populär popular ['pɒpjələ]
Post *(Briefe etc.)* post [pəʊst]
Post(amt) post office ['pəʊst ɒfɪs]
Poster poster ['pəʊstə]
Postkarte postcard ['pəʊstkɑːd]
Praline chocolate ['tʃɒklət]
Präsident/in president ['prezɪdənt]
Preis
  1. *(Kaufpreis)* price [praɪs]
  2. *(Kosten)* cost [kɒst]
  3. *(Gewinn)* prize [praɪz]
preiswert cheap [tʃiːp]
Prinz prince [prɪns]
pro: pro Ballon per balloon [pɜː], [pə] **10 Pfund pro Woche** £10 a week
probieren try [traɪ]
Problem problem ['prɒbləm]
Profit profit ['prɒfɪt]
Prospekt brochure ['brəʊʃə]
prüfen check [tʃek]

Pullover pullover [ˈpʊləʊvə]
pünktlich on time [ɒn ˈtaɪm]
Puzzle jigsaw [ˈdʒɪgsɔː]

Q

Quiz quiz [kwɪz]

R

Rad (*Fahrrad*) bike [baɪk] **Rad fahren** cycle [ˈsaɪkl]; ride a bike
Radiergummi rubber [ˈrʌbə]
Rap rap [ræp]
rappen rap [ræp]
Ratte rat [ræt]
Raum (*Zimmer*) room [ruːm]; (*freier Raum*) space [speɪs]
Realität reality [riˈælɪti]
Recht haben be right [raɪt]
rechte(r, s): auf der rechten Seite on the right
rechts right [raɪt]; on the right
Rede talk [tɔːk]
Redewendung phrase [freɪz]
Redner/in talker [ˈtɔːkə]
Regel rule [ruːl]
Regen rain [reɪn]
Regenhose rain trousers (*pl*) [ˈreɪn traʊzəz]
Regenjacke rain jacket
Region region [ˈriːdʒən]
regnen rain [reɪn]
regnerisch rainy [ˈreɪni]
reichen: 50 Pence reichen (auch) 50 p will do
Reise trip [trɪp] **eine Reise machen** do a trip
reisekrank travel-sick [ˈtrævlsɪk]
reisen travel [ˈtrævl]
reiten ride [raɪd] **auf einem Pony/ein Pony reiten** ride a pony (*das*) **Reiten** riding
relaxen chill [tʃɪl]
rennen run [rʌn]
Reporter/in reporter [rɪˈpɔːtə]
repräsentieren represent [reprɪˈzent]
reservieren book [bʊk]
Reservierung reservation [rezəˈveɪʃn]
Restaurant restaurant [ˈrestrɒnt]
retten save [seɪv]
Rezept (*Kochrezept*) recipe [ˈresəpi]
richtig right [raɪt] **das ist richtig** that's right
Rock skirt [skɜːt]
Rock(musik) rock (music) [ˈrɒk mjuːzɪk]
Rollstuhl wheelchair [ˈwiːltʃeə]

Rolltreppe escalator [ˈeskəleɪtə]
rosa pink [pɪŋk]
rot red [red]
rotblond ginger [ˈdʒɪndʒə]
Rücken back [bæk]
Rucksack rucksack [ˈrʌksæk]
Rückseite back [bæk]
rufen shout [ʃaʊt]; call [kɔːl]
Rugby (*Ballsportart*) rugby [ˈrʌgbi]
ruhig calm [kɑːm]; quiet [ˈkwaɪət]
Ruine ruin (*oft auch pl: ruins*) [ˈruːɪn]
Rundfahrt tour [tʊə]
Rundgang (durch) tour (of) [tʊə]
runter down [daʊn]

S

Sache thing [θɪŋ]
Saft juice [dʒuːs]
sagen say [seɪ] **sagen wollen** (*meinen*) mean [miːn]
Sahne cream [kriːm]
Salat (*Gericht/Beilage*) salad [ˈsæləd]
Salz salt [sɔːlt]
sammeln collect [kəˈlekt]
Samstag Saturday [ˈsætədeɪ], [ˈsætədi]
Sandwich sandwich [ˈsænwɪtʃ]
Sänger/in singer [ˈsɪŋə]
Satz sentence [ˈsentəns]
sauer sein feel fed up [fed ˈʌp]
Schachtel packet (of) [ˈpækɪt]
Schaf sheep, (*pl*) sheep [ʃiːp]
schauen look [lʊk]
Schauer shower [ˈʃaʊə]
Schauspiel drama [ˈdrɑːmə]
schauspielern act [ækt]
Scherz joke [dʒəʊk]
scherzen joke [dʒəʊk]
schicken send [send]
schießen (*mit dem Fuß*) kick [kɪk]
Schiff ship [ʃɪp]; boat [bəʊt]
Schild sign [saɪn]
Schlaf sleep [sliːp]
schlafen sleep [sliːp]
Schlafparty sleepover [ˈsliːpəʊvə]
Schlafsack sleeping bag [ˈsliːpɪŋ bæg]
Schlafzimmer bedroom [ˈbedruːm]
Schlagzeug drums [drʌmz]
Schlamm mud [mʌd]
Schlange snake [sneɪk]
schlau clever [ˈklevə]
schlecht bad [bæd]
schließen close [kləʊz]
schließlich at last [ət ˈlɑːst]; in the end [ɪn ði ˈend]
schlimm bad [bæd]

Schlittschuhlaufen ice skating [ˈaɪs skeɪtɪŋ]
Schluss end [end] **zum Schluss** in the end
Schlussverkauf sale [seɪl]
schmal narrow [ˈnærəʊ]
schmerzhaft sore [sɔː]
Schnauze (*Tier*) mouth [maʊθ]
schneiden cut [kʌt]
schnell quick [kwɪk]
Schokolade chocolate [ˈtʃɒklət]
Schokoriegel chocolate bar [ˈtʃɒklət bɑː]
schon: Warst du schon mal …? Have you ever been …? [ˈevə]
schön beautiful [ˈbjuːtɪfl]; fine [faɪn]; nice [naɪs] **Schön, wieder zusammenzusein.** Nice to be together again. **Ich wünsche dir einen schönen Tag. / Schönen Tag noch.** Have a good day.
schottisch, aus Schottland Scottish [ˈskɒtɪʃ]
Schottland Scotland [ˈskɒtlənd]
schrecklich terrible [ˈterəbl]
schreiben write [raɪt] **schreiben an** write to
Schreibtisch desk [desk]
schreien scream [skriːm]
Schuh shoe [ʃuː]
Schuld: jm. die Schuld geben (an) blame sb. (for) [bleɪm]
Schule school [skuːl]
Schüler/in student [ˈstjuːdnt]
Schulheft exercise book [ˈeksəsaɪz bʊk]
Schulklasse class [klɑːs]
Schulleiter/in principal [ˈprɪnsəpl]
Schulmensa canteen [kænˈtiːn]
Schulsport PE (physical education) [piː ˈiː], [fɪzɪkl edʒuˈkeɪʃn]
Schulter shoulder [ˈʃəʊldə]
Schuluniform uniform [ˈjuːnɪfɔːm]
Schwanz tail [teɪl]
schwänzen (*Schule*) skive [skaɪv]
Schwänzer/in (*Schule*) skiver [ˈskaɪvə]
schwarz black [blæk]
Schwein pig [pɪg]
schwer
1. (*Gewicht; Regen*) heavy [ˈhevi]
2. (*schwierig*) difficult [ˈdɪfɪkəlt]; hard [hɑːd]
Schwester sister [ˈsɪstə]
schwierig difficult [ˈdɪfɪkəlt]; hard [hɑːd]
Schwierigkeiten trouble [ˈtrʌbl]
Schwimmbad swimming pool [ˈswɪmɪŋ puːl]

schwimmen: schwimmen gehen go swimming ['swɪmɪŋ] *(das)* **Schwimmen** swimming

sechs six [sɪks]

Second-Hand-Laden second-hand shop [sekənd 'hænd]

See *(Binnensee)* lake [leɪk]; *(die See, das Meer)* sea [si:]

sehen look [lʊk]; see [si:] **Lass(t) uns (mal) sehen.** Let's see. **Sieh mal, Adam.** Look, Adam.

sehr very ['veri] **ich bin sehr besorgt** I worry a lot [ə 'lɒt] **jn. so sehr vermissen/mögen/lieben** miss/like/love sb. so much [səʊ 'mʌtʃ]

Seife soap [səʊp]

Seifenoper soap [səʊp]

Seilrutsche zip wire ['zɪp waɪə]

sein be [bi:]

sein/e *(besitzanzeigend)*
  1. *(zu „he")* his [hɪz]
  2. *(bei Dingen und Tieren)* its [ɪts]

Seite page [peɪdʒ]

selbst *(sogar)* even ['i:vn]

selbstverständlich of course [əv 'kɔ:s]

senden send [send]

Sendung programme ['prəʊgræm]

September September [sep'tembə]

setzen: sich setzen sit [sɪt]; sit down

Show show [ʃəʊ]

sich *(Reflexivpronomen)*
  1. *(zu „he")* himself [hɪm'self]
  2. *(zu „she")* herself [hɜ:'self]
  3. *(zu „it")* itself [ɪt'self]
  4. *(zu „them")* themselves [ðəm'selvz]

sicher sure [ʃʊə]; *(gefahrlos)* safe [seɪf]

Sicherheit security [sɪ'kjʊərəti] **in Sicherheit** safe [seɪf]

sie
  1. *(weibliche Person)* she **für sie** for her [hɜ:] **sie/sich selbst** herself [hɜ:'self]
  2. *(bei Dingen und Tieren)* it [ɪt] **sie/sich selbst** itself [ɪt'self]
  3. *(Plural)* they [ðeɪ] **für sie** for them [ðem], [ðəm] **sie/sich selbst** themselves [ðəm'selvz]

Sie *(höfliche Anrede)* you [ju:] **Sie/sich selbst** *(Singular)* yourself [jɔ:'self] *(Plural)* yourselves [jɔ:'selvz]

sieben seven ['sevn]

singen sing [sɪŋ]

sitzen sit [sɪt]

Skateboard skateboard ['skeɪtbɔ:d]

Skateboardfahren skateboarding ['skeɪtbɔ:dɪŋ]

Skilaufen *(Sport)* skiing ['ski:ɪŋ]

Sklave, Sklavin slave [sleɪv]

SMS text (message) ['tekst mesɪdʒ] **eine SMS schicken** text [tekst]

Snack snack [snæk]

so so [səʊ] **So viel kostet das nicht.** It's cheaper than that. **so viel wie** as much as

Socke sock [sɒk]

Sofa sofa ['səʊfə]

sogar even ['i:vn]

Sohn son [sʌn]

sollen: du solltest you should [ʃʊd]

Sommer summer ['sʌmə]

Sonne sun [sʌn]

Sonnenbrille sunglasses *(pl)* ['sʌnglɑ:sɪz]

sonnig sunny ['sʌni]

Sonntag Sunday ['sʌndeɪ], ['sʌndi]

Sonst noch etwas? Anything else? ['eniθɪŋ]

Sorgen: sich Sorgen machen (wegen, um) worry (about) ['wʌri]

sorgfältig careful ['keəfl]

Sorte: Welche Sorte (von) …? What sort of …? [sɔ:t]

Spanien Spain [speɪn]

Spaß: es macht Spaß, mit ihnen zusammenzusein they're fun [fʌn] **Klingt, als ob es Spaß macht.** Sounds fun. **Viel Spaß!** Enjoy yourself/yourselves. [ɪn'dʒɔɪ]

spät late [leɪt] **Wie spät ist es?** What's the time?

später later ['leɪtə]

Speiseeis ice cream [aɪs 'kri:m]

Speisekarte menu ['menju:]

Spiegel mirror ['mɪrə]

Spiel game [geɪm] **Spiele spielen** playing games [pleɪɪŋ 'geɪmz]

spielen play [pleɪ]

Spielzeug toy [tɔɪ]

Spitze: an der Spitze (von) at the top (of) [tɒp]

Sport sport [spɔ:t]; *(in der Schule)* PE (physical education) [pi: 'i:], [fɪzɪkl edʒu'keɪʃn]

Sportart sport [spɔ:t]

Sportgeschäft sports shop ['spɔ:ts ʃɒp]

sportlich sporty ['spɔ:ti]

Sportschuh trainer ['treɪnə]

Sprache language ['læŋgwɪdʒ]

sprechen speak [spi:k] **sprechen mit** speak to **sprechen über** talk about [tɔ:k] **Wer spricht (da)?** *(am Telefon)* Who's speaking?

springen jump [dʒʌmp]

Stadion stadium ['steɪdɪəm]

Stadt *(Großstadt)* city ['sɪti]; *(Kleinstadt)* town [taʊn]

Stadtmitte centre ['sentə]

Stadtplan map [mæp]

Stammbaum *(der Familie)* family tree

Star star [stɑ:]

stark strong [strɒŋ]

staubsaugen hoover ['hu:və]

stehen stand [stænd] **stehen bleiben** stop [stɒp]

Stelle place [pleɪs]

stellen put [pʊt]

sterben die [daɪ]

Stiefbruder stepbrother ['stepbrʌðə]

Stiefel boot [bu:t]

Stiefmutter stepmum ['stepmʌm]

Stiefschwester stepsister ['stepsɪstə]

Stiefvater stepdad ['stepdæd]

Stift pen [pen]

still calm [kɑ:m]; quiet ['kwaɪət]

stimmen: das stimmt that's right **das stimmt nicht** that's wrong **Was stimmt nicht mit …?** What's wrong with …?

stimmen für jn. vote for sb. [vəʊt]

Stolz pride [praɪd]

stolz (auf) proud (of) [praʊd]

Strand beach [bi:tʃ]

Straße *(in Ortschaften)* street [stri:t]; *(Landstraße zwischen Orten / Straße in Orten)* road [rəʊd]

Strauch bush [bʊʃ]

Streichelzoo pets corner ['kɔ:nə]

Streifenhörnchen chipmunk ['tʃɪpmʌŋk]

streng strict [strɪkt]

strikt strict [strɪkt]

Student/in student ['stju:dnt]

Stuhl chair [tʃeə]

Stunde hour [aʊə]; lesson ['lesn]

Stundenplan timetable ['taɪmteɪbl]

suchen look for ['lʊk fə]

Süden, Süd- south [saʊθ]

südlich south [saʊθ]

Südosten, südöstlich south-east [saʊθ'i:st]

Südwesten, südwestlich south-west [saʊθ'west]

Summe total ['təʊtl]

Supermarkt supermarket
['su:pəmɑ:kɪt]
Suppe soup [su:p]
süß cute [kju:t]
Süßigkeiten sweets [swi:ts]
Szene scene [si:n]

T

Taekwondo tae kwon do
[taɪ kwɒn 'dəʊ]
Tag day [deɪ]
Tag Rugby *(kontaktlose Rugby-Variante)* tag rugby ['tæg rʌgbi]
Tagesausflug day out [deɪ 'aʊt]
Tageszeitung newspaper
['nju:zpeɪpə]
Talkshow talk show ['tɔ:k ʃəʊ]
Tante aunt [ɑ:nt]
tanzen dance [dɑ:ns] *(das)*
Tanzen dancing
Tänzer/in dancer ['dɑ:nsə]
Tasche bag [bæg]; *(an Kleidungsstücken)* pocket ['pɒkɪt]
Taschendieb/in pickpocket
['pɪkpɒkɪt]
Taschengeld pocket money
['pɒkɪt mʌni]
Taschenrechner calculator
['kælkjuleɪtə]
Tasse cup [kʌp] **eine Tasse Tee** a cup of tea
Tatsache fact [fækt]
Tauchen *(Sport)* diving ['daɪvɪŋ]
Taxi taxi ['tæksi]
Team team [ti:m]
Technik technology [tek'nɒlədʒi]
Technologie technology
[tek'nɒlədʒi]
Tee tea [ti:]
Teenager teenager ['ti:neɪdʒə];
teen [ti:n]
Teenageralter: Kinder im Teenageralter teenage kids ['ti:neɪdʒ]
Teil part [pɑ:t]
teilnehmen: an etwas teilnehmen take part in sth. [teɪk 'pɑ:t]
Telefon telephone ['telɪfəʊn];
phone [fəʊn]
Telefonanruf *(phone)* call
['fəʊn kɔ:l]
Telefonnummer phone number
['fəʊn nʌmbə]
Temperatur temperature
['temprətʃə]
Tennis tennis ['tenɪs]
Test test [test]
teuer expensive [ɪk'spensɪv]
Theater theatre ['θɪətə] **Theater spielen** act [ækt]

Theaterstück play [pleɪ]
tief deep [di:p]
Tier animal ['ænɪml]
Tiger tiger ['taɪgə]
Tisch table ['teɪbl]
Tischtennis table tennis
['teɪbl tenɪs]
Toast(brot) toast [təʊst]
Tochter daughter ['dɔ:tə]
Toilette toilet ['tɔɪlət]
Toilettenpapier: Rolle Toilettenpapier toilet roll ['tɔɪlət rəʊl]
toll great [greɪt]
Tor gate [geɪt]
Tour tour [tʊə]
Tourist/in tourist ['tʊərɪst]
tragen *(Kleidung)* wear [weə]
Trampolin trampoline ['træmpəli:n]
Transporter *(Lieferwagen)* van
[væn]
Transport(wesen) transport
['trænspɔ:t]
Traum dream [dri:m]
traurig sad [sæd]
treffen; sich treffen meet [mi:t]
treten kick [kɪk]
Trick trick [trɪk]
Trimester term [tɜ:m]
trinken drink [drɪŋk]
trocknen dry [draɪ]
Trommeln drums [drʌmz]
trotzdem still [stɪl]
Tschüs. Bye. [baɪ]; See you.
T-Shirt T-shirt ['ti:ʃɜ:t]
tun do [du:] *(etwas wohin)* **tun**
put [pʊt] **(viel) zu tun haben**
be busy ['bɪzi]
Tupfen *(Leopard)* spot [spɒt]
Tür door [dɔ:]
Türkei Turkey ['tɜ:ki]
Turm tower ['taʊə]
Turnen gymnastics [dʒɪm'næstɪks]

U

U-Bahn underground
['ʌndəgraʊnd]; *(in London)* the
Tube [tju:b]
üben practise ['præktɪs]
über
1. about [ə'baʊt] **schreiben über**
write about
2. *(quer über)* across [ə'krɒs]
überall(hin) everywhere ['evriweə]
überfliegen *(Text)* skim [skɪm]
überprüfen check [tʃek]
überqueren cross [krɒs]
überrascht surprised [sə'praɪzd]
Überraschung surprise [sə'praɪz]

Überwachungskamera(s) CCTV
[si: si: ti: 'vi:]
Überwachungssystem CCTV
[si: si: ti: 'vi:]
üblich usual ['ju:ʒʊəl]
Übung exercise ['eksəsaɪz]
Übungen machen do exercises
Übungsheft exercise book
['eksəsaɪz bʊk]
Uhr clock [klɒk] **5 Uhr morgens/ vormittags** 5 am [eɪ'em] **5 Uhr nachmittags/abends / 17 Uhr**
5 pm [pi:'em] **um 1 Uhr / um 13 Uhr** at one o'clock [ə'klɒk]
Uhrzeit time [taɪm]
um: um 1 Uhr at 1 o'clock
umschauen: sich umschauen (in)
look around [ə'raʊnd]
umziehen *(an einen neuen Wohnort)* move house [mu:v]
umziehen nach move to
uncool uncool [ʌn'ku:l]
und and [ænd], [ənd] **Und du?**
What about you?
Unfall accident ['æksɪdənt]
unfreundlich unfriendly [ʌn'frendli]
ungefähr about [ə'baʊt]
ungesund unhealthy [ʌn'helθi]
Unglück *(Katastrophe)* disaster
[dɪ'zɑ:stə]
unglücklich unhappy [ʌn'hæpi]
unheimlich *(beängstigend)* scary
['skeəri]
Uniform uniform ['ju:nɪfɔ:m]
uninteressant uninteresting
[ʌn'ɪntrəstɪŋ]
Unit unit ['ju:nɪt]
unordentlich messy ['mesi]
Unrecht haben be wrong
unrichtig false [fɔ:ls]
uns us [ʌs], [əs] **uns selbst**
ourselves [aʊə'selvz]
unser/e our ['aʊə], [ɑ:]
unsicher unsure [ʌn'ʃʊə]
Unsinn rubbish ['rʌbɪʃ]
unten: nach unten down [daʊn]
unter under ['ʌndə]
Unterführung subway ['sʌbweɪ]
Unterhaltung *(Gespräch)* chat
[tʃæt]
unterrichten teach [ti:tʃ]
Unterrichtsstunde lesson ['lesn]
Unterschied difference ['dɪfrəns]
unterschiedlich different ['dɪfrənt]
unterstreichen underline
[ʌndə'laɪn]
Urlaub holiday ['hɒlədeɪ]
USA (= Vereinigte Staaten von Amerika) US (= the United

States) [ju: 'es], [junaitid 'steits];
USA [ju: es 'ei]

usw. (und so weiter) etc.
[et'setərə]

V

Vater father ['fɑ:ðə]

Vati dad [dæd]

verändern; sich verändern
change [tʃeɪndʒ]

Veränderung change [tʃeɪndʒ]

Verbandkasten first-aid kit
[fɜːst 'eɪd kɪt]

verbringen: Zeit verbringen (mit)
spend time (on) [spend]

verdienen: : Geld verdienen
make money

Verein club [klʌb]

Vereinbarung deal [diːl]

Vereinigte Staaten US (United
States) [ju: 'es], [junaitid 'steits]

Verfasser/in writer ['raitə]

vergessen forget [fə'get] **Ich habe
meine Hausaufgaben vergessen.**
I forgot my homework. [fə'gɒt]
nicht vergessen remember
[rɪ'membə]

Vergnügen: Viel Vergnügen!
Enjoy yourself/yourselves. [ɪn'dʒɔɪ]

verhalten: sich verhalten behave
[bɪ'heɪv]

Verkauf sale [seɪl]

verkaufen sell [sel]

Verkäufer/in salesperson, (pl)
salespeople ['seɪlzpɜ:sn], ['seɪlzpiːpl]

Verkehrsampel traffic lights (pl)
['træfɪk laɪts]

Verkehrsmittel transport
['trænspɔ:t]

verkehrsreich busy ['bɪzi]

verlassen: jn. verlassen leave sb.
[liːv]

verlieren lose [luːz]

vermissen miss [mɪs]

vermisst missing ['mɪsɪŋ]

verschieden different ['dɪfrənt]

verschlafen (müde) sleepy ['sliːpi]

verschwenden waste [weɪst]

Verschwendung waste [weɪst]

**Verspätung: mein Bus hat Ver-
spätung** my bus is late [leɪt]

verstehen understand [ʌndə'stænd]

versuchen try [traɪ]

vertreten (repräsentieren) represent
[reprɪ'zent]

verwundert amazed [ə'meɪzd]

Video video ['vɪdiəʊ]

Videochat video chat ['vɪdiəʊ tʃæt]

viel(e) a lot of [lɒt]; lots of ['lɒts əv]
viel much [mʌtʃ] **So viel kostet
das nicht.** It's cheaper than that.
Viele Grüße, ... (Briefschluss)
Best wishes ['wɪʃɪz] **Viel Glück!**
Good luck. [lʌk] **Wie viele ...?**
How many ...? ['mæni]

vielleicht maybe ['meɪbi:]; perhaps
[pə'hæps]

vier four [fɔ:]

Viertel (Nachbarschaft) neighbourhood ['neɪbəhʊd]

Vogel bird [bɜ:d]

voll full [fʊl] **voller ...** full of ...

Volleyball volleyball ['vɒlibɔ:l]

von
1. from [frɒm] **eine SMS von
Mama** a text from mum **von
Montag bis Freitag** from
Monday to Friday
2. of [ɒv], [əv] **von den Ferien**
of the holidays
3. by [baɪ] **(geschrieben) von
Sam Holmes** by Sam Holmes

vor (räumlich) in front of
[ɪn 'frʌnt əv]; (zeitlich) before
[bɪ'fɔ:] **vor zwei Jahren** two
years ago [ə'gəʊ]

vorbei: am Geschäft vorbei
past the shop [pɑ:st]

Vorbild role model ['rəʊl mɒdl]

Vordergrund foreground
['fɔ:graʊnd]

Vorführung show [ʃəʊ]

vorige Woche last week
[lɑ:st 'wi:k]

Vorschrift rule [ru:l]

vorsichtig careful ['keəfl] **vorsichtig fahren** drive carefully
['keəfəli]

vorstellen: Stell dir nur vor!
Wait for this. (infml) ['weɪt]

Vortrag talk [tɔ:k] **einen Vortrag
halten** give a talk

**Vorwurf: jm. Vorwürfe machen
(wegen)** blame sb. (for) [bleɪm]

**vorziehen: etwas einer Sache
vorziehen** prefer sth. to sth.
[prɪ'fɜ:]

W

wählen pick [pɪk]

wahr true [tru:]

Wald wood [wʊd]

Wand wall [wɔ:l]

Wanderer/Wanderin walker
['wɔ:kə]

wandern walk [wɔ:k] (das)
Wandern hiking ['haɪkɪŋ]

wann? when? [wen] **Wann hast
du Geburtstag?** When's your
birthday?

warm warm [wɔ:m]; hot [hɒt]

warten (auf) wait (for) [weɪt]

warum? why? [waɪ]

was? what? [wɒt] **Was ist
mit dir?** What about you?

Wasser water ['wɔ:tə]

Wasserkocher (elektrisch) kettle
['ketl]

Waveboarden street surfing
['stri:t sɜ:fɪŋ]

Website website ['websaɪt]

Wechsel change [tʃeɪndʒ]

wecken wake [weɪk]

Weg way [weɪ]; (Feldweg) track
[træk] **jm. den Weg beschreiben**
tell sb. the way **jn. nach dem
Weg fragen** ask sb. the way

weg away [ə'weɪ]

Wegbeschreibung(en) directions
(pl) [də'rekʃnz]

weggehen go away [gəʊ ə'weɪ];
leave [li:v]

wehtun: Ihr Bein tat weh.
Her leg was sore. [sɔ:] **Mir tut
der Hals weh.** I have a sore throat.
[sɔ: 'θrəʊt]

Weide field [fi:ld]

weil because [bɪ'kɒz]

weinen cry [kraɪ]

weiß white [waɪt]

weit far [fɑ:] **100 Meter weit**
for 100 metres

weitere more [mɔ:]

welche(r, s)? which? [wɪtʃ];
what? [wɒt] **welcher See?**
which lake? **Welche(s) sind ...?**
What are ...?

Welt world [wɜ:ld]

wem? who? [hu:]

wen? who? [hu:]

weniger less [les] **immer weniger**
less and less

wenn (falls) if [ɪf]; (zeitlich) when
[wen] **erst, wenn sie 13 sind**
not (...) until they're 13 [ən'tɪl]

wer? who? [hu:]

Werbung advert ['ædvɜ:t]

werden
1. **kalt werden** get cold
2. (Zukunft) will [wɪl] **das Wetter wird gut sein** the weather
will be good **es wird nicht** it
won't (= will not) [wəʊnt]
3. (Plan, Vorhaben) be going
to ['gəʊɪŋ tə] **ich werde fragen**
I'm going to ask

werfen throw [θrəʊ]
Werktag weekday ['wi:kdeɪ]
Westen, West- west [west]
westlich west [west]
Wettbewerb competition
[kɒmpə'tɪʃn]
Wetter weather ['weðə] **Wie ist das Wetter?** What's the weather like?
Wettstreit *(im Rap)* battle ['bætl]
wichtig important [ɪm'pɔːtənt]
wie like [laɪk] **genau wie Berry** just like Berry **so viel wie** as much as
wie? how? [haʊ] **Wie geht's?** How are you? **Wie ist das Wetter?** What's the weather like? **Wie nennt man …?** What do you call …? **Wie spät ist es?** What's the time?
wieder again [ə'gen]
Wiedersehen: Auf Wiedersehen. Goodbye. [gʊd'baɪ]
wild (lebend) wild [waɪld]
Willkommen in Plymouth! Welcome to Plymouth. ['welkəm]
Wind wind [wɪnd]
windig windy ['wɪndi]
winken wave [weɪv]
Winter winter ['wɪntə]
wir we [wiː] **wir selbst** ourselves [aʊə'selvz]
wirklich real [rɪəl] **wirklich nett** really nice ['rɪəli]
Wirklichkeit reality [ri'æliti]
wissen know [nəʊ]
Witz joke [dʒəʊk]
Witze machen joke [dʒəʊk] **Du machst wohl Witze! / Spitzenwitz!** You're joking!
WLAN *(kabellose Datenübertragung)* Wi-fi ['waɪ faɪ]
Woche week [wiːk] **eine Woche / sechs Wochen Urlaub** a week's/six weeks' holiday
Wochenende weekend [wiːk'end]
Wochentag weekday ['wiːkdeɪ]
wo(hin)? where? [weə]
wohltätige Organisation charity ['tʃærəti]
Wohnblock block of flats [blɒk əv 'flæts]
wohnen live [lɪv]
Wohnung flat [flæt]
Wohnzimmer living room ['lɪvɪŋ ruːm]
Wolke cloud [klaʊd]
wolkig cloudy ['klaʊdi]

wollen want [wɒnt] **kaufen wollen** want to buy
Wort word [wɜːd]
Wörterbuch dictionary ['dɪkʃənri]
Wörterverzeichnis: alphabetisches Wörterverzeichnis dictionary ['dɪkʃənri]
Wortnetz network ['netwɜːk]
wunderschön beautiful ['bjuːtɪfl]
Wurst sausage ['sɒsɪdʒ]
Würstchen sausage ['sɒsɪdʒ]
wütend angry ['æŋgri]

Z

zahlen pay [peɪ]
zehn ten [ten]
Zeichen sign [saɪn]
Zeichentrickfilm cartoon [kɑː'tuːn]
zeigen show [ʃəʊ]
Zeile line [laɪn]
Zeit time [taɪm] **Hast du um ein Uhr Zeit?** Are you free at one o'clock? [friː]
Zeitschrift magazine [mægə'ziːn]
Zeitung newspaper ['njuːzpeɪpə]; paper ['peɪpə] **Zeitungen austragen** do a paper round
Zelt tent [tent]
Zentrum centre ['sentə]
zerbrechen break [breɪk]
zerbrochen broken ['brəʊkən]
Zeug *(Kram)* stuff [stʌf] **dummes Zeug** *(Unsinn)* rubbish ['rʌbɪʃ]
ziehen nach *(umziehen)* move to [muːv]
Zimmer room [ruːm] **Zimmer mit Frühstück** bed and breakfast (B&B)
Zirkus circus ['sɜːkəs]
Zoo zoo [zuː]
zu
1. *(örtlich)* to [tu], [tə] **zu Hause** at home **bei Ellie zu Hause** at Ellie's house **Er legt sie zu den anderen Dingen.** He puts it with the other things. **zum Beispiel** for example
2. zu klein too small **zu spät** late [leɪt]
3. Zeit zu essen time to eat
4. *(geschlossen)* closed [kləʊzd] **zu sein** be closed
Zucker sugar ['ʃʊgə]
zuerst first [fɜːst]
Zug train [treɪn]
zugreifen: Greift zu! *(z.B. beim Essen)* Help yourselves.
Zuhause home [həʊm]

zuhören listen ['lɪsn]
Zuhörer/in listener ['lɪsənə]
Zukunft future ['fjuːtʃə]
zumachen close [kləʊz]
zurück back [bæk]
zurücklassen leave [liːv]
zusammen together [tə'geðə] **Schön, wieder zusammenzusein.** Nice to be together again.
zusammenzucken *(vor Schreck)* jump [dʒʌmp]
zustimmen agree with [ə'griː]
zwei two [tuː]
Zweibettzimmer twin room [twɪn 'ruːm]
zweimal twice [twaɪs]
zweite(r, s) second ['sekənd]
zwischen between [bɪ'twiːn]
zwölf twelve [twelv]

First names (Vornamen)

Abigail [ˈæbɪɡeɪl]
Alec [ˈælɪk]
Alex [ˈælɪks]
Alexander [ˈælɪkzɑːndə]
Alfie [ˈælfi]
Ali [ˈɑːli]
Alice [ˈælɪs]
Amy [ˈeɪmi]
Andy [ˈændi]
Angelo [ˈændʒələʊ]
Arif [ˈɑːrɪf]
Becky [ˈbeki]
Burak [ˈbjʊrək]
Cal [kæl]
Ciara [ˈkɪərə]
Dan [dæn]
Dara [ˈdɑːrə]
Darren [ˈdærən]
Dave [deɪv]
Duncan [ˈdʌŋkən]
Edward [ˈedwəd]
Evie [ˈiːvi]
Habib [haˈbiːb]
Hamish [ˈheɪmɪʃ]
Hannah [ˈhænə]
Jamie [ˈdʒeɪmi]
John [ˈdʒɒn]
Josh [ˈdʒɒʃ]
Jodie [ˈdʒəʊdi]
Jordan [ˈdʒɔːdn]
Julia [ˈdʒuːliə]
Kara [ˈkɑːrə]
Karan [kɑːˈræn]
Kate [keɪt]
Liam [ˈliːəm]
Livvy [ˈlɪvi]
Luigi [luˈiːdʒi]
Luke [luːk]
Marcus [ˈmɑːkəs]
Marty [ˈmɑːti]
Mehdy [ˈmedi]
Molly [ˈmɒli]
Natasha [nəˈtæʃə]
Noah [ˈnəʊə]
Pinar [ˈpɪnə]
Rob [rɒb]
Robert [ˈrɒbət]
Roger [ˈrɒdʒə]
Ruby [ˈruːbi]
Sammy [ˈsæmi]
Sandra [ˈsɑːndrə]
Sarah [ˈseərə]
Serena [səˈriːnə]
Simon [ˈsaɪmən]
Talia [ˈtɑːliə]
Tally [ˈtæli]
Tarik [ˈtɑːrɪk]
Tasha [ˈtæʃə]

Family names / Surnames (Familiennamen)

Atkinson [ˈætkɪnsən]
Blake [bleɪk]
Bantam [ˈbæntəm]
Bell [bel]
Burns [bɜːnz]
Butler [ˈbʌtlə]
Chung [tʃʌŋ]
Dolby [ˈdɒlbi]
Fitzwarren [fɪtsˈwɒrən]
Grant [grɑːnt]
Hall [ɔːl]
Harper [ˈhɑːpə]
Henson [ˈhensn]
Johnson [ˈdʒɒnsn]
Jonas [ˈdʒəʊnəs]
Jones [dʒəʊns]
Keating [ˈkiːtɪŋ]
Macdonald [məkˈdɒnəld]
Malone [məˈləʊn]
O'Brien [əʊˈbraɪən]
O'Connor [əʊˈkɒnə]
Smith [smɪθ]
Taylor [ˈteɪlə]
Webster [ˈwebstə]
Whittington [ˈwɪtɪŋtən]

Place names (Ortsnamen)

Aberdeen [æbəˈdiːn]
Albert Dock [ˌælbət ˈdɒk]
Battersea Park
    [bætəsi ˈpɑːk]
Baker Street
    [ˈbeɪkə striːt]
Brick Tower
    [brɪk ˈtaʊə]
Britannia Vaults
    [brɪˈtænjə ˈvɔːlts]
Buckingham Palace
    [bʌkɪŋəm ˈpæləs]
Cairngorms [keənˈɡɔːmz]
Cam River [kæm ˈrɪvə]
Camden Market
    [kæmdən ˈmɑːkɪt]
Catbrook [ˈkætbrʊk]
the Cavern Club [ˈkævn]
Chelsea [ˈtʃelsi]
Chipping Campden
    [tʃɪpɪŋ ˈkæmdən]
Clava Cairns
    [klɑːvə ˈkeənz]
the Cotswolds
    [ˈkɒtswəʊldz]
Covent Garden
    [kɒvənt ˈɡɑːdn]
Culloden [kəˈlɒdn]
Dores [dɔːz]

Dublin [ˈdʌblɪn]
Dyers Lane [daɪəz ˈleɪn]
Edinburgh [ˈedɪnbərə]
Fulham Broadway
    [fʊləm ˈbrɔːdweɪ]
Glasgow [ˈɡlɑːzɡəʊ]
Glenfinnan [glenˈfɪnən]
Grafton Street
    [ˈɡrɑːftən striːt]
Hammersmith
    [ˈhæməsmɪθ]
Ha'penny Bridge
    [heɪpəni ˈbrɪdʒ]
Heathrow Airport
    [hiːθrəʊ ˈeəpɔːt]
Hogwarts [ˈhɒɡwɔːts]
Hyde Park [haɪd ˈpɑːk]
Inverness [ɪnvəˈnes]
Kingcomb Lane
    [kɪŋkəʊm ˈleɪn]
Knightsbridge
    [ˈnaɪtsbrɪdʒ]
Laggan [ˈlæɡən]
Leadenhall [ˈlednhɔːl]
Leaky Cauldron
    [liːki ˈkɔːldrən]
Leeds [liːdz]
Liverpool [ˈlɪvəpuːl]
Loch Ness [lɒx ˈnes]
Mallaig [ˈmæleɪɡ]
Manchester [ˈmæntʃɪstə]
Mersey [ˈmɜːzi]
Mickleton [ˈmɪkltən]
the Millennium
    Bridge [mɪˈleniəm]
Moore Street [ˈmʊə striːt]
O'Connell Street
    [əʊˈkɒnl striːt]
Odeon [ˈəʊdiən]
Oxford Street
    [ˈɒksfəd striːt]
the River Liffey [ˈlɪfi]
the River Tay [teɪ]
Slains Castle
    [sleɪnz ˈkɑːsl]
Stamford Bridge
    [stæmfəd ˈbrɪdʒ]
Stephen's Green
    [stiːvnz ˈɡriːn]
St James's Park
    [sənt dʒeɪmzɪz ˈpɑːk]
St Paul's Cathedral
    [sənt pɔːlz kəˈθiːdrəl]
the Strand [strænd]
Stratford-upon-Avon
    [strætfəd əpɒn ˈeɪvn]
Temple Bar [templ ˈbɑː]
the Thames [temz]
Toxteth [ˈtɒkstəθ]

Trafalgar Square
    [trəfælɡə ˈskweə]
Waterloo Station
    [wɔːtəluː ˈsteɪʃn]
Wembley [ˈwembli]
Westminster
    [ˈwestmɪnstə]
Wimbledon [ˈwɪmbldən]
Woodlands [ˈwʊdləndz]

Other names (Andere Namen)

Arsenal [ˈɑːsnəl]
Arthur Conan Doyle
    [ˈɑːθə ˈkɒnən dɔɪl]
The Beatles [ˈbiːtlz]
Billy Eliot [bɪli ˈeliət]
Braveheart [ˈbreɪvhɑːt]
Cavern Club
    [ˈkævən klʌb]
George Harrison
    [dʒɔːdʒ ˈhærɪsən]
Harrods [ˈhærədz]
the Jacobite Steam Train
    [dʒækəbaɪt ˈstiːm treɪn]
the Jeanie Johnston
    [dʒiːni ˈdʒɒnstən]
John Lennon
    [dʒɒn ˈlenən]
Kenny Dalglish
    [keni dælˈɡliːʃ]
Leo Burdock's
    [liːəʊ ˈbɜːdɒks]
Lochside B&B [ˈlɒxsaɪd
biːəndˈbiː]
MacBean's [məkˈbiːnz]
Madame Tussaud's
    [məˈdɑːm tuːˈsəʊdz]
Maggie's Lodge
    [mæɡiz ˈlɒdʒ]
Milo [ˈmaɪləʊ]
Paul McCartney
    [pɔːl məkˈkɑːtni]
Queen Elizabeth II
    [kwiːn iˈlɪzəbəθ ðə
    ˈsekənd]
Ringo Star [rɪŋɡəʊ ˈstɑː]
Sean Connery
    [ʃɔːn ˈkɒnəri]
Shamrock Rovers
    [ʃæmrɒk ˈrəʊvəz]
Shannon Rovers
    [ʃænən ˈrəʊvəz]
the Titanic [taɪˈtænɪk]
Urquhart Castle
    [ɜːkət ˈkɑːsl]
Wally [ˈwɒli]

Illustrationen

Beehive Illustration, Cirencester (**Pete Smith**: S. 71; S. 73; S. 74; S. 75; S. 88); **Roland Beier**, Berlin (Umschlaginnenseite 2 Ireland castle icon (M)); **Carlos Borrell**, Berlin (Umschlagseite 2 British Isles (M); **Jeongsook Lee**, Heidelberg (Umschlagseite 2 icons außer Irleand castle (M); S. 124; S. 135; S. 149; S. 150; S. 151; S. 153; S. 154; S. 155; S. 156; S. 157 no parking, unten; S. 159; S. 160; S. 162; S. 164 two girls; S. 165); **David Norman**, Meerbusch (S. 31; S. 32; S. 34; S. 35; S. 40; S. 44; S. 50 (u. 103); S. 54; S. 55; S. 58 unten; S. 60; S. 82 oben; S. 100 unten); **Dorina Tessmann**, Berlin (S. 9; S. 12 Bild G; S. 1415; S. 20 Bild A-C; S. 28; S. 29; S. 30; S. 36; S. 41 (u. 102); S. 42 (u. 90); S. 53 table; S. 58 oben; S. 61 (u. 109); S. 63; S. 81 (u. 114); S. 82 Bild 1–8 (u. 115); S. 92; S. 93; S. 102; S. 114; S. 126; S. 129; S. 131; S. 133; S. 134; S. 136; S. 137)

Titelbild

Shutterstock.com/Bernhard Richter

Bildquellen

Susan Abbey & Frank Donoghue, Nenagh (S. 29 farm (M)); **Alamy**, Abingdon (S. 4 Mitte re.: Cultura Creative (RF)/Monty Rakusen; S. 6 unten li.: Incamerastock/ICP-UK; S. 8 Bild 5: Mattia Bicchi; S. 11 unten: Greg Balfour Evans; S. 12 Bild A: Jack Sullivan. "Billy Elliot the Musical logo courtesy of Billy London Limited"; S. 12 Bild C: Stuart Kelly. Used by courtesy of Transport of London and National Rail, Bild D: Travelshots.com/Peter Phipp; S. 13 unten re.: Alex Segre; S. 17 Bild B: London Entertainment. The image shown depicts wax figures created and owned by Madame Tussauds; S. 19 oben (M) (u. 39 u. 59 u. 79): Steve Cavlier; S. 25 oben: Hugh Threlfall; S. 28 unten: Graham Toney; S. 29 oben: PetStockBoys/The Art Of Animals.co.uk, girl holding lamb (M): Cultura Creative (RF)/Monty Rakusen; S. 32 girl holding lamb (M) (u. 99): Cultura Creative (RF)/Monty Rakusen, river (u. 99): Robert Read Thames Portfolio; S. 43 oben: Peter Titmuss; S. 49 Bild H oben: Paul Thompson Images/Chris Ballentine; S. 66 oben: Image Source7/Gary John Norman; S. 69 Bild F: Elizabeth Leyden, Bild G: newsphoto; S. 72 RockNess: Ross Gilmore, Lochside B&B: Senarb Commercial; S. 78 Bild 2 sports: Sam Strickler; S. 80 oben: PhotoAlto/James Hardy; S. 84 Bild A: South West Images Scotland; S. 85 oben li.: Nifro UK, re.: Simon Price; S. 86 Mitte: Radharc/Images/JoeFox; S. 87 Mitte li.: Image Source Plus/IS773; S. 88: Radharc Images/JoeFoxDublin; S. 89 Grafton Street: B.O'Kane, O'Connell Street: plpix, The Jeanie Johnston: Ruth Grimes, Moore Street: Barry Mason, Temple Bar: Radharc Images/JoeFoxDublin, Molly Malone: World Pictures, Stephen's Green: Barry Mason, The Ha'penny Bridge: incamerastock, Dublin Bay: Adrian Muttitt; S. 107 unten li.: PhotoAlto/Laurence Mouton; S. 110 Bild G: Oote Boe Ph; S. 118 oben u. unten: theatrepix, Mitte: UpperCutImages/Image Studios, S. 119 oben li. u. Mitte: theatrepix; S. 146 fast food stand: Peter Erik Forsberg/Lifestyle; S. 147 tractor (M): Juice Images, unten: Alvey & Towers Picture Library); **avenue images**, Hamburg (S. 28 Mitte: agefotostock/Olaf Protze); **Chelsea Football Club** (S. 12 Bild B logo, football player. Used by permission of Chelsea Football Club); **Corbis**, Düsseldorf (S. 24 oben li.: Simon Marcus, unten: Maurizio Rellini/Grand Tour/Grand Tour; S. 49 Bild G: Terra/Paul Thompson; S. 56: Paul Cunningham; S. 64 oben li.: Bettmann; S. 121 unten: The Mariners' Museum); **Cornelsen Schulverlage** (S. 4 oben re.; S. 10 Sam, Ruby, Tally; S. 11 oben; S. 19 Bild A-F; S. 29 crossroads, church, market, high street, gate, wood, pub, hill, farm; S. 30 oben re.; S. 37 oben; S. 39 scene 1–6; S. 59 a competition Bild A-D, who said what? Bild A-C; S. 79 Bild A-D); **Fotolia.de** (S. 52 unten Mrs Fox (M): Farina3000; S. 117 unten re.: OSCAR; S. 146 baker's: contrastwerkstatt); **Getty Images**, München (S. 8 Bild 1: AWL Images/Julian Love; S. 17 Bild C: Getty Images Entertainment/Fred Duval. The image shown depicts wax figures created and owned by Madame Tussauds; S. 77 unten: Taxi/Photo and Co); **Glow Images**, München (S. 24 oben Mitte, re.; S. 123 oben re.; S. 128 oben re.: Image Source); **International Slavery Museum** (S. 49 Bild E: © Redman Design); **Picture Alliance**, Frankfurt/Main (S. 95: EMPICS Sport; S. 113 re.: Costa/Leemage); **iStockphoto.com** (S. 4 Mitte li. (u. 28): Matthew Dixon; S. 6 unten re.: lubilub; S. 21 Bild A, B: hohl; S. 48 Bild B: hmproudlove; S. 53 oben li.: mbrowe; S. 66 unten: mauro grigollo; S. 70 unten: tbradford; S. 78 Bild 2 Nessie: ARTPUPPY; S. 83 unten: Claudiad; S. 84 Bild E mountain biking: pale62; S. 86 oben: lubilub; S. 97: ozgurdonmaz; S. 106: wdstock; S. 110 Bild A: Creativeye99, Bild C: atiatiati, Bild D: lucentius; S. 119 unten: Mimadeo; S. 120 unten: theatrepix; S. 123 kilt: jeangill; S. 137 tourists: erlucho; S. 138: ARTPUPPY; S. 139: AdobeDweller; S. 141: mammothis; S. 142: Pickledjo; S. 143 oben: IgorZakowski; S. 144: Peter Bajohr; S. 145 unten: Shannon Toth; S. 146 tram station: onfilm, chemist's: sjlocke, newsagent's: Giorgio Fochesato, ice rink: CEFutcher, skate park: Brad Ralph; S. 157 oben: bobash); **Liverpool One** (S. 4 unten li u. S. 91 li.: Used by courtesy of Liverpool One); **Madame Tussauds**, London (S. 17 Bild D. The image shown depicts wax figures created and owned by Madame Tussauds); **Mauritius**, Mittenwald (S. 48 Bild C: age fotostock, S. 146 youth centre: Maskot); **Mersey Ferries** (S. 64 oben re.: Used by courtesy of Mersey Ferries); **National Museums Liverpool** (S. 48 Bild A u. S. 91 re.: Used by permission); **O2 Arena London** (S. 12 Bild E: used by courtesy of The O2); **dpa Picture-Alliance**, Frankfurt/Main (S. 8 Bild 3: Jan Haas; S. 9 Bild 7: dpa; S. 21 Bild D: Robert Haas; S. 49 Bild H oben: empics; S. 51 Ben's father: Image Source; S. 69 Bild E: Adina Tovy/Robert Harding World Imagery, S. 77 oben: APA/picturedesk.com/Karl Schöndorfer; S. 84 Bild D: Arco Images/F.Scholz; S. 95: EMPICS Sport; S. 121 oben li.: landov, oben Mitte: Illustrated London News Ltd/Mary Evans Picture Library; S. 123 unten: United Archives/TopFoto); **Thomas Schulz**, Teupitz (S. 13 oben girl (M), step 2–3; S. 23 unten; 33 unten; S. 41 unten; S. 98; S. 105); **Transport for London** (S. 136 tube map © Transport for London – map used by permission of Pulse Creative Limited); **Shutterstock.com** (S. 4 oben li.(u. 8 Bild 3): S. Borisov, unten re.: East; S. 6 oben li.: Rob van Esch, oben re. (u. 70): Jorg Hackemann; S. 8 Bild 2: Mypokcik/London Uderground Roundel ® Transport for London. Reproduced by kind permission of Transport for London; S. 9 Bild 6: QQ7; S. 12 Bild F: pcruciatti; S. 13 oben London Eye (M): cycreation, unten li.: Ovchynnikov Oleksii; S. 17 Bild A: Jaguar PS. The image shown depicts wax figures created and owned by Madame Tussauds; S. 18 li. (u. 96): Horst Petzold, re. (u. 96): SergeBertasiusPhotography; S. 21 Bild C: Joerg Beuge; S. 22: Lance Bellers; S. 23 Bild A: Kamira, Bild B: Bikeworldtravel, Bild C: Paul Cowan; S. 25 unten unhappy emoticon (u. 45 u. 65 u. 85): Dawn Hudson, happy emoticon (u. 45 u. 65 u. 85): In-Finity; S. 26 oben: HENX, unten: CREATISTA; S. 27 Bild 2: Mark William Richardson, unten footsteps: Helga Chirk; S. 28/29 Hintergrund: carstests; S. 29 block of flats: David Hughes; S. 30 oben li.: Yuri Arcurs, dog: Mat Hayward, van: Sally Wallis; S. 33 oben: auremar, Mitte (M): Dobroslawa Szulc; S. 37 unten: Yuri Arcurs; S. 38 Bild A: Linn Currie, Bild C (u. 43): Nuno Andre; S. 41 oben: Yanik Chauvin; S. 46 unten li.: Vera F, oben re.: Fotokostic; S. 47 oben icons: Ziven, unten: egd; S. 48/49 skyline: YurkaImmortal; S. 50 Ben: East; S. 51 Bild A: Nattika, Bild B: Nata-Lia, Bild C: Oleksiy Mark, Bild D: Dudarev Mikhail, Bild E: margouillat photo, Bild F: Madlen, Bild G: Ian 2010, Bild H: Kesu; S. 52 oben u. unten Ben (M) : East, oben u. unten classroom (M): Tanchic; S. 61 Ben (u. 109): East; S. 62 Bild 1: gualtiero boffi, Bild 2–6, 8: Sarunyu_foto, Bild 7: Carsten Reisinger; S. 65 Kelly: Pressmaster, Jordan: Nolte Lourens, Evie: Alan Bailey; S. 68/69 Hintergrund tartan: Brandon Bourdages; S. 68 Welcome to Scotland button thistle (M): armvector, Scotland map: AndOcean, Bild A: Rob van Esch, Bild B: Grant Glendinning, Bild C: Zdenek Krchak, monster sign: Jeff Morin, Bild D: Pinon Road; S. 69 Bild H clouds (M): Archipoch, flag of Wales, Scotland, England (M): Maxx-Studio; S. 70 Bild A: Stuart Monk, Bild B: Mat Hayward, Bild

Liedquelle

infinitive	simple past	past participle	
be	was / were	been	sein
begin	began	begun	beginnen, anfangen
break	broke	broken	brechen, zerbrechen
bring	brought	brought	bringen, mitbringen
buy	bought	bought	kaufen
catch	caught	caught	fangen, erwischen
come	came	come	kommen
cost	cost	cost	kosten
cut	cut	cut	schneiden; (Rasen) mähen
do	did	done [ʌ]	tun, machen
drink	drank	drunk	trinken
drive [aɪ]	drove	driven [ɪ]	(mit dem Auto) fahren; (an)treiben
eat	ate [et, eɪt]	eaten	essen
fall	fell	fallen	fallen, hinfallen
feel	felt	felt	fühlen; sich fühlen
fight	fought	fought	kämpfen
find	found	found	finden
fly	flew	flown	fliegen
forget	forgot	forgotten	vergessen
get	got	got	bekommen; holen, werden; (hin)kommen
give	gave	given	geben
go	went	gone [ɒ]	gehen
have	had	had	haben
hear [ɪə]	heard [ɜː]	heard [ɜː]	hören
hurt	hurt	hurt	verletzen; wehtun
keep	kept	kept	behalten
know [nəʊ]	knew [njuː]	known [nəʊn]	wissen; kennen
leave	left	left	abfahren; (weg)gehen; zurücklassen
lose [uː]	lost [ɒ]	lost [ɒ]	verlieren
make	made	made	machen
mean [iː]	meant [e]	meant [e]	bedeuten; meinen, sagen wollen
meet	met	met	treffen; sich treffen; kennenlernen
pay	paid	paid	bezahlen
put	put	put	(etwas wohin) tun, legen, stellen
read [iː]	read [e]	read [e]	lesen
ride [aɪ]	rode	ridden [ɪ]	reiten; (Rad) fahren
ring	rang	rung	läuten, klingeln; anrufen
run	ran	run	rennen, laufen
say [eɪ]	said [e]	said [e]	sagen
see	saw	seen	sehen
sell	sold	sold	verkaufen
send	sent	sent	schicken, senden
sing	sang	sung	singen
sit	sat	sat	sitzen
sleep	slept	slept	schlafen
speak	spoke	spoken	sprechen
spend	spent	spent	ausgeben (Geld); verbringen (Zeit)
stand	stood	stood	stehen; sich (hin)stellen
take	took	taken	nehmen; mitnehmen; dauern, (Zeit) brauchen
teach	taught	taught	unterrichten, lehren
tell	told	told	erzählen, berichten
think	thought	thought	denken
throw	threw	thrown	werfen
understand	understood	understood	verstehen
wear [eə]	wore [ɔː]	worn [ɔː]	tragen, anhaben (Kleidung)
win	won [ʌ]	won [ʌ]	gewinnen
write	wrote	written	schreiben